The Grandes Dames

by

STEPHEN BIRMINGHAM

SIMON AND SCHUSTER · NEW YORK

Published by Simon and Schuster
A Division of Gulf & Western Corporation
Simon & Schuster Building
Rockefeller Center
1230 Avenue of the Americas
New York, New York 10020
SIMON AND SCHUSTER and colophon are trademarks of
Simon & Schuster
Designed by Eve Metz
Manufactured in the United States of America

1   3   5   7   9   10   8   6   4   2

Library of Congress Cataloging in Publication Data

Birmingham, Stephen.
The grandes dames.
1. Women—United States—Biography.   2. Upper classes
—United States—Biography.   3. Biography—19th century.
4. Biography—20th century.   I. Title.
CT3260.B55   305.4′2′0922   [B]   82-745
ISBN 0-671-25585-1   AACR2

*Grateful acknowledgment is made to Little, Brown & Company for the excerpt from
Ellery Sedgwick's* The Happy Profession, *1946.*

PICTURE CREDITS
Bettmann Archive: 3, 9, 23, 41, 42, 43; Cecil Beaton/Opera News: 44; Chicago Historical Society: 27; Cincinnati Historical Society: 52, 53, 55, 56; Culver Pictures: 15,
38, 39; Florida Photographic Archives/Strozier Library, F.S.U.: 5; Henry E. Huntington Library and Art Gallery: 30, 31, 33, 34, 35, 36, 37; Historical Pictures Service,
Chicago: 24; The Historical Society of Pennsylvania: 6, 7; Hon. James H.R. Cromwell: 1, 2, 4; Houston Chronicle: 50, 51; Isabella Stewart Gardner Museum: 8, 12, 13,
14; I Tatti: 10; Library of Congress: 11, 28, 48, 54; Longue Vue Collection: 17, 18, 19;
Metropolitan Museum of Art: 25; Mrs. Max Ascoli: 16; The Museum of Fine Arts,
Houston: 49; Museum of the City of New York: 32; Opera News: 40, 45; The Times-
Picayune: 20; Toni Frissell/LIFE © Time Inc.: 21; The University of Texas at Austin:
46, 47; UPI: 22, 26, 29.

FOR MY MOTHER
IN MEMORY

Contents

Contents

Foreword

WHEN I FIRST MENTIONED to friends and acquaintances that I was writing a book about American *grandes dames*—that special and increasingly rare breed of women who flourished between the Mauve Decade of the nineteenth century and the Second World War as high priestesses of uppercase Society, Culture, Philanthropy and Civic Duty—it suddenly seemed that everyone knew at least one, if not several. "You should include my grandmother!" was a familiar response, or it might have been a greataunt, or the great-aunt's best friend. Everyone, it seemed, had his or her favorite Mrs. Worthy or Lady Bountiful, whose singleminded mission in life was to provide Uplift and Example. It began to seem as though to compile a full roster of candidates for *grande dame*–ship would require a volume the length of the Manhattan phone book.

The arena, I found, was crowded with controversy. Who, for example, would qualify? How did one tell the true *grande dame* from the *poseuse?* Was it *essential* that a *grande dame* be rich? Wouldn't Mother Teresa be the ultimate *grande dame?*

Well, yes; but no, not really. The most successful *grandes dames* were not saintly creatures. They were tough. They were not sufferers, but fighters. They could be wily and manipulative and, clad in the armor of a righteous cause, they were stronger than all the hosts of Error and no more scrupulous than the average ward boss.

Take my own mother. My mother was not rich, and yet I am sure she considered herself a *grande dame* in the little Connecticut town where she lived and held a certain sway, though of course she never referred to herself as one. (*Grandes dames* never do.) On the other hand, she had been splendidly educated at Wellesley College and had emerged from that experience convinced, as most Wellesley alumnae are, that Wellesley had taught her all there was to know about everything. (A Wellesley friend of mine once said, "It's true. If there's anything wrong with you, Wellesley fixes it. If you don't walk properly, Wellesley corrects that. If you don't speak correctly, Wellesley teaches you how. If you can't swim when you enter Wellesley, you will have to swim a length of the pool before you graduate.")

My mother's chosen fields of civic duty, in our little town, were improving the local schools and straightening out local politics. As *grandes dames* often do, she made enemies, whom she simply ignored. Some found her autocratic, overbearing, opinionated and mule-stubborn, as indeed she was. She stood serenely above the criticism, buoyed up by her supreme self-confidence. Wellesley, you see, had made her an expert in many matters: plumbing, electrical circuitry, and automobile repair were useful ancillary skills. I remember, as a child, hearing of the first explosion of an atomic device over Hiroshima and, as we discussed the frightening new era we were entering, hearing Mother airily explain that she could have built an atomic bomb from what she had learned in chemistry class at Wellesley. All she would have needed was the money to buy the necessary parts. (*Grandes dames*, as the reader will perhaps discover, could also be eccentric.)

But here, of course, was the major difference between my mother—along with close members of their own families of whom readers of this book may be reminded—and the women taken up in the chapters that follow. She lacked the financial wherewithal, which these women had, to build wings of museums, to pay for a season of symphony, to support a struggling opera company through a Great Depression, to build a school, or a library, or a hospital, or a whole "model town" designed to lift the poor out of the slums. As a result, my mother's sphere of influence was a few square miles of New England countryside. She was a Legend in Her Lifetime only to her neighbors. And so, yes. A *grande dame* can be a much grander *dame* if she is very, very rich.

Many of the names dealt with in this book—Stotesbury, Dodge, Rosenwald, Huntington, Gardner, Belmont, Rockefeller—are nationally known. They stand for banking and industrial efficiency, government service, patronage of the arts, science, education, and vast philanthropy. In many cases the women who bore these names were also well known, but perhaps less understood. They were not, in Aline Saarinen's phrase, merely Proud Possessors. They saw to it that their money and possessions (or at least a goodly share) went to the public weal. They did not collect great art merely to adorn their drawing rooms but actually saw themselves as *custodians* of masterpieces which would eventually pass to the public. They also represent a naïve, almost-forgotten era—before a foundation's board decided who got what, before corporate giving, before government social welfare programs—when philanthropy was considered an individual matter, and a duty. It was an era when a rich woman felt that she personally owed something to her city and, rightly or wrongly, selected a personal way to pay her debt.

It was an era when Eva Stotesbury could say with great seriousness (as she once did to her young son), "Great wealth carries with it great responsibilities," and not be laughed at. It was an era when the word "charity" did not have a defensive edge to it, and when one could speak of "the deserving poor" without fear of reproach. (It was simply assumed that some of the poor were not deserving, an almost treasonous thought today.) And it was an era when great entertainments were put on for their own sake, not as fund-raisers, promotions, or tax write-offs. And, oddly, it was really not all that long ago.

A second question I was asked while working on this book was: How are you selecting which American *grandes dames* to write about? The answer has to be: Very arbitrarily.

There are, meanwhile, a number of individuals who were especially helpful to me in my research, and I would like to express my thanks to each of them. For the sections on Eva Cromwell Stotesbury, I am indebted to her son, the Hon. James H. R. Cromwell of New York, and her former secretary, the late Mrs. Katherine MacMullan of Philadelphia; for reminiscences and impressions of Edith Rosenwald Stern, I wish to thank Mr. Edgar B. Stern of Aspen, Colorado, Philip and Helen Markel Stern of New York, and Mrs. Marion Rosenwald Ascoli and Mr. Steven Hirsch, both of New York. The section of the book devoted to Isabella Stewart Gardner owes much to the impressions of Mr. Edward Weeks of Boston. In Houston, I would like to thank Misses Charlotte Phelan and Terry Diehl of the Houston *Post* for access to that newspaper's files, as well as Mrs. Barbara Dillingham for personal anecdotes. In Cincinnati, several people were helpful to me in trying to capture the elusive personality of the shy philanthropist Mary Emery. These would include Mrs. Elizabeth Livingood McGuire, Mr. Warren W. Parks, Mr. Robert Ashbrook, Mr. Millard Rogers of the Cincinnati Art Museum and Mr. Steven Plattner of the Cincinnati Historical Society. Miss Lee Scott of Packer Collegiate Institute, Brooklyn, New York, was helpful in supplying Mrs. Emery's school records. Helping to round out the figure of Eleanor Belmont were Mr. August Belmont of Easton, Maryland, Mrs. Patricia Shaw of New York, and Mr. Thomas Lanier of the Metropolitan Opera Guild.

Three other people deserve a special word of thanks: my friend Dr. Edward Lahniers, psychologist *par excellence*, who read the entire book in manuscript and offered analysis and interpretation of the characters involved; my friend and agent, Mrs. Carol Brandt, who guided the project from the outset with her usual cool aplomb; and my friend and editor, Mr. Frederic Hills of Simon and Schuster, who was first to propose that this was a project worth undertaking.

While all of the above had a hand in shaping the book, I alone must be held responsible for any errors or shortcomings.

—S.B.

PART ONE

Little Eva

vs.

Philadelphia

"A SENSE OF PERSONAL THEATRE"

THERE ARE SEVERAL QUALITIES that would seem to be required of a woman before she can be admitted to the hierarchy of Great Ladies, or *grandes dames*, a member of that vanished breed—the Great American Matriarchy —which ruled American society from the 1880s to the Second World War. One would certainly be toughness—physical and emotional toughness—the ability to fly serenely in the face of criticism, malice, and jealousy. To be a *grande dame* required thick skin. It also required, on the opposite end of the scale, a naïve, almost childlike, faith in oneself and one's infallibility. Luck was involved too, and, of course, money. Looks and manners—and that elusive ingredient charm—all helped, but were not essential. Most important, perhaps, was what author James Maher has described as "a sense of personal theatre." This is the sense which, if one is blessed with it, assures its possessor that, when she has entered a room, something important has happened. A curtain has risen, and the pink spotlight has fallen on the face of the star. It picks her out from the others, and follows her as she moves. The audience is hushed, expectant. Tilting her head just slightly to acknowledge the packed auditorium, she smiles. Then she speaks. Her timing and inflection are perfect. The drama, which is her creation, has begun.

Lucretia Bishop Roberts seemed to have been born with this sense of personal theatre. There was, for example, the matter of her name. She was a beautiful child, with light wavy hair, enormous gray eyes, a cupid's bow mouth, a beautifully shaped, slightly turned-up nose. Her skin was fair and flawless, her cheekbones were high and her cheeks were dimpled. Surely this pretty girl did not deserve to be named Lucretia, calling to mind as it did Lucretia Borgia, the famous poisoner. She also disliked her girlhood nickname, Lulu. No, this girl with the face of an angel, resembling paintings of the first woman in the Garden of Innocence, was more appropriately an Eva. And Eva was what Lucretia Roberts became. Later, when she became one of the wonders of her era, Eva would explain that her mother had given pet names to all her children, and that Eva had been hers. But one wonders. Every great star in the theatre tries to choose a name appropriate to her particular aura as she perceives it. And so Lucretia became Eva.

She had been born in Chicago in 1865, of parents who were by no means rich but were nonetheless respectable. Her father, James Henry Roberts, was an attorney who liked to recall the days when he had ridden the judicial circuits in southern and central Illinois with an older lawyer named Abraham Lincoln. In Chicago, Mr. Roberts's law partner was Melville W. Fuller, and the firm had a number of important clients, among them the Illinois Central Railroad. Fuller, in particular, was active in Illinois state politics, and from 1863 to 1865 was a member of the State House of Representatives. In 1888, by President Grover Cleveland's appointment, Fuller was named to succeed Morrison R. Waite as Chief Justice of the United States Supreme Court. According to a Roberts family legend, Cleveland had given both Fuller and Roberts equal consideration, and the two partners had flipped a coin to see which man would go to Washington. Roberts had lost. The story is undoubtedly apocryphal, but as a young woman Eva Roberts learned to believe that somehow fate had cheated her family of a magnificent destiny. While her father's partner went on into the pages of American history textbooks, her father remained James Roberts, Esq., successful attorney at law.

In 1889, Eva accompanied her father to Albuquerque, New Mexico, where he was arguing a particularly bitter case involving one of the many railroad "wars" that had become a commonplace of the era. The opposing counsel was a New York lawyer named Charles Thorn Cromwell, and with the senior Mr. Cromwell was his son, Oliver Eaton Cromwell. In the little frontier town, Eva Roberts and Oliver Cromwell met and fell in love. It was a match that displeased both sets of parents. Charles Cromwell and James Roberts were not only representing opposing sides of the case; they were also bitter enemies, had been for years, and were complete opposites in terms of personality. Cromwell was foul-mouthed, hard-drinking, and uncouth. Eva's father was courtly, abstemious, and devout. When Eva and Oliver Cromwell announced their intention to marry, Eva's father reportedly warned her, "Daughter, you must faithfully attend church every Sabbath to arm yourself against the godless Cromwells." Eva and Oliver were married in Albuquerque later that year, and their honeymoon was spent in a local hotel. She was twenty-four and he was forty-one.

Godless the Cromwells might be, but they were socially very well connected. Oliver Eaton Cromwell was a direct descendant of *the* Oliver Cromwell, Britain's Lord Protector. In New York, his father had belonged to all the best clubs, including the Union and the New York Yacht Club, and the Cromwell yachts had won a number of important racing trophies. When Oliver brought his beautiful young bride to New York in 1890, he and Eva sailed into the *Social Register* and into the waiting arms of New York's reigning hostess, Mrs. William Astor, and her chief lieutenant, Ward McAllister.

Mrs. Astor and McAllister had codified and delineated New York society ten years earlier. A list, Mr. McAllister explained, had to be made of those who "counted" in New York, as opposed to those who did not, and that list consisted of no more than four hundred people. Besides, the capacity of Mrs. Astor's ballroom was four hundred, and thus the phrase "the Four Hundred" became fixed in the press and made its way into the American vernacular. (For years society reporters tried to get McAllister to reveal the names of who the chosen Four Hundred were, and when he finally complied it seemed that his arithmetic was off: his list consisted of only three hundred and four names.)

Though Caroline Astor unquestionably considered herself the grandest of New York's *grandes dames*—and would continue to do so long after Ward McAllister had ceased to be useful to her (cruelly, she held a large gala on the eve of her former mentor's funeral)—it would be incorrect to suppose that she served as a role model for Eva's later career in society. Caroline Astor was a plain, stiff, frosty woman who rarely smiled and was often rude. It is possible, too, that she was not very bright. A story persists that once, boarding a streetcar and asked to deposit her fare, Mrs. Astor said, "No, thank you. I have my own favorite charities." (But how could this be true? She had her own carriages and coachmen and would never have needed to use a public conveyance.) She was usually overdressed, nearly always in black, the better to show off her extravagant amounts of jewelry, and she invariably wore a very obvious black wig. Furthermore, she gave terrible parties, and why New York society groveled before Caroline Astor's pointed feet for nearly a quarter of a century is, in retrospect, a little hard to understand. Her own sense of personal theatre was based on intimidation rather than enchantment.

For her evening entertainments, Caroline Astor had set rigid, grueling rules. Gaiety was frowned upon, as was any conversation that smacked remotely of intelligence or wit. Within Mrs. Astor's gilded inner circle, the talk was almost studiedly irrelevant, and its topics were restricted, as historian Lloyd Morris put it, to "thoughtful discussions of food, wines, horses, yachts, cotillions, marriages, villas at Newport and the solecisms of ineligibles." Anything that might be remotely considered an idea was eschewed at the Astor dinner table, and during the day Mrs. Astor's set had the dinners of the previous evenings to discuss. Actors, opera singers, musicians, composers, and people connected with the theatre in any way were considered socially disreputable. Writers, painters, and sculptors were not deemed worth discussing—or buying—until they had been respectably dead for a number of years. Politicians were vulgar, nor were educators or even clergymen regarded as fit for inclusion in fashionable society. The only "working" people to whom the Four Hundred gave the nod were high-ranking members of the military, and the Astor-McAllister list included at least five generals and two colonels and their respective ladies.

Mrs. Astor and her friends' one concession to the arts was to attend the opera at the old Academy of Music on Monday and Friday nights during the winter season. But the dictates of fashion precluded any real appreciation of the music, as fashion required that one not enter one's box until the end of the first act. Then, during the second interval, one made conversation with one's friends in the neighboring boxes. Then, before the house lights dimmed for the third act—so that the departure could be observed by the less fortunate in the stalls below—one grandly left the opera and went home.

At Mrs. Astor's Fifth Avenue house, the evenings were equally ritualized. Foregathering for dinner was at seven, and an invitation to dinner with the Astors meant arriving at *seven*, not a moment later. If too early, one waited in one's carriage outside the door and alighted to ring the bell at clockstroke. This meant that all the guests arrived at once, and proceeded into the house in single file. The gentlemen wore white tie and tails, and the ladies long gowns and their best jewels. The ladies took their wraps to a downstairs cloakroom, and the gentlemen took theirs upstairs. In the gentlemen's cloakroom, white envelopes were arranged on a silver tray, a gentleman's name on each envelope. Inside was a card with a lady's name on it—the lady he was to escort in to dinner. The ladies and gentlemen then reassembled downstairs, and there their hostess received them in her black wig and black dress which might be adorned with "the costliest necklace of emeralds and diamonds in America," or "the finest sapphire."

When the receiving line broke up, a butler appeared with a tray, and cocktails were served. There was never a choice of drinks. Mrs. Astor preferred something called a Jack Rose, and a Jack Rose was therefore what was offered, one to a guest in a small sherry-sized glass. A maid then entered with a tray of canapés, again one apiece. No one would have dreamed of asking for a second canapé, much less a second drink. In exactly fifteen minutes dinner was announced. At the table were printed place cards and menus, each embossed with the Astor crest, outlining the courses through the appetizer, soup, fish, meat or game, salad, cheese and fruit, dessert and coffee, with perhaps a lemon *sorbet* somewhere in the middle "to cleanse the palate." Of course, each course was adorned with an appropriate wine.

Dinner lasted two hours, and through it all, in addition to keeping track of what one was saying to one's dinner partner, it was necessary to keep an attentive eye on the hostess to catch the exact moment when she "changed the conversation." When Mrs. Astor shifted the focus of her attention from the dinner partner on her right to the person on her left, the entire dinner table had to turn heads with her. At approximately half past nine, Mrs. Astor rose, and the table did likewise. The ladies and gentlemen then separated—the men to the library for brandy and cigars, the ladies to the adjacent drawing room for a ladylike glass of mirabelle liqueur and gossip. In the library, the consumption of brandy was usually rapid and enthusiastic; it was the first chance the men had had all evening for solid alcoholic stimulation. Then, in exactly half an hour a butler opened the doors between the two rooms, and the gentlemen joined the ladies for another thirty minutes. At half past ten, Mrs. Astor rose again, the signal that the party was over.

The new Mrs. Oliver Cromwell had almost immediately become pregnant, and her first child, a daughter, was born in 1890. Two more children followed, both boys. Though her face was still smooth and beautiful, childbearing thickened Eva's figure somewhat. Still, it was not a matronly figure, and, with the aid of corsetières, she was able to achieve the hour-glass silhouette that was very much the fashion of the day—full-bosomed, full-hipped, with a tightly cinched-in waist. Ward McAllister died in 1893 and, though she did not yet realize it, Caroline Astor's star was beginning to set on the New York social horizon; her last important ball was held in the spring of 1897. Now it was possible for Eva Cromwell to do some important entertaining of her own.

Like many of his male contemporaries in Mrs. Astor's group, Oliver Cromwell's occupation was somewhat loosely defined. His father had died and left him a rich man. He was "in finance" and he "kept an office" —consisting of a secretary, a stock ticker, and a telephone—downtown, where he "managed his investments." Unlike the Philadelphia financier Edward T. Stotesbury, whom Eva would meet later on, Oliver Cromwell did not seem to have a lucky streak. Then, too, as America entered the twentieth century, panics on Wall Street began to occur with alarming frequency. In 1903 there was the so-called rich man's panic, caused by manipulators in U.S. Steel stock, when Steel plunged from $58 to $8 a share, taking most of the market with it. Then, four years later, the panic of 1907 threatened to wreck the whole fabric of the financial community. (Acting almost singlehandedly in October of that year, J. P. Morgan managed to avert a depositors' run on a number of leading U.S. banks; among the handful of financiers Morgan turned to were John D. Rockefeller, E. H. Harriman, and Edward Stotesbury.)

Through all these vicissitudes, Oliver Cromwell plunged ahead in the stock market, sending good money after bad and displaying all the desperate traits of a compulsive gambler. Alarmed, Eva begged her husband to move the family to Washington, on the probably naïve assumption that if she could physically remove him from the Wall Street area she could curb his speculative fever. It is also possible that she had begun to weary of the tedious predictability of New York parties, for which Mrs. Astor's continued to set the tone. And so the move to the capital was made.

In Washington, of course, Eva had many important social contacts. Her father's former partner was Chief Justice, and Washington, under the cheerful administration of President Teddy Roosevelt—sparked by the spirited antics of his irrepressible daughter Alice—was a merry place. Alice Roosevelt and Eva's daughter Louise were about the same age, and were invited to many of the same parties, and Eva and Oliver Cromwell were an immediate social success. They were taken up by the international diplomatic set, and it was here that Eva began to blossom into full flower as a hostess. Her parties were much gayer and less constrained than Mrs. Astor's. Guests chattered in both French and English. Champagne flowed. The hostess's personality was as sparkling and effervescent as Caroline Astor's had been dour and flat, and Eva was able to demonstrate another extraordinary talent: the ability, in a roomful of hundreds of people, to remember the name of every guest and, in most cases, the names of their children. Her sense of personal theatre was beginning to emerge.

Then, in 1909, tragedy struck. Oliver Cromwell suffered a series of strokes, the third of which was fatal. He had been sixty-one, and Eva was a widow at forty-four. The press reported that Eva had inherited "three houses" and an "ample fortune," but two of the three houses had never existed, and the fortune—though there was enough for Eva to live on comfortably—was far from ample. It had been seriously drained by her husband's financial misadventures. Eva went into deep mourning and seclusion.

Early in the spring of 1910, at the suggestion of friends who were concerned about her continuing depression, Eva Cromwell decided to take a trip to Europe with her nineteen-year-old daughter. The trip was intended to take Eva's mind off her loss. It would "give her something to do." It was assumed, of course, that Eva's brilliant social career was over.

In fact, it was just beginning.

2

PHILADELPHIA, MEET MRS. CROMWELL

By 1910, Edward T. Stotesbury was already known as "the richest man at Morgan's." The *wunderkind* who had started his banking career as a lowly janitor-clerk had not disappointed those men who first spotted his financial genius and promoted him upward, Anthony J. Drexel and J. Pierpont Morgan. Officially, Stotesbury was now the resident senior partner of Drexel and Company of Philadelphia, but he was also a senior partner of J. P. Morgan & Company in New York—"Morgan's man in Philadelphia," as he was often called. Actually, of course, the Morgan and Drexel banks were themselves a partnership, making Stotesbury a double partner. It was not as confusing as it sounded: Morgan ran New York and Stotesbury ran Philadelphia. When necessary, the two men used each other's services.

Stotesbury had been born in Philadelphia of an Episcopalian father and a Quaker mother, and he had been raised in the stern discipline of the Society of Friends. He was a short, dapper man, proud of his trim figure and carefully clipped moustache, and in dress—outside the office, at least —he was something of a fashion plate, favoring high collars, flowing foulard neckties, English-cut tweed jackets, and spotless white flannel trousers. As a young man he had started collecting watches, and as he grew wealthy this collection had become a truly princely one. He had also made himself an expert on gems and precious stones, and this collection too had become valuable. Horsemanship was another enthusiasm, and he maintained a stable of handsome trotting horses. In the office, of course, he was bankerly and sober, all business and humorless. Socially, on the other hand, he could be gracious and charming and even, in his dignified way, amusing.

He had been married quite young, in 1873 at age twenty-four, to a pretty Quaker girl named Fanny Butcher. Eight years later, in 1881, Fanny Stotesbury had died after giving birth to their second child. He had been left a widower at thirty-two, with two small daughters, one of them an infant. From that time he had lived alone in his big dark house on Walnut Street, "south of Market," where fashionable Philadelphia lived. Young and handsome, single and rich, he was a popular extra man at Philadelphia dinner parties. Even though he had often let it be known that he would never marry again, the newspapers, noting his imposing eligibility, were always "linking" Edward Stotesbury's name with this young woman or that. In his roguish way, by never denying these persistent romantic rumors, he encouraged them. Early in 1909 the second of his two daughters married. Now, save for the servants, he was truly alone in the Walnut Street house. It must have seemed very large and very empty.

Accompanying Eva Cromwell to her European sailing in 1910 was William Eldridge, an old family friend and the godfather of her younger son. Friends had long suspected that Eldridge might have had a romantic interest in Eva, though he was far too much of a gentleman to admit it, and on that chilly spring day, after Eldridge had got Eva settled in her stateroom and the two were strolling on the deck waiting for the whistle to signal that it was time for all visitors to go ashore, an event occurred —coincidence, luck, trick of fate—that would remove Eva from William Eldridge's future forever. Whom should Eldridge spot, also strolling on the deck, but his old friend Ned Stotesbury, the Philadelphia banker, who was on his way to Europe on business. Eldridge promptly introduced the two, and suggested that they might enjoy each other's company on the voyage. Thus the widower of twenty-nine years and the widow of just a few months were thrown together in that most romantic of settings, an ocean crossing. Ned Stotesbury, from all reports, was immediately smitten.

For Eva, meeting Ned Stotesbury must have involved a sense of *déjà vu*. He was almost exactly the same age her husband had been when he died. And though he was shorter than Cromwell—a shade shorter, in fact, than Eva—there was otherwise a strong physical resemblance. Also, with his proper manners and his pious Quaker ways—he still occasionally used "thee" instead of "you"—Ned Stotesbury may have reminded Eva of her father. In any case, before the pair debarked at Cherbourg to go their separate ways, they had fallen in love.

Obviously, for Eva's sake, a "decent interval" had to elapse between her first husband's death and the announcement of her remarriage. This came some eighteen months later, in early December of 1911.

Obviously, too, some noses would be placed permanently out of joint by this news in Philadelphia, where there were plenty of attractive widows who would have been not at all reluctant to accept a proposal from the city's richest citizen. While the newspapers proclaimed the engagement in banner headlines, Philadelphia society braced for an "outsider" and an upstart. Who, after all, *was* this Mrs. Cromwell? She was associated with three cities which Philadelphia had always held in low esteem. Born in Chicago, she had dazzled social New York and political Washington. With no Philadelphia credentials whatsoever, she had snapped up Philadelphia's richest single man. Eva Cromwell, if she was aware of it, might have been alerted to the opposition she would soon encounter by a headline in the *Bulletin* which soothingly reassured its readers that

MRS. CROMWELL IS "ENTIRELY CHARMING"

as though to put down rumors that she was only partly charming. The story went on, in the same patronizing vein, to predict that the new Mrs. Stotesbury would be "every bit as popular" in Philadelphia as she had been in New York and Washington. Did the *Bulletin* reporter slyly realize that this sort of thing was certain to raise the hackles of Old Philadelphia? Philadelphians were not going to be told whom they would and would not like.

"Philadelphians" here is used advisedly. In *Philadelphia Gentlemen: The Making of a National Upper Class*, the historian E. Digby Baltzell writes, "Within the fashionable and sometimes snobbish world of Proper Philadelphia . . . there are, of course, a few 'old families' who consider themselves, and are reverently so considered by many others, to be 'first families.' In the local upper-class vernacular, these 'first families' are known simply as 'Philadelphians.' One may have been born in Philadelphia, and one's ancestors may have been born there since colonial times, without ever presuming to call oneself a 'Philadelphian,' at least within the city's loftiest circles. This rather esoteric use of the term 'Philadelphian' is altogether confusing to the outsider." In other words, not all Philadelphians are *Philadelphians*; that distinction is left for the few.

Obviously, Eva Cromwell was not a *Philadelphian*. Neither, for that matter, was her future husband, even though, as Baltzell points out, he was born there. For one thing, no individual of the Quaker persuasion, no matter how industrious or prosperous he might be, was ever admitted to the ranks of Philadelphianism: this was a rule of thumb, unalterable as the course of the Schuylkill River. Furthermore, Philadelphia would never forget that Edward Stotesbury, though he might be the richest man in town, had started his career as a $16-a-month clerk; he was a man who *worked*. One of the earliest standards for admission to the *Social Register* was this: "One must not be 'employed'; one must make application; and one must be above reproach."

Even on this last score Ned Stotesbury had a black mark against his name, having managed, innocently enough, to offend the city's most prestigious family, the Biddles. When Anthony J. Drexel was still head of the bank, his daughter Emily had married Edward Biddle, and Drexel had brought his son-in-law into the business, giving him a partnership. Fiske Kimball, in his memoir of the Stotesbury family, wrote of an episode that occurred not long afterward, and that illustrated the high esteem in which Mr. Drexel held young Stotesbury:

> One day . . . Biddle came to Drexel saying, "Your clerk has insulted me. Either he or I must go." "What clerk?" croaked Drexel. "Stotesbury." "Then you'd better go." And go Edward Biddle did.

It was a gesture that cost Edward Biddle many millions of dollars.

At least two Philadelphia institutions exist only for Philadelphians in the Baltzell sense. One is the Philadelphia Assembly, a debutante ball—but really much more than that, since so much weight and importance are attached to Assembly invitations—which was established as an annual event in 1748, making it the oldest organized ball in the United States. Both of Edward Stotesbury's daughters, by virtue of having married Philadelphians, had been rewarded with Assembly invitations. Edward Stotesbury himself had never been invited.

The second is the Philadelphia Club, the oldest men's club in America, membership in which, as Digby Baltzell puts it, is "the hallmark of gentlemanly antecedents and business accomplishment." In Philadelphia, Edward Stotesbury belonged to many clubs, including the Merion Cricket Club, the Philadelphia Cricket Club, the Philadelphia Art Club, the Radnor Hunt, the Germantown Cricket Club, the Racquet Club, the Rabbit Club, the Rose Tree Hunt, the Pennsylvania Club, the Corinthian Yacht Club, the Philadelphia Country Club, the Huntingdon Valley Country Club, the Bachelor Barge Club, the Farmers' Club, and the Union League Club. As a clubman, he was unquestionably popular, and he served five full terms as president of the Union League.

But two club invitations, the top two, eluded him: the Rittenhouse Club and the Philadelphia Club. Then at last came an invitation to join the lesser of the two, the Rittenhouse. With this, Ned Stotesbury may have felt that he was finally making some real headway against Philadelphia snobbery because, after all, the Rittenhouse was considered the final steppingstone into the Philadelphia. Everyone taken into the Rittenhouse was eventually taken into the Philadelphia; it would only be a matter of time. But the ultimate invitation that should have been forthcoming never came. Edward T. Stotesbury had been snubbed. It was Philadelphia's pointed way of telling him that he could come just so far toward joining the ranks of Philadelphians. But no farther. Ever.

Between the December 1911 announcement of the Cromwell-Stotesbury nuptials and the January 18, 1912, wedding itself, newspapers across the country—and particularly in Philadelphia—were crammed with details of the impending event. The wedding was described as "socially important" and "one of the most important in this country . . . in several years." Wisely, probably, Eva chose to be married in the drawing room of her Washington house on New Hampshire Avenue. It is doubtful whether Philadelphia would have been able to choke it down. It was certainly a glittering occasion. President William Howard Taft was among the guests. J. P. Morgan, away in Europe on business, had sent regrets, but his wife, son, and daughter were there to represent him and so was his gift, a diamond necklace set in platinum with a center pendant "the size of a robin's egg," according to the *Bulletin*. It was said to have cost $500,000. Ned Stotesbury's gift to his bride was a $100,000 sapphire necklace, plus a rope of pearls so long that, if worn as a single strand, it would have extended to the floor. During the engagement Ned Stotesbury had also spent some $2,000,000 refurbishing the Walnut Street house for Eva's arrival. If the sheer expenditure of money is any indication of the extent of one's devotion, Ned Stotesbury adored Eva.

Following the ceremony, the newlyweds boarded a private "palace" railway car for Palm Beach, where they dallied for about a month, staying at the Breakers Hotel. In the newspapers the honeymoon was reported to be "quiet," but even the quietness and uneventfulness of it was chronicled daily in the press. Desperate for Stotesbury news, even the stately *New York Times* was driven to write about how, during the Stotesburys' Palm Beach stay, two new dances, the Bunny Hug and the Turkey Trot, "took the fashionable colony by storm." The Stotesburys, it was assumed, were ipso facto taken by storm.

Meanwhile, Philadelphia waited. The trouble was, there was no clear consensus on how the new Mrs. Stotesbury should be treated. Would it be simplest merely to snub her? That might prove unwise, as Mrs.

Stotesbury appeared to have powerful friends—United States Presidents, the nation's most powerful banker—at her beck and call. Perhaps it would be better to test her, put her through a social probationary period, let her show her colors, reveal the extent of her ambitions. The mood of the city grew tense as the news came, early in February, that the bridal pair were winding up their Florida stay and preparing to return home.

In most successful dramas of the early twentieth century, the curtain did not rise to reveal the heroine, the star, sitting on a sofa in center stage. It rose, instead, on a butler and a parlor maid discussing the peccadilloes of the mistress of the house, who was expected home at any moment from some long journey and some unusual experience. The maid might go to the window, part the curtains: Could this be she arriving now? No, it was only a porter delivering trunks. A sound of voices offstage: This must be she at last. No, it is only the Australian cousins who have come to ask her an important favor. The cousins enter, fuss and wring their hands. What can be keeping her? The maid makes a few last passes at the furniture with her feather duster. The butler straightens his tie and arranges the sherry glasses. The audience, teased and tantalized with suspense beyond endurance, strains forward in its seats. Then, all at once, through the door she sweeps and stands there, looking up at the key light.

This was the way Eva Stotesbury orchestrated her entrance into Philadelphia, her "debut" before its society. She and Ned Stotesbury slipped into town quietly, unnoticed by the press, secured themselves in the newly decorated Walnut Street house, and only after they had arrived let Philadelphia learn that Eva was there and waiting in the wings for her proper cue. That came on February 12, when it was learned that the Stotesburys had taken seats for the opera that evening. In the event, the house was packed, but not for the performance. Society reporters, each eager to scoop the next, filed their stories in advance of the event. One wrote that Eva was twenty minutes early, another that she was half an hour late. Actually, unlike Mrs. Astor, Eva and Ned arrived precisely on time.

"Scores of opera glasses" were immediately trained upon her. Her appearance, according to the press, drew "audible" comments. Her majestic figure was swathed in a dress of white satin "with a net of silver and crystal spangles." Over this she threw a long purple opera cloak with heavy swags of white fox fur at the collar and cuffs. On her bosom lay the Stotesbury pearls, looped in four coils, and above these, at her throat, were the Morgan diamonds. But the climax of her costume was a diamond tiara, "the most beautiful ever seen at the Metropolitan Opera House, or at the Academy of Music, for that matter," declared the *Bulletin*. The *Inquirer*'s headline was typical: MRS. STOTESBURY IS SEEN AT OPERA. The *Inquirer* went on to predict that the new Mrs. Stotesbury would "doubt-less . . . assume a commanding position in local society corresponding to that she occupied . . . in Washington."

The *Inquirer* was wrong. Diamonds and pearls alone could not make a Philadelphian, nor could all the breathless publicity in the world. Philadelphia would have the last word on Eva, one way or the other. Did Eva Stotesbury realize even then, as the necks craned and the opera glasses were trained on her, and as, during the intervals, opera goers jammed into the narrow aisle behind the Stotesbury box for an even closer look at her, that those in "a commanding position in local society" were viewing her as an interloper, a creature from a strange and hostile planet?

A few days later, however, she must have known. It was announced that neither Edward Stotesbury nor his bride would be receiving invitations to Philadelphia's 1912–13 Assembly season.

3

THE RING-MISTRESS

ONE OF THE MANY unusual things about Philadelphia is that it is a city that doesn't mind making fun of itself. When a New Yorker is chided or ridiculed about his city, he springs angrily to its defense. So does a Chicagoan, San Franciscan, or Houstonian. A Philadelphian merely smiles pleasantly and says, "But that's the way we are here."

A number of funny stories Philadelphians tell on themselves are repeated so often over the years that one wonders whether any of them was ever true. Take, for example, the one about the Philadelphia debutante who, standing in the receiving line at the Assembly, suddenly feels the elastic in her panties give way and feels the garment slip to her ankles. Undeterred, she stoops, picks the garment up, stuffs it in her purse, and continues shaking hands. This story is intended to illustrate Philadelphian *sang-froid*. The only trouble is that so many former Philadelphia debutantes insist it occurred at their debut that one can only conclude it may have been an annual event, or the elastic in Philadelphia is particularly flimsy stuff.

There are also a number of stories about how Eva and Ned Stotesbury got to the Assembly that year, because, in the end, they went. One version has it that the Stotesburys simply crashed the party, and that the invited guests were so flabbergasted by their temerity that no one knew what to do about it. Another tale insists that Ned Stotesbury threatened, "If my wife and I are not invited to the Assembly, I'll call in all the commercial paper in Philadelphia and ruin everybody." A second version of the threat is that Stotesbury said, "If we're not invited, I'll move Drexel and Company and all its business to New York." Still another has it that, if not invited, he threatened to fire "all his aristocratic young clerks."

According to a fifth tale, Stotesbury resorted to bribery, saying to one of his brokers, who had powerful Assembly connections, "If you'll get us an invitation, you'll be the next head of Drexel's."

Whatever actually occurred, the point of all the stories is the same: pressure was applied; the Stotesburys were not wanted at the Assembly, but they wangled their way in anyway. Somehow, the Philadelphians had been forcefully reminded that they needed the Stotesburys as much as the Stotesburys needed them. A bargain was struck—which is of course a little different from "acceptance" of the Stotesburys.

A postscript to the various Stotesbury-Assembly stories is that Ned and Eva were so thrilled with their invitation that they at once had it framed and hung under a spotlight in the entrance foyer of Whitemarsh Hall. This, however, could not possibly have been true because Whitemarsh Hall did not exist until a number of years later.

And through the thorny undergrowth of tales, one wonders: Why did Edward Stotesbury, for it must have been he, act in such a way as to insure that word of the grudging invitation would travel through the catty annals of Philadelphia society for the next half-century? All the stories varied the same theme—and did nothing to enhance the Stotesburys' position but, rather, forever tarnished Eva's reputation. The only plausible explanation must be that Ned loved Eva so much that he would have done anything to get her invited to the city's most exclusive party. But he underestimated Philadelphians' long memories.

Eva Stotesbury, meanwhile, was not a limited woman. She realized soon enough that she not only had caught Philadelphia's biggest fish but also had moved back with him into enemy territory. Wisely, she saw that she needed another ally besides her doting husband, and her choice was a clever one. She did not choose a member of Philadelphia's genteel society to be her aide, mentor, and amanuensis. She selected, instead, a forthright young Irishwoman named Mrs. Edward J. MacMullan.

Katherine MacMullan was from Philadelphia, but she was by no means a Philadelphian. Her background—or so it was said—was humble, though no one knew for sure because Katherine MacMullan preferred to keep her background out of the conversation. No one knew for certain, either, what had become of Mr. MacMullan, unless, as a local wag suggested, "She ate him." All that was certain was that Katherine MacMullan was a striking-looking woman, with flaming red hair, an aquiline nose, boundless energy, and an Irish temper. She was twenty-some years younger than Eva Stotesbury and, as an outsider looking in, she had studied the rites and rituals of Philadelphia's ruling class for years. She knew who liked whom, who hated whom, and she knew where several embarrassing family skeletons were buried. She understood the politics of social maneuvering, especially as it was done in Philadelphia, and knew that there were more subtle forms of intimidation than threats and bribery. "My rules are simple," she once said. "Manners. Good manners. Rudimentary good manners are all I ask. There's little enough elegance left in the world. Are a few good manners too much to ask for?"

Eva Stotesbury had no need for lessons in good manners, but when Katherine MacMullan first offered her services to Eva, in the loosely defined capacity of social secretary, she did provide a few other inside tips. She knew, for example, that whereas Washington's society might be based on government, and New York's on money, Philadelphia's was essentially about food. Philadelphians took special pride in their chefs and menus, and were fond of supposing that the meals served in Philadelphia's private homes were among the finest in the world. Furthermore, there were certain regional dishes—terrapin and canvasback duck among them —that were special favorites. Finally, Katherine MacMullan—"Mrs. Mac," as Eva was soon calling her—knew that Philadelphians prided themselves on "giving the most beautiful parties of any city in the country," even though, as Mrs. Mac liked to say tartly, "They don't." Eva Stotesbury's social star would rise or set, Mrs. Mac advised, depending on the quality of her entertainments.

Later, Katherine MacMullan would confess to having been "as nervous as a cat with kittens" when diagramming the seating arrangement for Eva Stotesbury's first large party, planning the menu, overseeing the table settings, the flowers, and the music. Nervous she may have been, but it didn't show in the evening that resulted. Spurred, no doubt, by curiosity about the redecoration of the Walnut Street house, society turned out in force, and the party was pronounced a complete success.

One of Mrs. MacMullan's "inventions" for that first evening was a rearrangeable dinner-seating chart. She cut a large piece of poster board to represent the Stotesbury dining table, and around the edges of the board she made little slits representing the chairs. Cards bearing the guests' names could then be inserted in the slits. Thus the hostess could inspect the seating plan and, if she wished, reseat her table simply by shifting the cards around. After each dinner the charts were dated and filed for reference. Also filed with each seating chart were such important bits of information as what the menu had been; which gown, shoes and jewels the hostess had worn; and what flowers had been used in the

centerpieces. Soon Katherine MacMullan and Eva Stotesbury were working so well together that the relationship became almost symbiotic. Quite
often Eva had no idea who might be coming to her dinners until Mrs.
Mac had given her a quick pre-party briefing.

Soon, as Eva's *arbiter elegantiarum*, Katherine MacMullan had made
herself indispensable. One of her rules was that, on the afternoon of a
party, the hostess herself should have absolutely nothing to do except
take a nap, followed by a long hot bath in salts, followed by dressing for
dinner. Katherine MacMullan turned into a furious list maker, listing in
detail the menus and flowers and guests of each of Eva's parties, so that
there would never be an exact duplication. She also catalogued Eva's
dresses and jewels, so that what the hostess wore would never be repeated
for an occasion involving the same people, and the elaborate seating charts
were filed and indexed so that no two guests would ever be seated together
a second time at a Stotesbury party. Mrs. Mac could also be peppery
with her boss, and Eva grew to enjoy the occasional scoldings. "She's
such a bear!" Eva would exclaim happily when Mrs. Mac would tell her
which necklace should be worn with which gown. One of Eva's difficulties was a particular diamond and emerald tiara, so heavy with stones, she
said, that whenever she wore it she got a stiff neck. "You deserve to suffer
with that much jewelry on your head," said Mrs. Mac. "Either attach a
few helium balloons to it or wear it without complaining!" The same tiara
had a tendency to list to one side and fall over Eva's ear. And so Katherine
MacMullan stationed herself behind Eva at parties and, whenever the
tiara began to slip, nudged it back into place again.

Emboldened by her early success, Mrs. Mac began to develop more
imaginative ideas for parties, and Eva's "theme evenings" became the talk
of Philadelphia. If Philadelphia prided itself on splendid parties, Eva
reasoned, she would produce parties more splendid than Philadelphia had
ever seen. And the Stotesbury-MacMullan parties were just that—theatrical productions. Katherine MacMullan, for example, frequently introduced wildlife into her décors, releasing flocks of white doves, or, in one
instance, four hundred canaries. Once a herd of peacocks, plumes fanned
regally, was paraded across the Stotesbury ballroom.

As the fame of Eva's parties grew, so did the span of her social horizon.
Seated dinners for forty were her usual dos, and she often gave as many
as three a week. There were also frequent teas and receptions, for as
many as six hundred and fifty people. House parties were common, too,
and guests were brought in from Washington and New York by private
trains. Soon it was estimated that the Stotesburys entertained, on an

average, two hundred people a week and that, all told, a hundred thousand guests had crossed the threshold of their house. Eva had become one of the most extraordinary hostesses in the world, and even the State Department began turning to her for advice on protocol and the proper way to entertain visiting foreign dignitaries. Through it all, Eva's composure was complete, as, bejeweled, she spoke to everyone, remembering every name. "A nervous hostess makes an unhappy guest," she used to say.

Does this mean that Eva Stotesbury had a hundred thousand friends? Alas, it does not. Many on Eva's long list of guests were among the most cynical and hypocritical people in the city. "It was sad," Katherine MacMullan recalled many years later, "but I could see perfectly well what was going on. The way people would grovel to her for her invitations, go to her house and gorge themselves on her wonderful food, and then start disparaging and ridiculing her the minute they got outside the door, talking about how the Stotesburys were vulgar and *nouveaux riches*. Often they didn't even wait to get outside the door. They'd come in, shake her hand, kiss her cheek, and say, 'My dear, you look absolutely ravishing tonight,' and three minutes later they'd be whispering with their friends, 'Have you ever seen such a pretentious necklace?' It was disgusting, I thought."

Was Eva herself ever aware of this? "Oh, yes," said Mrs. MacMullan. "She knew it, and it amused her in a grim sort of way. She had no illusions about what people said. She knew that it was simply jealousy. She had more money than they did, that was all it was, and she spent it better than they did, and she and he dressed better than they did and looked better than they did. She had no use for the whole idea of Philadelphia 'society'—actually, she considered many of those people a dangerous and destructive element in the city. In her own way, she succeeded in exposing those people for what they were. That gave her a certain sense of power. After all, no matter what they said about her, they were still dancing to her tune. It was a circus, and she was the ring-master."

Ned Stotesbury had begun buying paintings before he met Eva, and he owned a number of Gainsboroughs and Romneys. As a wealthy collector he quite naturally came to the attention of the legendary art dealer and supersalesman Joseph Duveen. Duveen, as he had managed to do with other rich men of the era, had become Stotesbury's mentor of taste in art and, in the process, was selling him a number of costly pieces. Now it was natural that Duveen should take Eva under his protective wing as well. Soon he was guiding her in purchasing paintings and sculpture as well as furniture, tapestries, rugs, china, crystal, gold and silver services, bibelots, and other *objets d'art*. It wasn't long, under the guidance of Duveen's suave persuasion, before Eva had acquired more art and furniture than the Walnut Street mansion would comfortably hold. It was Duveen who now began persuading Eva that the scale of her entertaining demanded a larger proscenium—a truly princely residence, a palace. With more space for her activities, of course, there would be more rooms for Joseph Duveen to fill. Eva's two-story ballroom on Walnut Street was already the biggest in the city. This did not mean, however, Duveen suggested, that she did not deserve a bigger one.

Eva mentioned Duveen's suggestion to her husband, who immediately liked the idea. Late in 1915 he purchased three hundred and sixty-five acres in semisuburban Chestnut Hill, and architects began submitting sketches. Joseph Duveen, as usual, had made his suggestion at precisely the right psychological moment. J. P. Morgan had been appointed purchasing agent for the Allies, and the profits of the firm were enormous. In the years 1915 and 1916, for example, Ned Stotesbury's personal income had topped $7,000,000 a year. The supply of money now appeared to be endless. Why shouldn't his beloved Eva be given her personal Taj Mahal—the biggest, grandest, costliest, most beautiful estate Philadelphia (or almost any other place) had ever seen? It was only fitting.

4

MORE STATELY MANSIONS

"I STAY HERE," Eva Stotesbury once confided to a friend, "only because of Ned. Philadelphia is Ned's town. I really don't like it much." Perhaps she felt that she had earned the city's most imposing castle as due compensation for the way Philadelphia had treated her. Or perhaps, in the five years—from 1916 to 1921—that it took to build Whitemarsh Hall, with Eva supervising every detail, Eva was merely busying herself with a project that kept her mind off Philadelphia.

Whitemarsh Hall was six stories tall and had three basements. There were two mahogany-paneled passenger elevators, and a dozen more for freight and service. There were a hundred and forty-seven rooms scattered across a hundred thousand square feet of floor space, and if that much floor space is difficult to envision, it amounted to approximately two and a half acres. In volume, the house comprised 1,500,000 cubic feet. There were forty-five bathrooms. To communicate from one part of the house to another a commercial telephone switchboard and operator were required. In the cavernous basements were bakeries, laundries, a tailor shop, a barber shop, a carpenter's shop, a gymnasium, even a movie theatre. Forty-five live-in servants were required to staff the house, and other full- or part-time "dailies" came in from the village. Whitemarsh Hall employed a full-time carpenter and a full-time electrician. Eva even had her own resident hairdresser and couturier, and each house guest was assigned his or her personal chauffeur. There was garage space for eighteen automobiles. Servants' rooms were supplied for house guests' servants. Outside, to care for the three hundred acres of formal gardens, seventy gardeners were employed.

In the background of this huge creation lurked Joseph Duveen. He had recommended the architect, Horace Trumbauer; the landscape designer, Jacques Gréber of Paris; and the interior decorator, Sir Charles Allom of London, who had helped George V and Queen Mary redo some of the principal rooms at Buckingham Palace and Windsor Castle. Duveen's firm had also supplied most of the furniture, rugs, and tapestries, a collection of five hundred paintings, and monumental sculptures by Pajou, Tassaert, and Lecomte, as well as two Clodion groups whose only matching pairs were in the Louvre. One fifty-three-foot Isfahan carpet which lined the Great Hall, or ballroom, had cost Eva $90,000. Eva once said of Duveen, "I can never be grateful enough to him. He taught me how to live"—a remark that was widely ridiculed in Philadelphia, where people added, "And he also taught her how to spend." Eva Stotesbury countered this with a little joke of her own. Admitting that she had little business sense, she said, "The only successful financial transaction I ever made in my life was when I married Mr. Stotesbury."

Whitemarsh Hall was opened with a great party in October 1921. The entire social and banking community of Philadelphia turned out for it, plus many guests from New York and a handsome sprinkling of titled foreigners. Forty extra footmen, it was said, had been hired to serve the party, and in the corner niches of one of the two rotundas, four bars were set up—one for cocktails, one for whiskey, one for champagne, and one for other sorts of drinks—a lavish thumb to the nose at Prohibition. Four orchestras—two seated, and two strolling—played for dancing, and, as he often did, Ned Stotesbury, who had been a drummer boy in the Civil War, took a few turns on the drums.

Still, for all the gaiety and splendor, there were the usual sour comments. The Philadelphia aesthete Fiske Kimball, director of the Art Museum, appraising Mr. Duveen's work, said, "The furnishings made an impression of great magnificence. One scarcely realized how few of them were actually antique." Kimball also found fault with the flowers: "On an estate where flowers grew luxuriantly in parterres and green-houses, the roses in the drawing room . . . were silk, sprayed with perfume. Everywhere were English portraits, chiefly by Romney and Lawrence, which Duveen had unloaded on the Stotesburys at enormous prices." Other details of the evening sound like canards. It was said, for example, that Eva—who was so good at attaching names to faces—moved among her guests with "a typewritten catalogue" of the paintings in her hand in order to name the artist, title, and provenance of each piece. It was also said that, at the outset of the evening, guests were paraded past glass cases where her entire jewelry collection was displayed. (Eva never displayed her entire collection of jewelry to any guest, though, as we shall see, her husband did on one occasion.)

Not even Ned Stotesbury was spared the criticism. Philadelphian Nathaniel Burt wrote that Ned banged on the drums "when he got drunk," and that Stotesbury was the kind of man "who would give himself a testimonial dinner and then clap at the speeches," even though Stotesbury never did such a thing.

Naturally, the burning question on everyone's lips was how much Whitemarsh Hall had cost. No one could be so crass as to ask the host and hostess, and in the press the estimates varied wildly. It is also likely that Ned Stotesbury did not know exactly—it was to be his beautiful monument to Eva and her entertainments, and he had given her virtually a blank check. Perhaps the best estimate comes from Horace Lippincott, who was a close friend of Ned Stotesbury and who mentions a figure of around three million dollars, exclusive of furnishings and décor. These, of course, were pre–First World War dollars. It was a very expensive house.

And, though Philadelphians went right on accepting Ned's and Eva's invitations, the Philadelphia consensus was that it was all too much. Philadelphians preferred a more restrained expensiveness. To understand what Philadelphians admired, one would have had, just a few years back, to spend an evening in rural Penllyn, not far from Chestnut Hill, with the elderly Miss Anna Ingersoll.

Ingersolls, as they say, have been in Philadelphia forever—at least since Revolutionary times, when the first Ingersoll came down from Salem, Massachusetts, and settled there. They have produced seven generations of Philadelphia lawyers, bankers, civic leaders, and gentlemen. According to Philadelphia legend (and there is no way of ever knowing whether any of the legends occurred quite as told), Miss Anna, who was very beautiful and popular in her youth, never married because the young man she was in love with was a Jew. This made marriage out of the question, of course, and so, forbidden to marry the man she loved, Miss Anna chose to remain a spinster. (The man she loved, it is said, never married either.)

Penllyn is something of an Ingersoll family compound, and various Ingersoll houses are scattered across the rolling hills. Driving down the long graveled drive to Miss Anna's big old graystone house, one used to be able to see, in the rear-view mirror of one's automobile, a gardener appear with a rake to smooth the gravel that had just been disturbed by the passing of the car.

Tea with Miss Anna in her portrait-hung drawing room (all portraits of Ingersolls, of course, nothing that had been plucked from an English Stately Home by a voracious Joseph Duveen) in that not-so-long-ago day —we are talking here of the mid-1960s—was a merry, gossipy affair: who married whom, the Coxes, Chews, Peppers, Newbolds, Morrises, Ingersolls, Cadwalladers, and Pughs. The difference between the Pughs and the Pews, the Cadwalladers and the Cadwaladers, is far more than a matter of spelling. Sitting behind her huge silver tea service, pouring tea, offering tiny watercress sandwiches, bread-and-butter sandwiches on the thinnest bread, and little English biscuits from a Fortnum & Mason box, Miss Anna was a lively octogenarian. One by one her various relatives— brothers and their wives, cousins, nieces, nephews—would drop by for an afternoon visit with Miss Anna. Without missing a beat, tea time turned into the cocktail hour, with one of Miss Anna's brothers splashing a little domestic vermouth into the mouth of a Gilbey's gin bottle and shaking the mixture vigorously. The result, martinis at room temperature, was then poured from the gin bottle into empty glasses held in eager hands.

Dinner was equally unpretentious. Though the silver, laid with xylophone precision about the dinner plates, was of the heaviest—three-pronged forks, pistol-handled knives—and gleamed with that special deep, creamy luster that can be achieved only in old silver that is polished after every meal, the napkins were of a ten-cent-store paper variety. Also, though the dining table was of museum-quality wood, it was possible to spot, among the heavy silver epergnes and candelabra, a ketchup bottle and a French's mustard jar. This, after all, is Old Philadelphia. Because it knows who and what it is, it has no reason to apologize for anything.

At the mention of Eva Stotesbury's name, Anna Ingersoll's expression grew thoughtful—pleasantly thoughtful. "Oh, I knew Eva well," she said, choosing her words with great care. "I liked her *very* much. She was absolutely charming, and she gave wonderful parties. She was so—gracious, always. But, you see . . . well, she married Ned Stotesbury, of course. And Eva was very . . . very ambitious."

That, then, was Eva's fatal flaw: ambition. In Philadelphia, ambition had become a pejorative term.

James Henry Roberts Cromwell, the younger of Eva's two sons by her first marriage, was only ten years old when his father died, and since the age of eight he had attended the Fay School, a private boys' academy in Massachusetts. It was natural, after his mother's remarriage, that Jimmy Cromwell should call Ned Stotesbury "Father."

As head of—among other things—the Philadelphia & Reading Railroad, Ned Stotesbury had told his young stepson about a special railroad car, which was hitched on in front of the engine and was used to transport the railroad's directors on inspection tours of coal-mining operations in the northeastern part of the state. The coal companies were some of the railroad's most important customers, and Jimmy had begged his father to take him on one of these excursions. Finally, when Jimmy was fifteen, Stotesbury invited the boy along, saying, "Just don't get underfoot, and make yourself as inconspicuous as possible." And so Jimmy joined his father and the other members of the board for a trip to Mauch Chunk, the county seat of Carbon County, Pennsylvania, in the heart of the anthracite country.

"I had never seen poverty before," Jimmy Cromwell recalled many years later. "I was horrified. I had always assumed that everyone lived in houses like Whitemarsh Hall, but here were miners living in tiny shacks. The children had no shoes or stockings. The people were in rags—unwashed and sickly. In two of the little shanties we went in, coal was stored in the bathtubs." On the ride home, Jimmy seemed so unusually pensive that Stotesbury said to him, "What are you being so glum about?"

At home, Jimmy mentioned the experience to his mother, who quickly said, "You must speak to your father about this." The boy did so, and, after closing the study door and sitting the young man down, Ned Stotesbury began a long and rambling lecture that was as serious—and ultimately as confusing—as any parental explanation of the facts of life. "I want to explain this," Stotesbury began. "What you have seen is the price of competition. For example, in our coal business we're having trouble competing with oil as a fuel. Oil is cutting into our business, cutting into our profits. . . ." On and on he went for the better part of two hours, Jimmy Cromwell remembered, outlining his own capitalist theories on the American free enterprise system.

Later, Eva took her son aside and asked, "What did he tell you?" As best he could Jimmy Cromwell recounted what his father had said to him. "There is something I would like to add to that," his mother said at last. "Great wealth carries with it great responsibilities. It is the best part of the Christian ethic to take care of the underprivileged and less fortunate. Don't forget that if you don't, you may lose all your luxuries, because revolution is an indictment of the ruling class." It was an era, after all, when concepts like "wealth," "responsibilities," and "class" could all fit comfortably in the same sentence. Then Eva added, "Perhaps this will inspire you to devote your life to some form of public service."

Several years later, Jimmy Cromwell was dancing at the Washington's Birthday costume ball in Palm Beach, which officially marked, in those days, the end of the winter season. His fancy was caught by a young lady who had come dressed as a ballerina and who, he could not help noticing, had lovely legs. He presented himself to her. She was Delphine Dodge, the only daughter of Mr. and Mrs. Horace Dodge of Detroit, who were in the automobile business. A romance and courtship followed, and a wedding was announced for June 20, 1920.

The marriage was spectacular news: two enormous American fortunes were joining hands, and the union seemed absolutely dynastic—at least on the surface. Actually, the Dodges had no real social position in Detroit, and did not rank with such pre–internal combustion families as the Joys, Newberrys, and "old" Fords, no kin to Henry. Horace Dodge was a self-taught, self-made man, and his wife, Anna, was the daughter of a rough old Scottish sailor. Both Mr. and Mrs. Dodge had trouble speaking the King's English correctly, and Anna Dodge used to startle acquaintances by saying, "I helped make this fortune, too. I used to get up at six in the morning to fix Dad's breakfast and pack his lunch pail." Mrs. Dodge always called her husband "Dad," and he called her "Mother." Needless to say, the Dodges were overjoyed at the prospect of their daughter's union with not one but three important American families, the Cromwells, the Robertses, and the Stotesburys.

Naturally, Eva and Ned were invited to visit Rose Terrace, the Dodge estate in Grosse Pointe on the shore of Lake St. Clair. The house was large and the grounds were extensive, but Anna Dodge had had no Joseph Duveen to guide her hand and shape her taste. The furniture was heavy and ugly, the paintings on the walls were still-life reproductions, and the rooms were cluttered with pretentious bric-à-brac and a great deal of Tiffany glass. Next, Eva and Ned invited their future in-laws to Whitemarsh Hall, where the Dodges were goggle-eyed at what they saw. Horace Dodge, in particular, was impressed with Eva's jewelry, and begged to be shown it all. Ned Stotesbury—who even before meeting Eva had begun collecting precious stones—thereupon produced tray after tray of glittering gems.

Not long before the wedding Mr. Dodge took his future son-in-law aside. "Jim," he said, "I'm worried about Mother." "What about her?"

Cromwell wanted to know. "Well, Mother doesn't have the kind of pearls your mother has. In the church, people are going to notice that sort of thing. Where does your mother buy 'em?" Cromwell mentioned Cartier. "Never heard of him," Dodge said. "But get me an appointment with this fella." And so Cromwell arranged a meeting between Pierre Cartier, Horace Dodge, and himself.

At the meeting, Cartier—whom Mr. Dodge persistently called "Mr. Car-*teer*"—produced several trays of pearl necklaces. "No, no, Mr. Car-*teer*," said Mr. Dodge. "I want something bigger than that for Mother. Something to match Mrs. Stotesbury's pearls." Finally Cartier said, "Monsieur Dodge, I do have one very fine set. They belonged to the Empress Catherine." "Never heard of her," said Mr. Dodge, "but let's see 'em." Cartier then brought out a magnificent strand of pearls the size of robin's eggs. "That's more like it," said Mr. Dodge. "How much?" "Ah, Monsieur Dodge," said M. Cartier, "that necklace is one million dollars." "I'll take it," said Dodge, pulling out his checkbook and writing a check for $1,000,000.

Meanwhile, Anna Dodge had been carefully studying Whitemarsh Hall. Later she would hire Eva's architect and decorator and transform Rose Terrace in the image of the Stotesbury house.

Throughout the 1920s Eva and Ned Stotesbury entertained like mad. Eva liked to say that she had taught her husband "how to play," another comment that was greeted sneeringly in Philadelphia; the term "playboy" had come into fashion, carrying derisive overtones, and the image of a millionaire in his seventies cavorting across an endless series of ballrooms made Ned Stotesbury seem something of a caricature of the type. And it was true that, though Ned was at his office at Drexel's every morning at eight, most of the Stotesburys' evenings were spent in some form of fun. The wardrobes of jewels, furs, and gowns increased, and both Ned's and Eva's names now appeared regularly on "best-dressed" lists.

In the 1920s, however, one began to sense a note of hysteria, of barely controlled desperation, in Ned and Eva's social activities. It was as though they had seen that they had gone too far, but it was now too late to turn back, and all they could do was go even farther. The Stotesburys built another huge villa in Palm Beach, where "for lack of competition"—as Philadelphia chronicler Nathaniel Burt rather snidely put it—the Stotesburys became the winter colony's acknowledged social leaders and where their El Mirasol (The Sunflower) was the resort's largest house. (The name struck some people as odd and inappropriate; El Mirasol was the name of the Albuquerque hotel where Eva and her first husband had spent their honeymoon.)

In 1925 the Stotesburys decided to move on to the summer colony of Mount Desert Island, Maine, where Bar Harbor had long been a favorite resort for Old Philadelphians, and here Eva's behavior drew even more criticism. The house they bought had belonged to Alexander Cassatt, who had been president of the Pennsylvania Railroad, but when she toured her new acquisition Eva announced that it wasn't big enough. There were only fifteen servants' rooms; she needed forty. So she ordered the house torn down and a larger structure erected in its place, instructing her architect to have the place ready for occupancy the following summer. But when she returned in 1926, to find the place completed and furnished to the last detail, she walked through the result and it *still* wasn't big enough. Her husband, it seemed, wanted her to live on an ever-grander scale. "It won't do," she said. "Tear it down and build it over again, and this time I'll stay here and see that it's done properly." In the end, what was achieved was Wingwood House, the largest example of Colonial-style architecture in the State of Maine.

It was curious, because this sort of thing was not at all what Eva had originally said she wanted—"a cozy little retreat," "a cottage," where she and Ned could relax and enjoy each other's company away from the heavy social duties of Palm Beach. Instead, she had built another palace. But once again the *éminence grise* behind her actions was Joseph Duveen. Duveen had acquired roomfuls of English furniture from a titled Britisher and had succeeded in selling it all to the Stotesburys. Another expanded house was the only solution to where to put it.

"Of course Duveen overcharged her outrageously," Jimmy Cromwell, a tall, spry man in his eighties, says today. "But at least my mother knew she was getting good goods. I don't think Father ever read a book in his life, but Mother was always researching. If she was buying English furniture, she would read every book she could find on the subject. If she was buying a particular painter, she would dig up everything she could find on him. I used to tease her and call her the American Clipper, because she usually had a pair of scissors in her hand to cut out clippings from newspapers and antique and art magazines. Mother loved to *create* things. But what a lot of people who criticized her for being ostentatious never realized was that it wasn't *she* who insisted on living on that magnificent scale. It was he. Father was the show-off—not my mother. He was of a generation of men who wanted to show the whole world how important they were. And of course his firm was making so much money that

—well, today it would be downright embarrassing. His theory was: If you've got it, flaunt it."

Now, with a summer place in Maine and a winter place in Palm Beach, and with Katherine MacMullan in tow from place to place, Eva opened Whitemarsh Hall only for the late-spring and early-autumn seasons. At Bar Harbor, of course, it was assumed that the Stotesburys intended to establish themselves as the social leaders there as well. But this was something that the Old Philadelphians of Bar Harbor were not prepared to allow Eva and Ned to do. One by one, Chestons, Clarks, Lippincotts, Ingersolls, Newbolds, Morrises, and Thayers began moving out of Bar Harbor and reestablishing themselves at quieter, folksier Northeast Harbor, on the opposite side of the island. In fact, Wingwood House and the Stotesburys are often cited as the cause for the demise of Bar Harbor as a fashionable resort—though a great fire that ravaged Bar Harbor in 1947, and destroyed many of the summer mansions, also helped.

In the 1920s, of course, it was all right to be rich. Suddenly, it seemed, everyone was, and bankers traded stock tips with their bootblacks, and the extravagant doings of the wealthy were cheerfully, almost worshipfully, reported. In the 1920s, too, it was acceptable for a rich woman such as Eva Stotesbury to assume the role of a Lady Bountiful, which Eva did. Though she was generous to her Episcopalian church and to one or two other organized philanthropies, her favorite form of charity was what she called "the personal kind." She would, for example, personally deliver Thanksgiving turkeys to poor families of Philadelphia, and boxes of toys to their children at Christmastime. But when the Roaring Twenties ended in a roaring crash in October of 1929, and the nation awoke to a world of breadlines, being rich was no longer quite so fashionable, and women like Eva became—overnight—dreadful anachronisms. As the Depression deepened, Ned and Eva Stotesbury came under particularly vicious attack, led by a Philadelphia radio commentator named Boake Carter. In the terrible winter of 1932, Carter actually recommended over the air that a bomb be dropped on Whitemarsh Hall. The Stotesburys also heard that a band of starving citizens had been organized to besiege the house and put it to the torch. A terrified Ned and Eva, envisioning an angry proletarian mob storming their gates, immediately announced plans to close all their houses and move to Europe.

Meanwhile, all sorts of grim rumors circulated. Ned Stotesbury's fortune, once reckoned at $200,000,000, was now said to be down to $5,000,000. It was said that on the night before their departure all the Stotesbury servants had walked out on them while they sat at dinner. It was said that all the lights at Whitemarsh Hall had suddenly gone out, the implication being that the Stotesburys had been unable to pay their electric bill. Both stories were untrue. Fiske Kimball, visiting Ned and Eva on the morning of their sailing, found the house running as smoothly as always, the servants efficiently attending to the details of the trip, the lights working and the house electrician on duty. Looking about her magnificent estate for what might be the last time, Eva Stotesbury turned to her lawyer, Morris Bockius, and said with a certain gallantry, "Well, Morris, if we never come back we've had ten wonderful years of it." Later that year, however, they were back—not at Whitemarsh, but at Philadelphia's Barclay Hotel, where they gave their traditional New Year's Eve party in the hotel ballroom and danced, somewhat prematurely, to the strains of "Happy Days Are Here Again."

Fiske Kimball, meanwhile, had always assumed that the Stotesbury art collection would eventually go to the Philadelphia Art Museum, of which he was the distinguished head. Eva had often said, "We consider ourselves only the trustees of our collection for the public." But now, with New Deal taxes and increased inheritance levies—President Roosevelt's motto, it was said, was "Soak the rich"—eroding the fortunes of the wealthy, Kimball was apprehensive. By rights, he should have been sympathetic to the Stotesburys. An "outsider" himself, he had, like Ned Stotesbury, been rebuffed by the Philadelphia Club. (Kimball, furthermore, had made the fatal error of asking a friend to put him up for membership. When several months went by with no further word on the subject, Kimball approached the friend again. "I have tried," was the reply.) Instead, however, Kimball's attitude toward Ned and Eva was the fashionable one of toplofty condescension—at least when he was not in their presence. With them, of course, with his eyes on the collection, he was all smiles and flattery and blandishments. His hopes were revived in 1933, when Ned and Eva reopened Whitemarsh Hall and embarked on another season of entertaining as though unaffected by the Depression.

In 1936, when 38 percent of United States families had incomes of less than $1,000 a year—and when the Bureau of Labor Statistics had placed the poverty line at $1,330—the stock market suddenly enjoyed a sharp comeback. Capitalists cheered the fact that the Depression seemed at last over. Early in 1937, however, the market tumbled so precipitously that the crash of 1929–30 seemed almost minor. That winter, Eva—who Fiske noted waspishly "had been a very inactive member of our Committee"— invited Fiske and the members of the museum board to Whitemarsh Hall for lunch. Before sitting down, Kimball was alerted to the situation by one of Eva's secretaries, who murmured something about "these awful taxes, this awful Roosevelt, and the collection." During dessert, Eva sadly gave Kimball the bad news. Ned's will had had to be rewritten; in it, the collection was directed to be sold. "The collection may have to be my bread and butter," she said quietly.

Horace Dodge had died not long after his daughter's marriage to Jimmy Cromwell, and his widow had been devastated, seemingly unable to function without her husband at her side. Eva went immediately to her rescue, and for the better part of a year Anna Dodge lived with the Stotesburys at Whitemarsh Hall. If Philadelphia's reception to Eva had been frostily superior, it was as nothing compared with the way the city's worthies received the humbly bred and humbly spoken Mrs. Dodge. "But my mother simply didn't give a damn," says Jimmy Cromwell. "Mother was not a snob. She felt it was her *duty* to help take care of Anna." (It was a kindness which would one day be well repaid.) "Besides, Mother wasn't the only woman in Philadelphia who knew how to be a real lady. Two of her dearest friends in the city were Mrs. Alexander Biddle and Mrs. Alexander Van Rensselaer—who were hardly out of the bottom drawer. Both of them remained devoted to her to the very end." Jimmy Cromwell, who had started his business career with his stepfather's Drexel and Company, now turned his attention to the affairs of the Dodge Corporation. Among other things, he helped Anna Dodge orchestrate the sale of her Dodge stock, from which she realized $160,000,000. Eventually—though for a rather brief duration—Anna Dodge married a man named Hugh Dillman, and then embarked, throughout the Depression, on a career of spending that made anything the Stotesburys had done seem like child's play.

Jimmy and Delphine Dodge had been divorced in 1928, to his mother's sorrow, but the families had remained friends. Then, in 1935, Jimmy Cromwell made an even more spectacular marriage, to Doris Duke, whose father, James Buchanan Duke, had peddled tobacco with a team of two blind mules and parlayed this modest enterprise into the American Tobacco Company. Doris was only thirteen when her father died, and she inherited $70,000,000 along with a private railroad car named *Doris*. At the time of her marriage to Cromwell, she was twenty-three and, thanks to the shrewd management of her mother, Nanaline Inman Duke, Doris's fortune was worth $250,000,000.

Jimmy Cromwell had also, rather belatedly—he was thirty-six—embarked upon the career of public service his mother had envisioned for him. To the horror of his stepfather, Cromwell had become an ardent New Dealer and an active campaigner for Franklin D. Roosevelt and his programs of social and economic reform. Not surprisingly, there were arguments between the two men on this subject. "Roosevelt was anathema to him," Cromwell recalls. "I tried to point out to him that he should be grateful to Roosevelt. Few people realize how close the country was to revolution when the banks closed." One afternoon as stepfather and son sat in the study at Whitemarsh Hall, Ned Stotesbury put down his newspaper and said, "Jim, I have something to tell you. It's a good thing you married the richest girl in the world. Why? Well, you're not going to inherit anything from me. Your deity, Franklin D. Roosevelt, is ruining free enterprise. He's destroying my firm. I made all this myself. FDR is not going to waste it for me. *I* am."

Ned Stotesbury died at Whitemarsh on May 21, 1938, at the age of eighty-nine. Reportedly, he died with curses on his lips against Roosevelt and the New Deal, which he blamed for all the world's woes. Still, the Stotesburys had not spent the early 1930s in much discomfort, and, when Ned's estate was examined, it turned out that he had been true to his word. In the five years between 1933 and his death, it seemed, Ned Stotesbury had withdrawn from his account at Drexel's some $55,000,000 in cash—or more than $10,000,000 a year. How this extraordinary sum was spent, or wasted, is anyone's guess. It can only be assumed that $10,000,000 a year was the figure required to maintain the Stotesburys' standard of living. In light of these huge withdrawals, it was even more surprising that his estate ended up amounting to as much as $5,000,000, which was the figure finally placed on it. Looked at another way, he died with barely enough capital for another six months' expenses, and if he had lingered on until November he would have died penniless. The division of the money was straightforward. Two thirds was to be divided equally between the two daughters by his first marriage. One third, along with the houses and their contents, went to Eva. As he had promised, nothing went to any of Eva's three children. And it took Eva's lawyers only a moment to realize that the annual income from her inheritance would amount to less than a quarter of what it cost to maintain Whitemarsh Hall, not to mention the other houses.

In 1937 an advertisement for Whitemarsh Hall appeared in *Fortune*, listing all its splendors. No price was mentioned, and there were no takers. Oil-rich Arab sheiks would not discover America for another generation. Similarly, the Palm Beach and Bar Harbor houses were put up

Little Eva vs. Philadelphia

for sale, with similar results. In a little over a decade's time, all Eva's properties had become costly white elephants. A discouraged Eva was advised that the Whitemarsh property might be more salable if the building itself were demolished. It would cost almost as much to tear it down as it had to build it. She could not afford that, either.

Next, Eva turned to the sale of her art collection. From London, Duveen, her old friend and mentor and the man who had pocketed so much Stotesbury money in commissions and inflated prices over the years, reported that he was too ill to come to America to help her dispose of all the acquisitions he had helped her acquire. Knoedler's in New York was then turned to, and their report was equally gloomy. The art market was as depressed as everything else. Eva's paintings were mostly English, including many Romneys, and English painting was now out of fashion. Once more Fiske Kimball was invited to Whitemarsh Hall, where Eva told him, "I thought I must sell the sculpture, but, at the figures I am offered, I would much rather give it to the museum in memory of Ned." Fiske made his selections: four stone statues by Pajou, a marble by Tassaert that had once belonged to Frederick the Great, and the two Clodion groups whose only likes were in the Louvre. Fiske also asked for two sets of four plaster female figures bearing torches, which had stood in each of Whitemarsh Hall's two great rotundas, even though their authorship and provenance were unclear. (Later he would discover that at least one of the sets had decorated the inaugural ball of Madame du Barry at Louveciennes in 1771.)

Not until 1943 was Eva able to sell Whitemarsh Hall—to the Pennsylvania Salt Company for use as a research laboratory. The reported price was $167,000, including twenty acres of land. The following year, two auctions—one in Philadelphia and one in New York—attempted to sell the rest of Eva's art and furnishings. The Philadelphia auction was attended mostly by curiosity seekers. The New York auction was, in Fiske Kimball's words, "a butchery." One Romney, *The Vernon Children*, brought $22,000, but that was the highest price achieved in the sale. Nothing else brought more than $10,000, and the magnificent Isfahan carpet, for which Ned Stotesbury paid Duveen $90,000, was sold for only $5,000.

Through all these vicissitudes Eva remained cheerful and optimistic, never losing her well-bred composure and, if she was ever frightened or disheartened, never letting on. "There was never any bitterness, not even the sense of the stiff upper lip," says Jimmy Cromwell. "She was sweet and fun-loving as always, poking gentle fun at the vagaries of people—

47

people's little peculiarities always amused her." Through it all her two "top-drawer" Old Philadelphia friends, Mrs. Biddle and Mrs. Van Rensselaer, remained supportive and close, even though, it might be added, neither came forth with any offers of material assistance. That was left to plain old Anna Dodge, who came straight out of the bottom drawer to announce that she had a large and elegantly decorated house on Garfield Street in Washington which she never used. It was called Marly. Eva, she pointed out, knew and liked Washington and had lived there for several years. Why didn't Eva move to Washington and live in Marly? The rent would be nominal, just a token to make it all legal. Eva moved back to Washington not long after Ned's death. Anna Dodge also privately bought some pieces from Eva's art collection, for undisclosed prices.

With Marly to live in, and with the eventual sale of her properties and possessions—including most of her jewelry, though she refused to sell Ned's wedding pearls—she was able to live quite comfortably. The Bar Harbor house was eventually sold to a junk dealer for about $5,000; he tore the house down to salvage the lead in the plumbing, and then sold the waterfront property for a ferry dock, where thousands of tourists from Canada now seasonally disembark. Far away from touristy Bar Harbor, in the quiet remove of Northeast Harbor, Old Philadelphians, when they bemoan what has happened to Bar Harbor, still seem to be saying, "But we told you so."

Whitemarsh Hall still stands, more or less. After acquiring the house, the Pennsylvania Salt Company decided it would be prudent to sell the copper roof, which consisted of several tons of metal. With the copper roof gone, the weather came in. In the wake of the weather came the vandals. The gold-and-white paneling, the carved porticos, pediments, chimney pieces, and capitals have been ripped away. The draped statue that stood at the entrance has been beheaded. Only the façade of the great house remains, a silent and ghostly presence staring through broken windows at a banal array of middle-income suburban housing developments which have replaced the vast formal gardens. At the time of Eva's death, only El Mirasol in Palm Beach remained unsold, her last white elephant. Eventually that property was sold too, and the house razed.

And so there is only the shell of Whitemarsh Hall to provide a reminder of an era when to be a great hostess, to give glorious parties, to wear beautiful gowns and splendid jewels, to remember every guest's name, was—well, *enough*. Or almost enough, though not quite enough for Philadelphia, which would never forget that Eva was not a *Philadelphian*, that Stotesbury's was a twentieth-century fortune, and that Eva had more money than anyone else. "My private theory is that the strongest force in the world is the green-eyed monster, that it's the cause of all the evil we see around us," says Jimmy Cromwell. "And of course Philadelphia is a particularly stiff-necked place. It's why I came to New York as quickly as I could. Why should I sit around in Philadelphia waiting to be asked to join the Philadelphia Club, when my grandfather was a founder of the Union Club in New York? My second daughter was born in New York, which makes her a ninth-generation New York Cromwell. The Philadelphia caste system has, I know for a fact, hurt the city in terms of attracting commerce and industry. Many talented business executives refuse to relocate in Philadelphia because they know that they and their wives will be snubbed by the Old Guard. Philadelphia can't stand successsful outsiders."

But the final hypocrisy was that Philadelphia panted for invitations to Eva Stotesbury's parties. She may have been encouraged and abetted in her extravagances by her husband, but she was also encouraged by Philadelphia, where she was given no real competition, where she was permitted to have the field to herself. No one even attempted to outdo her; she was given free rein. Philadelphia's *only* grand parties were Eva's parties. And in the process she lifted Philadelphia entertaining to heights which it—and most other cities—had never seen and may never see again, far more imaginative and festive than anything ever achieved under the rigid and boring reign of Caroline Astor and her "Four Hundred." If the thousands of Philadelphians who accepted Eva's hospitality and were fed and wined at her table are any indication, she filled, for a while at least, a definite local need. Philadelphia would have been a much duller place without her. In a way, she was a rare municipal asset.

Eva's gifts were subtle ones, but they were at least two—that sense of personal theatre, and the gift of enjoying beautiful things. Trying to make the point that a great designer cannot create great designs without the support of a great patron, one of the designers from Lucien Alavoine et Cie, the Paris decorating firm that helped Eva with many of her most ambitious projects, despaired of trying to define Eva's talent and said simply, "Well, the point is . . . she was a great lady."

And she also had charm. In all the gossip about Eva Stotesbury that has survived, there is nothing connecting her with an unkind deed or word. "It's true," says Jimmy Cromwell. "Outside of the privacy of her own bedroom, about which I have no knowledge, I never heard her say anything that was disagreeable. She used to say, 'I try to make it a rule, and I try to abide by it, that if I can't say something nice about someone

I don't say anything.' To my knowledge, she and Father never quarreled. I never heard them raise their voices to one another. They were an ideal couple. She had a pet name for him—'Kickapoo.' Sometimes when he'd grumble about business or market conditions, she'd laugh and tweak his ear and say, 'Now, Kickapoo . . . we have a pleasant life, don't we?' "

"Gracious" is an adjective that meant more to Eva's generation than it did to later ones. Eva was always gracious. Hers were talents that did not transplant easily to Philadelphia, nor did they translate well into the 1930s and 1940s, but that was not her fault.

"If there was one person my mother ever really hated," says her son today, "and I even hate to use the term, it was Doris." During the Second World War, President Roosevelt appointed James H. R. Cromwell United States Ambassador to Canada, but Doris Duke Cromwell did not care for life in Canada and went to Hawaii, where she embarked upon the building of her famous estate, Shangri-La. After the war, Jimmy Cromwell decided to run for the United States Senate from New Jersey, where Doris Duke also maintained a large place. It was at this point, in the middle of his Senate campaign, that Doris Duke chose to return to the continental United States—pregnant, and accompanied by a new gentleman friend. "*Officially*, of course, the baby was mine," says Cromwell, "but everyone knew we'd been separated. Anyway, she lost the baby, but the incident ruined my campaign. I really believe that Doris shortened my mother's life by what she did. Mother would have loved to see a son in the United States Senate. But Doris saw to it that it didn't happen. That was the end of my campaign." The Cromwells were divorced in 1948.

"Of course the divorces saddened Mother," Cromwell says. "In my generation we became a particularly divorce-ridden family. She was especially upset by my sister's divorce from Douglas MacArthur." Louise Cromwell MacArthur, who is now dead, would go on to be divorced from three more husbands. James Cromwell's older brother, Oliver Cromwell, Jr., who lives in Switzerland, has been married and divorced twice. Jimmy Cromwell's third wife, the former Maxine MacFettridge, died. He now lives with his fourth wife, the Paris-born Germaine de Baume, in New York. "Mother always thought Doris was a cold person," he says. "She didn't approve of the way Doris treated her *own* mother. When Doris and I were leaving on our wedding trip, she said good-bye to her mother with a little peck on the cheek. And it was Nanaline who was responsible for tripling Doris's fortune! Of course Mother took our side in all the divorces, but they saddened her terribly, and the Doris thing shortened her life."

In the spring of 1946, in the middle of the "Doris thing," Eva Stotesbury had a heart attack at the Palm Beach house. Her doctor telephoned Jimmy Cromwell and urged him to plead with his mother to stay in bed until she had recovered. Eva wanted to be up and about. Cromwell hurried to Palm Beach to remonstrate with her, and he found her, even at the end and bedridden, perfectly groomed and coifed, the Stotesbury pearls looped at her throat, a gracious, regal Presence. "Just as I never saw her angry, never saw her lose her temper, I never saw her let her hair down," Cromwell says. In appearance she had not changed much from the Douglas Chandor portrait of her, painted in 1926—the same wide eyes, winglike eyebrows, smooth skin, dimpled cheeks, the slightly upturned nose and the pleasantly crooked, almost mocking smile.

Cromwell urged her to follow her doctor's orders. With a smile she said, "My dear son, I am yearning for my quiet grave. I don't want any part of your world, Mr. Roosevelt's world, or Mr. Stalin's world." Twelve hours later, on May 31, 1946—little more than eight years to the day after Ned's death—Eva died. She was eighty-one.

At the time of her death, some of her old acquaintances wondered what Eva was doing in Palm Beach so far out of season. (By then the Palm Beach season had been "officially" extended from February 22 to April 1.) But of course Eva herself—and she surely knew it—had gone out of season. Out of season, too, were the values and concepts she lived by: duty, responsibility, *noblesse oblige*, character, kindness, dignity, politeness, graciousness, grandeur, luxury, patronage of the arts, serenity, splendor, formality, gaiety. It was a season which would perhaps never pass across the American landscape again, and its fading had left Eva behind, an anachronism. Soon, El Mirasol would crumble before the wrecker's ball. The Washington house, Marly, Eva's last real home, would become the Belgian Embassy, all business.

Eva Stotesbury had made only one trip back to Philadelphia between Ned's death and her own. This was in 1939, to view the installation of the Stotesbury Collection at the Philadelphia Museum of Art. She had arrived from Washington twenty-seven years earlier in Ned Stotesbury's private railroad car. Now she was conveyed northward from the capital in an ordinary Pullman chair. On Fiske Kimball's arm she toured the Collection and pronounced herself satisfied with its new home. The two reminisced briefly about the glorious epoch of Whitemarsh Hall. No, she did not want to be driven out to see the house. She thanked Fiske Kimball for past kindnesses. Then she glanced at her watch. It was time to catch the train back to Washington. "This will be my last visit to Philadelphia," she told Kimball. "I never want to see it again."

And she kept that promise. Her will directed that she be buried in Chicago, with her parents and the other Roberts relatives.

PART TWO

New York Belle Among the Brahmins

5

"A TERRIBLE CUT-UP"

"ARE YOU A HAPPY WOMAN?" someone had the temerity to ask Mrs. John Lowell Gardner of Boston.

She froze her questioner with a look. "If I were not happy, do you think I would tell *you?*" she replied.

Those not familiar with the two cities often assume that Boston and Philadelphia are very much alike: ruled by a stiff-necked social aristocracy in which, if one cannot trace one's ancestry back to the Landing of the Mayflower, one is forever an outsider and a newcomer. Actually, the two cities are quite dissimilar in attitude and, even more important, in tone. Philadelphia, near the Mason-Dixon line, has always displayed some of the mentality of the Old South. Boston is a resolutely northern, Yankee city, toughened and made wisely cynical by icy winters and cold winds off the North Atlantic. Philadelphia is a city of marble and white columns. Boston is a city of weathered red brick.

There are other differences. Boston, replete as it is with all sorts of institutions of higher learning, is an intellectual city. Education and culture count for more than money. Wits count for more than pearls. As such, Boston is also a remarkably liberal city, and unconventional behavior is tolerated as long as it is accompanied by a certain amount of intelligence. This applies to sex as well, which is treated in a sensible way as nobody's business besides the persons' involved in it. Boston's many colleges and universities make it a particularly youthful town—the quest for knowledge seems to fill the streets. And so, compared with Philadelphia, Boston is sophisticated, tolerant, wicked—Bohemian, almost.

One of the most vivid exemplars of the Boston spirit was the late grande dame Mrs. Robert Homans, née Abigail Adams. She was a direct descendant of John Adams and John Quincy Adams, the second and sixth Presidents of the United States, respectively, as well as a niece of both Henry Adams and Brooks Adams, and until her death at near the century mark she was the reigning dowager of the ancient and distinguished Adams clan whose first American forebear immigrated to New England in 1636. She was a lady so free of the restraints of fashion that when she died she had not changed her hair style for over fifty years. "When it comes to style," she once said, "Boston doesn't have much. We all have what we call a hat. You know, they cover your head. My daughter makes me burn them now and then." Though Abigail Homans liked to call herself "the last of the old Adamses," she always insisted that Boston had "a regular society, a regime under which you live and do the things you ought to do." (Among the things she felt she ought to do was spend some time every day turning over her money to cultural, educational, and philanthropic causes with very little fanfare.) But the existence of such a regime never prevented Abigail Adams Homans from doing exactly as she liked. She once said, "If I stood in the Common on my head, people'd say, 'Oh, that's just Abigail Adams.' They wouldn't pay any attention. We're conventionally independent."

"Conventionally independent" is an interesting way to describe Boston. Mrs. Homans did not make it clear whether she meant independent *by* convention or independent *of* conventions, but she probably meant a little of both. She was certainly able to plunge forthrightly into situations that would daunt lesser folk. Once, when Beacon Street had become impassable in a blizzard, Mrs. Homans directed her taxi to stop in front of her husband's club, the stately Somerset on the lower slope of Beacon Hill, and requested a room for the night. The club politely explained that it had a rule against giving rooms to unescorted women, whereupon Mrs. Homans said, "Very well. In that case, I'll go out and get my taxi driver to share it with me." The story, which Boston loved to retell, contained just the right amounts of spunk, quick thinking, and naughtiness. Needless to say, Abigail Homans got the accommodations she wanted.

Conventionally independent also describes Mrs. John Lowell Gardner. Like Eva Stotesbury, Isabella Gardner came as an outsider to the city in which she gained her fame. As had not happened to Eva, Isabella Gardner would be warmly clasped to her adopted city's bosom. Unlike Eva, too, Mrs. Gardner was far from beautiful. In fact, she was altogether plain. Her hair was a hard-to-describe rusty color, and her eyebrows were sparse and pale. Her nose was long and crooked, and her face was long and thin, and tapered to a pointed chin. Her skin was chalky white—so white that the least exposure to the sun caused it to redden and freckle. She was a tiny woman, and in her childhood calisthenics had been prescribed by her family doctor as a remedy for her diminutive size. The calisthenics had made her spry and wiry, but they did not make her tall. Her eyes were her best feature; they crackled with intelligence and mischief. She was also proud of her slender arms and small, dainty hands, and, when it became fashionable for a woman to bare her back, Isabella Gardner proudly did so. "My back is flawless," she declared. And she could dance. Being small, weighing barely ninety pounds, she seemed to float like a feather in a dancing partner's arms. It was said of Isabella that she "danced her way into the hearts of men," and Isabella liked men.

She was born Isabella Stewart in New York City on April 14, 1840. Her father, David Stewart, was a second-generation Scottish American, an "importer of linens and laces." Not long after Isabella's birth, however, sensing the coming of what was called the Age of Iron, David Stewart founded the Stewart Iron Company. In iron, he prospered, and the family progressed to a series of more fashionable addresses in Manhattan. Isabella's grandmother Stewart, after whom she was named, was also a woman of property, who owned a large farm on Long Island and who, after her husband's death, managed her affairs shrewdly and became a moderately wealthy woman in her own right. Years later Isabella Stewart Gardner would enjoy telling friends of childhood visits to her grandmother's Long Island "plantation," where Grandmother Stewart "kept slaves." This cannot have been true, since slavery was abolished in New York State in 1841, but Grandmother Stewart probably did have a number of servants. In any case, young Isabella was a woman whom one never knew whether to believe or not.

Her mother's side of the family, meanwhile, was decidedly humble. Mrs. Stewart, the former Adelia Smith, was the daughter of a tavern keeper and stable owner. Isabella was able to get much more mileage out of her Stewart family connections. When she eventually arrived in Boston, a city which she knew placed great weight on ancestry, Isabella Stewart hired a "genealogist" to prepare an elaborate Stewart "family tree." The genealogist knew perfectly well what Isabella had in mind, and produced an imposing document, a long parchment scroll illuminated with gold leaf, which attested to the fact that her Stewarts were "The Stewarts of Appin," descended from King Fergus I, a contemporary of Alexander the Great. The family tree carried the Stewarts back to the twelfth century, and showed that Isabella shared an ancestor with Mary

Queen of Scots. Again, no one quite knew how seriously to take all this, or even how seriously Isabella took it herself. Once, to a Boston dowager who was discussing her pre-Revolutionary ancestors, Isabella commented, "Ah, yes. I gather they were much less strict about immigration in those days." Still, if anyone questioned her antecedents, Isabella could produce her illuminated scroll, and there they all were: King Fergus, Robert the Bruce, Queen Mary, the martyred Charles I, and Isabella.

Despite her regal first name, Isabella Stewart was always known in the family as Belle (though in later years she would sometimes fancifully sign her letters "Ysabella" in imitation of Isabella of Spain, or simply "Y"). She was educated in a private girls' school in New York, where she was taught all the subjects deemed proper for a young woman of the period: music, dancing, etiquette, the art of the curtsy, needlework, and French. She was quick at all her studies, and showed a particular aptitude for languages. It was this which prompted her parents, when she was sixteen, to take her to Paris for a year of study. Later it would be said of her that she "climbed out a window of a French convent and eloped with Jack Gardner," and Belle never denied stories like this. As the legends about her grew, she encouraged them. "Don't spoil a good story by telling the truth," was one of her favorite maxims. In fact, the school was a Protestant one and not a convent, and Belle's mother had had serious doubts about educating her daughter in a Catholic country. Before departing for Europe, she had read *The School Girl in France*, published in 1850, with its warnings about "the snares, pitfalls, and innumerable perils of a Popish school."

At her French finishing school, meanwhile, one of Belle's classmates was a Miss Julia Gardner of Boston, the daughter of Mr. and Mrs. John Lowell Gardner. Like Belle's parents, the Gardners had come to Europe to chaperone their daughter and protect her from Popish ways. The girls, it seems, had a much better time in Paris than their elders. Neither the Stewarts nor the Gardners spoke much French—Mr. Gardner always referred to the Bois de Boulogne as "the Boy"—and, naturally, the two American couples spent a good deal of time with each other. Belle Stewart and Julia Gardner also became close friends.

There was a uniquely American kind of mission involved here. In nineteenth-century America fortunes were being made on a scale that had never before been imagined, and that were difficult even for the men who made them to comprehend. The country was leaving the gentle Age of Innocence of which Edith Wharton wrote, and was entering what James Truslow Adams labeled the "Age of the Dinosaurs." The Dinosaurs, of course, were clumsy creatures, all mass and power and no grace. And, though new millionaires like David Stewart had learned to plow through the underbrush of commerce and finance to scavenge whatever plunder they could find, their progress was not always a pretty sight. It was clear that something was lacking, and that something was capital-C Culture.

Moreover, America seemed to offer little of it. Even in "artistic" Boston there was as yet no symphony orchestra, no art museum of any importance. Opera companies visited the city periodically, but the grandly named Boston Opera House was more often the setting for minstrel shows and vaudeville acts involving performing seals, bears, dogs, and monkeys. And so, for culture, rich Americans turned to Europe. In terms of education, England became the model, and private boys' boarding schools were springing up all over New England carefully fashioned along the lines of such British "public" schools as Harrow and Eton. England's example was also followed when it came to architecture, and English manor houses that had graced the hills of Kent and Sussex were copied and deposited, often incongruously, on the flatlands of Chicago. For art and music, however, the French and the Italian were most favored. Men like David Stewart and his wife may have realized that they would never really acquire Culture—in his case, the making and managing of money had left too little time for other pastimes, and in hers she was getting too late a start—but they were determined that their children, particularly their female children, should acquire this intangible asset. After all, Culture marked the difference between a woman and a lady. What the newly rich Dinosaurs were doing in the years just before, during, and after the Civil War, though they may not have realized it, was creating a cultural matriarchy that would dominate the American artistic community for nearly a hundred years.

In Belle Stewart's case, the mission was particularly successful. She was a quick study, and during her European sojourn she not only perfected her French but became equally fluent in Italian. She visited all the museums, castles, and cathedrals, listened to concerts and recitals, attended performances at the theatre and Paris Opéra, and became knowledgeable about European painting, sculpture, and music from the Renaissance onward. When the Stewarts sailed home to New York late in 1858 (Mother Stewart was pregnant again, and it was unthinkable that her child should be born on alien soil), Belle was eighteen, and considered herself a thoroughly cultivated, even sophisticated, young woman. There was a rumor, in fact, that she had enjoyed a "flirtation" with her young Italian instructor.

Belle Stewart had been more or less out of touch with her friend Julia Gardner when, early in 1859, an invitation arrived from Julia asking Belle up to Boston for a visit with her family. Belle's parents, who had found the Gardners "nice," agreed to let her go. In Boston, however, the Gardners were something a little more than "nice." They were not only socially prominent themselves, but were also dizzyingly well connected, through marriages, to other prominent families: the Peabodys,* the Endicotts, the Lowells, the Cabots, the Parkmans, the Lawrences, the Higginsons, and the Lees, whose cousins married other cousins. The Gardners of Boston were not to be confused with the Gardiners, another important New England family. To differentiate between the two, the Gardiners were known as "the one-eyed Gardiners," and the Gardners were "the blind Gardners." Naturally, each family claimed that the other "spelled it wrong," each insisting that the other's ancestors had had a lesser mastery of spelling. Both, meanwhile, claimed direct descent from the original "gardeners," Adam and Eve. The blind Gardners were in banking and shipping, and they were well fixed. (In Boston it was not considered proper to describe any family as "rich.") The family owned merchant vessels, had profited discreetly in the slave trade, and controlled a sizable amount of Boston real estate.

Julia Gardner had never made much of the fact that she had two unmarried brothers, Joseph and John Lowell Gardner, Jr. Both were bachelors, waiting for the right cousin to marry, and both were handsome—particularly John, whom the family called Jack. He was six feet tall, slender, with dark hair, deep-set eyes, and a drooping black moustache that gave him a brooding, poetic look. He was twenty-one years old, and after two years at Harvard he had entered the family business, where he had begun to show great promise. His father, in fact, while in Europe with his wife and daughter, had left young Jack in charge of things.

Both boys were immediately smitten with Belle. In the little Memory Album that Belle Stewart carried about with her, in which she pasted invitations, calling cards, and notes from friends, Joe Gardner wrote, "May your own path in life be always strewn with flowers as gay as those which spring up everywhere around you under the vivifying influence of your sunny glance." Even more smitten was his brother Jack. He danced with Belle. He strolled with her in the Common and on Beacon Hill. He showed her where land was being reclaimed from the Charles River,

---

* Julia Gardner's mother was a Peabody "of Salem," where it was said, "You are either a Peabody or a nobody."

which would become Back Bay and an extension of Beacon Street, and where he intended to build a house. Then he proposed to her.

A moment should be taken, perhaps, to explain why this extremely plain young woman should have exerted such a strong allure to the opposite sex. For one thing, there was her petite figure. American fashion was in a period of furbelows and flounces, bustles and hoop skirts, and the yards of bombazine seemed designed to deny the fact that women had breasts and hips and legs. In Paris, Belle's father had taken her to the *ateliers* and couturiers and bought her a number of expensive dresses from designers who were creating clothes that clung to women's bodies. Belle also liked to show off as much of her arms, throat, shoulders, and back as she could get away with. A friend once wrote, "Saw Belle last night . . . saw a *lot* of her!" And one of her many admirers, Dr. Henry J. Bigelow, wrote to her, saying he missed her and adding, "As it is, there seems to be no alternative but to sit . . . and think of the way your dress fits." For young men accustomed to dancing with partners in hoop skirts, the sensation of dancing with a woman in a slinky dress was evidently overpowering.

Then there was the matter of her wit, which would prompt yet another admirer to say, "Everyone who has ever talked with her declares that she is the most brilliant, charming, and attractive woman on earth"—high praise indeed. To be sure, Belle's European experience had enabled her to talk intelligently with men on many subjects, but that may have been secondary to her quick delivery. She may not have said things which, repeated, were actually funny, but her ripostes were so fast and blunt and opinionated that they provoked amusement. Once, for instance, when she was asked to contribute to the Boston Charitable Eye and Ear Infirmary, she replied, "I didn't know there was a charitable eye or ear in Boston." Later, another Boston woman tried to take credit for this comment, and Belle, hearing of this, announced, "The *mot* was mine. I will not give it up!"

In addition to her vivacity, she exhibited stubbornness and willfulness —qualities which came as a distinct surprise in an era of Victorian propriety and seemliness. She once said that the only person she envied was the Dowager Empress of China because, when someone displeased her, she could order, "Cut off his head." Finally, she loved mischief and scandal—even when it involved herself—and was known as "a terrible cut-up." Some of Belle's capers do not, in retrospect, seem very scandalous, but in their day they were enough to shock. For example, she liked to stay in bed until noon, something that in the 1860s was considered unladylike to the point of slatternliness. Once, too, when she was walking down the street, her shoes began to hurt so she simply took them off and continued in her stocking feet, unheard-of behavior. Finally, there was the shocking fact that she *smoked*. In Paris she had developed a fondness for Turkish cigarettes. Obviously she considered herself a free spirit, unbound by convention. Obviously too, for a girl who would never be remotely pretty, Belle Stewart had learned to make the most of what she had.

On the matter of marriage, however, she was conventionally prim. Jack Stewart, she told him, would have to ask her father. And so Jack journeyed to New York to ask David Stewart for his daughter's hand in marriage. David Stewart consented, and announced that his wedding gift to the couple would be to build them the house Jack Gardner envisioned in Back Bay. Isabella Stewart and John Lowell Gardner, Jr., were married on April 12, 1860, in Grace Church, New York City. Two days later, the bride would be twenty.

6

A PATRONESS IS BORN

THE FIRST FEW YEARS in the Massachusetts capital were not especially happy ones for the new Mrs. Gardner. Not long after her marriage to Jack, she began to enjoy, as they said, poor health, and for the rest of her life she would have a reputation for periodic bouts of sickliness. This was all very odd, because she was a strong and athletic young woman who would rather run than walk, who was an excellent figure skater, who loved to dance, and who was an accomplished horsewoman. Her ailing was even odder because doctors could find nothing whatever the matter with her. In the beginning, of course, she may have been suffering from homesickness, and there were several protracted visits to her family in New York, from which her husband would have to journey southward to retrieve her. But it was also true that Belle was a woman who liked to take, and keep, the center of the stage, and her illness may, unconsciously or not, have been her way of indicating that Boston was not paying enough attention to her.

In Boston the matrons of society made their ritual rounds of visiting, dropping off the required numbers of calling cards, in the morning. But Belle's habit of languishing in her bed till lunchtime meant that she was never "at home" to receive the ladies when they called, and this the women of Boston—who were not about to alter the custom of a lifetime to suit Belle, even if she *was* Mrs. John Lowell Gardner, Jr.—found off-putting. And there were some social activities from which Belle was excluded. By local custom also, each year's crop of debutantes formed, at the finish of their coming-out season, a Sewing Circle. The Sewing Circles sewed, ostensibly, for the poor, even though the most arduous tasks involved rolling hems on handkerchiefs. Belle, not having been a Boston debutante of any year, was ineligible to join any of the Sewing Circles. Later, to be sure, she would find a way to use this exclusion to her advantage. By simply adding eighteen to the year of any woman's Sewing Circle, it was possible to calculate her age. Belle's age—though she annually celebrated her April fourteenth birthday with a party—would always remain her secret. While the other women of Boston aged, Belle would manage to grow younger. Once, when asked about her memories of the Civil War, Belle replied, "Oh, but I was much too young to remember it"—though she was twenty-one at the time of the Battle of Bull Run.

Belle's health always markedly improved during the winter season of the Boston Assemblies, or Germans, at which elaborate cotillion figures were performed, interspersed with waltzing. At these dressy gatherings Belle Gardner quickly became a star. While waltzing, there was a practice that was known as "chandeliering." Chandeliering meant that the most accomplished couple on the floor maneuvered to the center of the ballroom, directly beneath the chandelier, and there proceeded to perform —their deepest dips, their most spectacular twirls—while the other guests moved back a little distance to admire the show. Belle Gardner was an expert when it came to chandeliering.

She was also always careful to arrive at the Germans late, so as to make a dramatic entrance in one of her clingingly revealing Paris gowns. Soon, other women were arriving late as well, but somehow they never managed to upstage Mrs. Jack Gardner, who always seemed to appear a few minutes later. Her trick, it eventually turned out, was to conceal her tiny self in the cloakroom behind the coats until all her rivals were accounted for on the dance floor. That was her cue to appear. There were other quaint traditions involving the Germans. A married woman, for instance, was expected to have only one brief "duty dance" with her husband. The rest of the evening she spent with other partners. In advance of each gala women received notes from gentlemen requesting that their names be placed on the women's dance cards. If a woman accepted a gentleman's request for a dance, custom dictated that the gentleman should send the lady a bouquet of flowers. The women then carried their bouquets of flowers to the dance, and a woman's popularity could quickly be ascertained by the number of floral offerings she carried in her arms.

Belle Gardner invariably made her entrance to the German with an armload of blooms. On at least one occasion an entire box at the ball had to be given over to Belle Gardner's collection of bouquets. She had, however, one rival who threatened to outdo her. After a dance at which

Belle and her competitor appeared to be running neck and neck, bets were discreetly placed among the gentlemen as to which lady might prove to be the winner at the next. The odds were running in Belle's favor, but no one could be sure, and the next gala was the subject of much excitement and anticipation. Somehow, Belle Gardner, who always had her ear to the ground when it came to gossip, got wind of the wagers. The night arrived, and the competition appeared, so overburdened with nosegays that it seemed likely she had added to her collection out of her own purse. The suspenseful minutes passed, while everyone waited for Belle. Then she appeared, in form-fitting black, her bare white arms outstretched to receive her courtiers, carrying not a single blossom.

One reason for Belle's periodic ailments was that she desperately wanted to have a child. Her Gardner in-laws were all proving remarkably fecund, and the Gardners had let it be known that they expected John Lowell Gardner, Jr., to produce John Lowell Gardner III, who would eventually produce John Lowell Gardner IV, and so on until the end of time. In those days, pregnancy, though regarded as a blessing, was also treated as an embarrassment and an illness. The minute the tiniest bulge began to show, a woman went into seclusion in her home, and if she had to go out did so only when swathed in shawls and lap robes to conceal her "delicate condition."

Every month, in her new house at 152 Beacon Street, Belle Gardner took to her bed to await that delicate condition. Month after month, she was disappointed.

Finally, in November 1862, after nearly three years of marriage, the condition appeared to manifest itself. When it was confirmed, Belle was overjoyed. She immediately went into her retirement; a nurse was hired and a nursery prepared. John Lowell Gardner III was born on June 18, 1863. The birth was difficult—Belle's small frame was not well suited to childbearing—but the baby was healthy and Belle recovered nicely, and for the next two years both Gardners doted on their little son, boasting to all who would listen of Jackie's latest accomplishment. The child learned to talk early, and Belle was convinced that Jackie was going to be a genius. Then, in the late winter of 1865, when he was not quite two, Jackie came down with a cold, which developed into pneumonia, and on March 15 he died. Belle was devastated. Moreover, part of the price paid for Jackie's hard birth had been her capacity to have another child. Belle would let no one touch her dead son, and bathed him and dressed him herself for his funeral. For the rest of her life she would refuse to speak of her son, though she kept a miniature of him, with his dates and a lock of his baby hair tucked in the back of the frame, in a closed case on her writing table. Later, when one of her relatives asked if she could name her baby John Lowell Gardner III, Belle assented, but only on the condition that the parents promise never to use the nickname Jackie. For her there was only one Jackie.

There followed two years of despondency and depression, and Belle was said to have suffered a "nervous breakdown." In those days it was almost fashionable for women who had endured tragedies such as Belle's to take to their beds more or less permanently and spend the rest of their lives in bed jackets, assisted feebly from bed to chaise longue and back to bed again by servants and long-suffering, indulgent husbands. It was an era, among other things, of the stylish invalid. Whether Belle Gardner would actually have taken to this sort of life seems, in retrospect, unlikely, and it is probable that, though she enjoyed all the care and sympathy that were lavished upon her for a while, she eventually grew bored with it. She was further prodded out of her torpid state by her doctor, who, in a common-sense way, pointed out to her that there was nothing really the matter with her, and that a great many women managed to live interesting and useful lives without children. The doctor prescribed a European trip and Belle assented. Still, Belle's sense of the dramatic was such that she could not depart Boston for Europe without creating a certain amount of fuss. An ambulance was summoned to 152 Beacon Street, and Belle was lifted into it, to be driven to the ship that was to carry the Gardners abroad. From the ambulance she was carried up the gangplank on a mattress. Interestingly, no mattress was required ten days later when the Gardners debarked at Hamburg, nor was an ambulance.

The Gardners embarked on an ambitious touring schedule that would keep them busily moving from capital to capital for months. They spent weeks in Sweden, more weeks in Norway, and more in Denmark. Then it was on to Russia—to St. Petersburg and Moscow—and from there to Vienna and night after night at the opera. From Vienna they went to Paris for two more months, filled with opera, theatre, museums, and shopping to replace the old couturier wardrobe. At one point Jack Gardner wrote home to say that all the travel had left him quite exhausted, but that Belle had recovered her energy to such an extent that she never seemed to tire at all.

In many ways, that year, 1867, was a watershed year for Isabella Stewart Gardner. Had her son lived, she might have become just another conventionally independent Boston matron, seeing her son through Harvard and then on into State Street law or finance or the family business. But with Jackie's death, the realization that she would never be a mother again, followed by the boredom of being an invalid, followed by the blood-stirring trip to Europe, she seemed to discover that her life had to point in some direction, that she had to do *something* to justify her existence. She was twenty-seven years old, getting too old to worry about how many bouquets she received from admirers at a party. She had to devote herself to a cause, an important cause, a cause that would last beyond her lifetime. The cause she chose was art, or, rather, Art.

In the back of her mind, a grand scheme had begun to appear in outline —vague at first, but more specific the more she thought about it. There had long been patrons of the arts in Europe, but they had all been men. The men of the European aristocracy, after all, had time and money on their hands. In their leisure, they could become connoisseurs. In America it was just the opposite. America's was a business aristocracy, and it was the wives of the rich who were idle. If great institutions of art and culture were to be developed and supported, patronesses of the arts would have to do it, and one of these was what Belle Gardner had decided to become. Her grand scheme, furthermore, included building her own museum, filling it with art, and giving it to the city of Boston. Her museum would be more than a great civic benefaction, a gift that would "uplift" and "inspire" the general public as, in those days, art was supposed to do. It would also insure that, long after she had gone, Boston would be re-minded of her existence. Years before it became a reality, she had picked the name for it: the Isabella Stewart Gardner Museum.

Returning to Boston in the autumn of 1867, Belle embarked upon a serious program of self-improvement. She set off across the Charles River to attend lectures at Harvard. She read avidly—in English, French, and Italian—anything she could find on the subject of art and artists. She read Dante in the original. She hired a young actor to give her speech and elocution lessons. In her upstairs sitting room at 152 Beacon Street, over tea, she began conducting what amounted to a *salon*, to which visiting painters, writers, and musicians were invited. All this was quite new to Boston, which still tended to believe that no writer was worth reading, no painter worth hanging, and no composer worth hearing until he had been respectably dead for a number of years. Belle Gardner actually had "finds"—young people of no particular fame or distinction, but whom she considered promising—whom she included in her intellectual after-noons. In London, she had met James McNeill Whistler, who was con-sidered a very controversial and radical painter at the time. Whistler had sketched Belle in pastels, and titled the portrait *A Little Note in Yellow*. At the same time, she had bought another Whistler sketch called *Violet Note*, a female nude. The pictures were the same size, and rumors circulated on Beacon Hill to the effect that Whistler had painted Belle in the nude. Though the nude had actually been a Whistler model, Belle liked the story and, to emphasize the point, hung the sketches side by side. By 1873, Belle was ready to buy her first important painting, by Emile Jacque of the French Barbizon School—a genre that was considered daring because it moved from interior still-lifes and formal portraits to the out-of-doors, to rural scenes of peasants and livestock, with much emphasis on sunlight and the weather.

Belle Gardner's approach to collecting was very different from Eva Stotesbury's. For one thing, Belle had nowhere near as much money to spend. For another, she was not buying art to feed the expanding ego of a husband who considered himself a latter-day Maecenas. For still another, she had no Duveen constantly trying to stuff her rooms with his wares. Eva, to be sure, also read art history books and periodicals, but only after the fact, becoming an authority on English antiques only to familiarize herself with what she had just bought. Of necessity, Belle Gardner bought selectively and carefully, only laying down her money when she was sure of what she wanted, sure of what she was getting, and sure that the price was right. If Eva Stotesbury bought indiscriminately, Belle Gardner tried, at least, to buy intelligently.

As Boston's new patroness of art and artists, Belle soon acquired one of her first big plums, the semiexpatriate American novelist Henry James. Belle had first met James in London—though their paths may have crossed earlier in Boston, when he was a still-unknown student at Harvard—and now, by 1882, James was a periodic guest at Belle's salons. He was working on a dramatic version of *Daisy Miller*, which at that point had been his most successful novel, and he spent two afternoons and evenings alone with Belle in her sitting room, reading the play aloud to her. She pronounced it brilliant (later, the critics would not). James, admiring the rapt attention she gave to his reading, and obviously enjoying her critical reaction, developed a kind of schoolboy crush on Belle and wrote her effusive letters in which he spoke of "the harmony of your presence" and "the melodies of your toilet." During these evenings *à deux* with Henry James, Belle's servants were instructed that the mistress of the household was not to be disturbed. Word of these "pretty little evenings," as James called them, reached the rest of Beacon Hill through backstairs gossip—the Irish servants of Boston all knew one another—and, naturally, there was talk.

It began to be noted that, while many of Mrs. Gardner's little gatherings contained members of both sexes, many more were attended by gentlemen only. It was further noted that Mrs. Gardner much preferred the company of *younger* men. There was the young actor, for example, who gave her private instruction in voice projection—he was young enough to have been her son. Henry James was also younger (though in fact only three years younger), and also quite apparent was the fact that Mrs. Gardner's husband didn't seem to mind.

The location of the Gardner salons had a lot to do with the talk. Rather wickedly, Belle always referred to the upstairs sitting room as "my boudoir." In Europe a sitting room can be called a "boudoir," but in Boston a boudoir was a bedroom, nothing else. Even though Belle's Beacon Street "boudoir" contained no bed, it was on the second floor of the house, where the principal sleeping rooms were, and it was considered just a few short steps from the tea table to the four-poster.

All this remained idle chatter and speculation, of course, as long as Jack and Belle Gardner continued to appear together at the Germans and other social functions. It was clear from Jack's admiring expression, as he watched his dainty wife glide across the dance floor in the arms of other men, that he was proud of her popularity and accepted her flirtatious ways. His business was continuing to prosper, and he was now beginning to shower her with important jewels—a long rope of pearls with a ruby pendant, a pair of large diamond clips that she often wore in her hair. Every year he replenished her wardrobe with expensive new gowns from Worth of Paris. It seemed obvious that he adored her.

In the case of Henry James, of course, Boston need not have worried. A lifelong bachelor, devoted to his mother, James had an absolute terror of predatory women, and his only women friends were chosen from the ranks of the securely and comfortably married. James, if not a homosexual, was an asexual creature. But in 1881 quite a different sort of man appeared on the Boston scene. He was Frank Marion Crawford—six feet tall, athletically built, matinee-idol handsome, brought up and educated in libertine Italy. Crawford was also enormously vain, and was often observed carefully posing in front of mirrors, admiring his face and his oarsman's physique. He had no visible means of support, but was well connected in Boston. An aunt was Julia Ward Howe, who wrote, among other things, "The Battle Hymn of the Republic." Crawford had journeyed from Europe to visit his American relatives and to pursue some vaguely defined career, and it wasn't long before he was a regular figure at Belle Gardner's boudoir afternoons. He also appeared on outings with her in her carriage. The two picnicked together in the Public Garden and lunched together in restaurants, where each seemed to have much of intense importance to discuss with the other. Many of their little confidences, furthermore, were communicated in Italian, to everyone's frustration since no one knew what they were talking about. Again backstairs gossip told of long do-not-disturb afternoons in Mrs. Gardner's boudoir, and the servants told one another of secret letters that were carried back and forth. Frank Crawford was twenty-seven. Belle Gardner was forty-one.

Up to now there had been just sly talk of Belle's "flirtations." But this was quite, quite different. Belle, of course, insisted that Frank Crawford was another of her "finds," a talented protégé whose gifts would one day take the world by storm, a budding artistic genius of some sort. To the gossips of upper-crust Boston, it seemed quite simple. Mrs. Jack Gardner was having an affair.

7

FLINGS

FRANK MARION CRAWFORD'S NAME TODAY, as a novelist, does not cause gasps of recognition. In *Bartlett's Familiar Quotations* he is given only a footnote, for having written, "What is charm? It is what the violet has and the camellia has not." Few people today read the swashbuckling, romantic, and purple-prosed novels that he produced in the 1880s and 1890s—*Mr. Isaacs: A Tale of Modern India*, *Dr. Claudius*, and *Children of the King*—but it is thanks to Isabella Gardner that these volumes were written.

When Crawford first met Belle, he talked of becoming an opera singer. He had a pleasant voice, but the trouble was that he could not stay on key. What he enjoyed most was going to parties, and his Boston relatives worried that his popularity and heavy social schedule would make him "too sensual." They also fretted about what seemed an unusual fondness for alcoholic stimulants, and blamed his lack of productivity on the fact that he had a key to his aunt's wine cellar. Belle's influence, to her credit, would change all that. During the early part of their two-year relationship, she noticed that Frank's drinking was causing him to gain weight. Belle herself disliked alcohol, but she disliked fat even more. Under the strict regimen of diet, exercise, and total abstinence from liquor which Belle put him on, he slimmed down. It was also Belle's suggestion, since he did not seem cut out for a career in opera, that he try his hand at writing a novel. The result was *Mr. Isaacs: A Tale of Modern India*, a shortish work designed to capitalize on the popularity of exotic romanticism. It was completed in the spring of 1882, promptly sold to Macmillan, and published in December of that year. Crawford gave Belle the first printed copy of the book, with a handwritten sonnet on the flyleaf.

At the time he wrote to her, "I think of it as someone else's work; as indeed it is, love, for without you, I should never have finished it."

Obviously it was thrilling for Belle to think of herself as the inspiration for a young novelist's first book. And Crawford possessed other attributes that attracted her to him. He flattered her, fawned over her, showered her with compliments and flowers. It is possible, too, that she saw him as a kind of surrogate for her dead son. As for Crawford, his feelings toward Belle are harder to fathom. His letters and notes to her were full of "love," and "my love," and "my dearest lady," but it is important to remember that this sort of effusiveness was fashionable at the time, and was perhaps not intended to be taken seriously. On the other hand, Crawford had grown up in Italy, where affairs with married women were not uncommon and no cause for alarm, provided they were managed discreetly. In Boston, noting the quaint custom by which married ladies received bouquets from other male admirers, Crawford may have assumed that Boston ladies routinely took lovers. Or he may simply, and rather cynically, have seen Belle as a lonely woman whose husband spent most of his time at his office and club, and found that she made a convenient sponsor who happened to like his work. Certainly he spent a great deal of time under her roof, eating her meals. When she made him expensive gifts—among them a gold watch—he accepted them. He had himself, it might seem, a good deal. As we shall see, there are indications that Frank Crawford was not a very nice fellow.

As to how Jack Gardner felt about the situation, there is no telling. On the surface, at least, he seemed unperturbed. No change in his behavior or demeanor was noted, though there are hints that he was growing a little tired of having Crawford almost constantly underfoot in his house. At one point Jack Gardner offered Crawford a job in his company, possibly to give the young man something to do besides read aloud to Belle from works in progress—Crawford immediately launched into a second novel—but the offer was refused. And whether Belle and Crawford ever had a sexual relationship is also a matter of conjecture. When Belle and her husband were "told" by her doctor that she could have no more children, this did not mean that a hysterectomy or other sterilizing operation—unknown in those days—had been performed. It simply meant that the doctor had advised the couple to refrain from activities that could result in childbirth. Assuming this, and assuming that Belle believed that if she conceived again it could cost her her life, her sexual frustration in a passionless marriage, and in an unconsummated new romance, might easily have added to her passion for Frank Crawford. Because passion it was on her part—it was obvious to everyone who saw them together. Clearly, Belle Gardner had fallen head over heels in love.

And the trouble was, it was not discreet. They rode together, strolled together, danced together, went to the opera and concerts together. *Town Topics*, the New York gossip sheet, soon got wind of the Boston romance, and began writing about it. Cleverly, to steer clear of libel, the paper referred to Belle as "a married belle." Everybody in Boston, of course, knew whom the paper was talking about.

Now, early in 1883, there were new plans afoot. A journey to the Orient was being planned, and the travelers would be Belle and Jack Gardner—and Frank Crawford. Picking up the tab for Crawford's ticket and expenses, naturally, would be the Gardners. At first Crawford seemed genuinely excited about the prospect of the trip, and he approached his uncle, Sam Ward, and invited him to join the jolly party and make it a foursome. Ward, however, sensing trouble ahead, was dubious about the whole idea, and declined. He had already expressed concern about what he called, in uncertain French, his nephew's "*affaire du coeur.*" The next news was that Jack Gardner would *not* be accompanying his wife and Crawford to the Far East. Some sort of crisis seemed to be brewing, and Crawford asked his cousin, Maud Howe, to join the tour as his and Belle's chaperone. Maud was also apprehensive, and the plans for the grand voyage remained in abeyance.

Meanwhile, in a number of hushed Back Bay drawing rooms, secret family discussions had begun. Matters were being weighed, arguments put forth, priorities considered. And in the course of these, while Belle Gardner was planning her wardrobe and packing for the trip with her young swain, Frank Crawford would be persuaded not only to withdraw from the tour but to slip out of Belle's life entirely, without warning and without adieu, and under cover of darkness. In one of his letters to Belle he had written, "There is only to be one goodbye between us, and I do not think it will be spoken aloud, nor written, for it will come when one of us two reaches the end, and it will be very long before that. Goodnight then, and sweet dreams. . . ." Now, however, he was planning a very different sort of departure.

In her biography of Isabella Stewart Gardner, Louise Hall Tharp hints that Jack Gardner may have issued some sort of ultimatum to Crawford which prompted him to behave as he did. There is, however, no real evidence of this. To have threatened Frank Crawford in any way would not have been Jack Gardner's style. Jack Gardner's position in Boston society was unassailable. So was his wife's. The Gardners were invulnerable to gossip. Jack Gardner knew he had married a spirited filly, and he had long ago given her her head. More than a domestic crisis in the Gardner household would be needed to understand why Frank Crawford chose to walk out on his adoring patroness in such an ungallant fashion.

To begin with, it is necessary to understand the new relationship that was developing between artists and American society. America in the 1880s was going through what would later be described as an artistic Renaissance. In the years immediately following the Civil War, the men who had made great fortunes—and their wives—had turned for Culture to Europe, where the great castles and châteaux and collections were systematically looted of the art treasures they contained. There was ample criticism of this, and new-rich American collectors were depicted by journalists almost as cartoon characters, waving sheaves of money in exchange for European Old Masters to decorate their mansions. The rich responded to the critics defensively. Breast-thumping patriotism was trotted out. America, it was argued, was now becoming the most powerful nation in the world. It was America's right, its Manifest Destiny, to acquire the finest things that the world had to offer, including art from Europe, where fortunes were declining. The architect Stanford White, when reproached for importing so much European art to adorn the houses he was designing for moneyed Americans, would use this argument, claiming that "In the past, dominant nations had always plundered works of art from their predecessors . . . . America was taking a leading place among nations and had, therefore, the right to obtain art wherever she could."

Edith Wharton was also sensitive on this issue, and in *The Custom of the Country* she used the forced sale of Boucher's famous Saint-Désert tapestries as a literary symbol for the transfer of power from a decadent old European aristocracy to the muscular new American plutocrats. Thus the looting was justified. America was merely taking what was justly her due.

But by the 1880s it had begun to seem possible that America could contribute artists of her own. This was a much more exciting notion than one that depended, abjectly, on borrowing taste and talent from across the Atlantic, and now, in another burst of patriotism, there was talk of the New American Masters in the arts. The rich were quick to jump on the bandwagon and to find, in the vision of an American Renaissance which would surpass anything that had occurred in Imperial Rome, Renaissance Florence, or Bourbon Paris, an outlet for any guilty feelings they might have had. The result of the new vision would be increased patronage of public buildings, monuments, painting, sculpture, poetry, and letters by American artists and writers. In the course of this Renaissance, the artists and writers themselves, especially if they were "attractive," would find themselves swept into the highest circles of perfumed society. Celebrities such as Henry James, Edith Wharton, Mary Cassatt, and Cecilia Beaux were already socially well placed. But under the new rules more raffish types such as John Singer Sargent, Stanford White, and Augustus Saint-Gaudens were also asked to all the best parties.

In Boston, the aristocratic Wards and Howes were particularly concerned about what was happening to the reputation of their cousin, Frank Marion Crawford. He was now a published novelist, which gave him the credentials of a serious artist. But the affair with Belle Gardner had gone on too long, and too many tongues were wagging. Furthermore, the gossip was not damaging Belle's social position—it was damaging his. By continuing in the public role of protégé of a wealthy older woman, Frank Crawford was in danger of not being taken seriously by Boston society. He was becoming a laughingstock, the butt of lewd jokes. Cousin Maud was particularly emphatic to her relative on this point. His position in society was something Frank Crawford cared more than a little about, and her arguments were obviously persuasive. Thus the plot evolved for Frank's secret escape from Boston.

If he even considered a farewell meeting with Belle, or a message to her, he was dissuaded from both courses. A meeting would have meant a confrontation and a "scene," and a message would have left Belle with something in writing that she might have used against him. He should leave, Cousin Maud told him, like a man, if not exactly like a gentleman, without a farewell or an explanation, and abandon Belle in the fashion of a bride left jilted at the altar.

On the night of May 12, 1883, dressed elegantly in dinner clothes, Crawford and Cousin Maud sat in her library hastily correcting proof for *A Roman Singer*, a magazine serial he had dashed off a few weeks earlier; Belle had assured him it was the finest thing he had ever written. That done, Frank and his belongings—including the various gifts from Belle —were hurried out into a waiting taxi and driven through the night to the pier, where he boarded a midnight boat that would carry him back to Italy.

The next afternoon, Frank and Belle were to have met at four, their customary hour. When he had not appeared by five, Belle sent her coachman out to make inquiries. She was told that Frank Crawford had left Boston "permanently"—she was not immediately told where he had gone —and would not be back.

She was devastated. Then heartbreak gave way to rage. She took his departure not only as an insult but as an act of cowardice and treachery. She felt betrayed. She immediately collapsed into another "nervous breakdown," and closed her door to all visitors.

Her husband, as he had done before—and as he would do many times again throughout their married life—came to her rescue with updated plans for extensive foreign travel. Within weeks, the Gardners had boarded a train for San Francisco, where they sailed for Yokohama. Then on to China, Cambodia, Java . . .

A kindly man, he wanted to give her something to repay her for her loss.

One of the lessons Belle Gardner might have learned from all this was that it was unwise for a patroness of the arts to let herself become emotionally involved with the artist she was patronizing. The lesson was certainly there, but it was one, alas, that she would never learn. Jack Gardner once patiently described his wife as "a little girl who never grew up," and this was accurate enough. Girlish she remained—her age always something of a mystery—and subject to schoolgirlish crushes. In London, in 1886, through Henry James, the Jack Gardners met John Singer Sargent. Sargent had already had a number of successful exhibitions at important salons in Europe, had been acclaimed as a major artistic talent, and was receiving commissions from prominent people for portraits. He had also, through no fault of his own, become notorious. In 1884 he had exhibited a portrait of Madame Gautreau in Paris under the title *Madame X*. The trouble was that everyone recognized Madame X as Madame Gautreau—who was fond of a particular lavender shade of face powder —and she was the mistress of the French Republican leader Gambetta. The portrait was not a flattering one. Madame Gautreau had been made to look, it seemed, like a whore, and Sargent had been accused of painting an anti-Republican political cartoon. The French press had raged at him for weeks over this, and, in the end, the controversy caused Sargent to angrily close his studio in Paris and move to England.

Belle Gardner admired the portrait of Madame Gautreau. Something in the lady's defiant stance and haughty, almost brassy look of challenge may have appealed to Belle's own sense of unconventionality. (Eventually she would see to it that a Sargent portrait of Gautreau came to her museum.) Belle also liked John Singer Sargent the man. There were disturbing similarities between Sargent and Frank Crawford. Like Crawford, Sargent was an American born and brought up by an American family in Italy. Like Crawford, Sargent was tall and dark and lean and handsome. As the painter Julie Helen Heyneman described him, he had "an air about him of singular freshness and calm, he had a look as of some serene and beneficent Jove." Like Crawford, Sargent was some years younger than Belle—sixteen years younger, in fact.

Naturally, Belle Gardner immediately wanted John Singer Sargent to paint her portrait. But unfortunately there was no time. The Gardners were due to sail for America within a few days. Before departing, however, she got Sargent to promise to paint her on his next trip to the United States.

Back home in Boston in the late autumn of 1886, Belle Gardner found no shortage of attractive young men. One was twenty-five-year-old Denis Bunker, who Belle quickly decided was a painter of great promise. Denis Bunker, whose family background was a little vague, had been born Dennis Bunker but, after studying art in Paris, had Gallicized his first name by dropping an "n," and become Denis. He liked to explain that his prosaic surname had probably originally been Boncoeur. Bunker, blond and handsome, had already had some experience as a rich woman's pet. He had been taken up by one of the great operatic sopranos of her day, who called herself Nordica (née Lillian Norton of Maine). Bunker had been Nordica's escort and constant companion for the better part of a year, but he had finally dropped her, claiming that she had become "*trop exigeante,*" too demanding. Now Belle Gardner filled Nordica's place, and presently Bunker was receiving commissions to do portraits of nearly all the members of the large Gardner clan.

Bunker also delighted Belle by introducing her to all sorts of little night spots and cafés that were frequented by students and theatre folk, and that Belle had never known existed. He also helped her arrange some Bohemian entertainments of her own. In those days women were not permitted to attend prize fights. With Bunker's assistance, Belle decided to correct this injustice. They hired a hall, a referee, a pair of local boxers and their trainers, and staged an invitation-only fight, to which all of Boston's society matrons were invited. The women-only audience cheered and stamped and practically stood on their seats with excitement through the event, loving it all the way through to the bloody end.

That Belle's unconventionality did not shock and scandalize Puritan Boston is interesting. If Belle had had children, of course, it might all have been different. Mothers might have cautioned their own children not to associate with Belle's, lest they pick up her worldly ways, and Belle herself might have been ostracized. But, as it was, Belle's behavior posed no threat. In fact, it was welcome; Belle dared to do all the things that Boston women had always wanted to do but had been afraid to try. In the winter of 1886–87, the boxing career of John L. Sullivan was at its height, and Belle Gardner was going through a kind of prize-fighter phase. That was the winter when she invited a group of her women friends to tea at 152 Beacon Street, where, she promised them, she would offer them a special treat. The treat was a young prize fighter, whom Belle had asked to strip down to his trunks and pose against a window, but behind a semitransparent screen, so that the ladies could admire his physique. The ladies, however, would have none of the screen, and demanded that the young man come out in full view to flex his biceps and ripple his pectorals before their wondering eyes.

The ladies of Boston had grown accustomed to the fact that, whenever Belle went out, she was usually accompanied by one or another of her youthful protégés. It seemed hardly worth noting that, as Belle approached fifty, the young men she sponsored got younger and younger. Again, she posed no threat, since she seemed to have no interest or designs whatever on the husbands of her contemporaries. Belle's young men were beautiful aliens, strangers from another place who had come for a while to nest with her. Most of them, like Denis Bunker, were witty and amusing, attentive to women's comforts and pleasures. They opened doors, kissed hands, ran little errands. If one of Belle's women friends wanted something from a shop, one of Belle's young men could be dispatched to fetch it for her. Some of the young men were even recognizably talented. One was named George Santayana; another was a fledgling poet, T. S. Eliot.

Another such was a twenty-one-year-old youth just out of Harvard. A young Jew, born in Lithuania, he had been brought up in the mean poverty of Boston's North End, but he had the face of a poet or, some said, an archangel. His nose was long and thin and aquiline, and his brown eyes were large and deep-set. His cheekbones were high and his lips so full that they were almost feminine. This extraordinary face was set off by a mane of long, wavy dark hair. He resembled the youthful Byron, and he exuded a kind of androgynous sexuality which women, and even some men, found almost disturbing. What his talent was, precisely, was not yet clear, but it was obvious, even then, that some exceptional future was in store for this young man. His name was Bernard Berenson, and Belle and a group of her friends set up a fund for him to travel and study in Europe.

It was late in 1887 when John Singer Sargent arrived in Boston to begin working on Mrs. Jack Gardner's portrait. In New York, *Town Topics* raised its eyebrows over the fact that Sargent had moved, bag and baggage, into the house of "the married belle." In fact, it was common practice for a portraitist to live in a client's house while he worked. Sargent, meanwhile, had become an artistic star of the first magnitude, and *le tout Boston* did its enthusiastic best to see to it that Sargent had no idle evenings. So did Belle and Jack Gardner, opening the doors often to guests who wanted to meet the celebrity of the moment, driving Sargent out for week-end rambles in the Massachusetts countryside. One week end they drove him up to visit the Groton School, where Gardner nephews had studied, and to meet the famous Rector, Dr. Endicott Peabody, who was a Gardner relative by marriage. A student at the school at the time was young Ellery Sedgwick, later to become the well-known editor of Boston's favorite magazine, *The Atlantic Monthly*. In Sedgwick's memoir, *The Happy Profession*, he describes the following scene from the Gardner-Sargent visit:

The time was a lovely Sunday morning in the late '80s. There were two hours before church, and I well knew the danger of running across a master and hearing his suggestion that there is nothing like a Sunday morning walk in God's sunshine. I had other views, and with a copy of *Ben Hur*, which had just burst on my excited world, I slipped into the gymnasium and, piling two wrestling mats, rolled them up in one corner, tucked myself securely behind them, and was lost to the world. For an hour I was buried in my book, when suddenly the gymnasium door was thrown wildly open and a woman's voice thrilled me with a little scream of mockery and triumph. Cautiously I peeked from behind my concealment and caught sight of a woman with a figure of a girl, her modish muslin skirt fluttering behind her as she danced through the doorway and flew across the floor, tossing over her shoulder some taunting paean of escape. But bare escape it seemed, for not a dozen feet behind her came her cavalier, white-flanneled, black-bearded, panting with laughter and pace. The pursuer was much younger than the pursued but that did not affect the ardor of the chase. The lady raced to the stairway leading to the running track above. Up she raced, he after her. She reached the track and dashed around it, the ribbons of her belt standing straight out behind her. Her pursuer was visibly gaining. The gap narrowed. Nearer, nearer he drew, both hands outstretched to reach her waist. In *Ben Hur* the chariot race was in full blast, but it was eclipsed. "She's winning," I thought. "No, she's losing." And then at the apex of my excitement, "He has her!" But at that crucial moment there came over me the sickening sense that this show was not meant for spectators, that I was eavesdropping and, worse, that I would be caught at it. There was not one instant to lose. The window was open. Out I slipped and slithered to safety.

For me that race was forever lost and forever won. The figures go flying motionless as on the frieze of the Grecian urn.

> *What men or gods are these? What maidens loth?*
> *What mad pursuit? What struggle to escape?*

I knew not then whether it was lost or won. What I did know was that the Atalanta of that Sunday morning was Mrs. Jack Gardner and Milanion Mr. John S. Sargent. It was that same year he painted the famous portrait of her with her pearls roped about her waist, her beautiful arms glowing against a background that might have been the heart of a lotus.

The portrait that resulted from Sargent's Boston stay is certainly extraordinary. Sargent painted Belle standing, full length. The design of the painting was a series of curves and ellipses. There are the curves of her hips and bosom, of the double strand of pearls at her waist. Then there is the downward curve of her white arms, joined loosely at the fingertips. Finally there is the curve of the heart-shaped neckline of her dress and the curve of the enigmatic half-smile on her face, giving the impression that she is just about to speak. The whorls of the floral tapestry which Sargent used as a backdrop appear to be a series of halos radiating about her face.

Mrs. Gardner's portrait went on exhibit at the St. Botolph's Club, a literary-artistic men's club in Boston, and drew considerable comment from the press. But from the published accounts one wonders whether any of the reporters had actually seen the painting. One reporter wrote that Belle's dress was white. The dress is black. Another claimed that the dress was cut very low at the back, but Belle's back is not even visible. Still another wrote that Sargent painted Belle dripping with diamonds. The only jewels are the pearls, and a ruby pendant at her throat. One report claimed that the dress was sleeveless; the dress, which was by Worth of Paris, has short sleeves. The most damaging comment was that Belle's dress was "very décolleté," though it is certainly no more low-cut than anything that was fashionable at the time. Still, rumors that Sargent had portrayed more of Belle's *poitrine* than was entirely proper continued to circulate, and one wag commented that Sargent had painted Mrs. Gardner "all the way down to Crawford's Notch." The reference was to a popular resort in the White Mountains, but was there another meaning intended here? Was the name of Frank Crawford also being slyly dragged into the controversy?

Word of the possible *double-entendre* got back to Jack Gardner. Usually serene, he was not amused. He would not tolerate his wife being made the butt of coarse jokes, and the portrait was withdrawn from exhibition. Despite many requests, the painting was never again shown publicly during Mrs. Gardner's lifetime, though Belle always insisted that it was the finest work Sargent had ever done. Today it hangs as one of the centerpieces of the Isabella Stewart Gardner Museum.

8

THE PALAZZO

BY THE 1890s, Belle and Jack Gardner had more or less established a fixed routine that involved spending alternate summers in Europe. Jack Gardner's shipping business was prospering—indeed, in that wonderful era of gaiety and extravagance, every American business venture seemed to prosper and the poverty that lay beneath it was successfully hidden—and Gardner could leave the day-to-day handling of the office to talented nephews. In 1891, Belle's father, David Stewart, had died, and this self-made man had left an estate valued at $3,500,000. Nearly half of this, about $1,700,000, went to Belle, an indication that she was the favorite of all his children. Though not imposingly rich from this inheritance, she was now very well off, and her money gave her a certain independence. She no longer had to turn to her husband for the pretty things she wanted to buy.

She was also acquiring a somewhat imperious and autocratic manner, and a habit of hurling expletives that were then unprintable at people who did not do exactly as she wished, though she usually said them in French or Italian. (Once, to an overtalkative dinner partner, she shouted *"Basta!"* —"Enough"— and word circulated that Mrs. Gardner had called a prominent Bostonian a bastard.) At regular intervals, when anything in the running of her household displeased her, she would fire all her servants, crying, "Out! Out!" The servants, however, soon learned that if they hid in the wings until the master of the house came home for the evening, he would straighten things out, and despite her periodic rampages, her servants remained remarkably loyal.

She also continued to enjoy her reputation for eccentricity and outrageous behavior, and whenever there was an opportunity to do something a bit outré, she seized it. For a Boston Symphony concert, she might wear diamonds in her hair, or she might wear a red ribbon advertising the Boston Red Sox. When a lioness at the Boston Zoo gave birth to twins, Belle succeeded in persuading the keeper to let her borrow the cubs for an afternoon's outing in her carriage, and she then brought them home to let them romp about her Beacon Street house. Later, at the zoo, she appeared in the lion's cage to play with the babies, and the rumor circulated that Belle had actually adopted the lions and brought them home to live with her. On another occasion, going to a picnic in the country by train, she asked—and was permitted, since she had hired the train—to ride up in the cab with the engineer, and spent the trip gaily pulling the whistle. She arrived at the party with her white Paquin gown covered with soot, but insisted that the adventure had been worth it. Such exploits inevitably made their way into gossip sheets like *Town Topics*, invariably exaggerated. The more distorted the accounts, the more Belle liked them. She loved reading about herself. And, as always, wherever she went she was surrounded by her adoring coterie of fresh-faced, flattering, bright young men.

Friends noticed, too, that Belle and Jack Gardner had fallen into a habit of bickering. It was just that—not real quarreling. They never said unkind things to each other, but whenever her husband voiced an opinion Belle would immediately take the opposite view. "Wrong!" she would cry in response to whatever statement he had just made, and he, in return, had given her the teasing nickname of "Busy Ella."

The Gardners had bought their first important painting in 1888 in Seville. It was a seventeenth-century *Madonna and Child* by Francisco de Zurbarán. Now, in 1894, the Gardners broke their every-other-summer routine by sailing for Europe with plans to spend more than a year, and their purpose was to buy art seriously. Learning of their arrival, Bernard Berenson, then twenty-nine, wrote a shy note to Belle wondering whether his former patroness still remembered him. The traveling fellowship to study art which Belle had helped establish had long since run out, but Berenson had decided to live more or less permanently in Italy and he was, he explained, in the process of making himself an expert on Italian Renaissance art. He was refining and perfecting techniques of art appraisal, such as examining canvases with microscopes and studying characteristics of individual brush strokes, to sift genuine Old Masters from the countless copies and forgeries that were being routinely palmed off on gullible rich Americans. Indeed, Belle Gardner remembered Berenson. Who could forget that classically beautiful face, those huge dark eyes? Berenson offered the services of his expertise to Belle. Thus a long relationship began.

It was not, however, altogether a smooth one. Berenson was opinionated, but so was Belle. Also, now that Berenson was in the art business, Belle was never entirely sure she trusted him. He was, after all, making a living from commissions charged to customers for whom he bought. Belle was aware that Berenson was Jewish, and a Jewish reputation for alleged sharp practice was a commonplace of the time. Belle, though not a Yankee by birth, had very much become one in spirit, and her Scottish heritage made her a woman who disliked being outsmarted on a deal. As their relationship developed, Belle would regularly send friends as envoys to visit Berenson to appraise his character and assess his integrity. "Well, what did you think of him?" she would then demand. "Is he on the up-and-up?" She was usually assured that Berenson seemed a thoroughly honest man, but she was never entirely convinced. He might, she said, not actually be deceitful in his dealings with her, but that did not mean he could not be deceived by others. Therefore, it was wise to keep checking on him about the authorship and provenance of the pieces of art he was recommending that she buy. In her approach to buying, she was the opposite of Eva Stotesbury, who looked on Joseph Duveen as a kind of teacher. In the case of Bernard Berenson, it was Belle who was the demanding schoolmistress and he the pupil who was required to show her that he had done his homework. With her exacting standards, of course, she was also helping to train Berenson to become what he would one day be acknowledged to be—the world's foremost expert on Italian Renaissance art.

For Berenson, this also meant that in Belle Gardner he had acquired a suspicious and difficult client. To his annoyance, she refused to let him be her exclusive dealer, as Eva Stotesbury let Duveen. Belle insisted on shopping from other dealers as well, which meant that Berenson was constantly competing with others for her attention and her business. Often, she would reject his recommendations, and send him scurrying off instead in search of an entirely different painting which might or might not be for sale. If the painting was unavailable, Berenson had Belle's temper to deal with. He cajoled her with blandishments and flattery, but nothing he undertook for Belle was ever easy.

Occasionally they saw eye to eye. This was the case with Botticelli's *The Tragedy of Lucretia*, which Berenson was able to acquire for Belle at the astonishingly low price of $16,500. It would be the first Botticelli ever to hang in an American collection. There were other important purchases. By the end of the Gardners' long European stay, Belle and Jack Gardner had bought nineteen paintings, nine by contemporary artists and ten Old Masters purchased through Berenson. Their collection was now beginning to have a focus. It would be Italian Renaissance and Dutch genre painting.

In Europe, too, Belle had made another interesting young acquaintance. Strolling through the Louvre, she had noticed a boy—he was no more than sixteen or seventeen—who was studying the pictures with particular concentration. She struck up a conversation with the youth and found him to be surprisingly knowledgeable about art for his age. Impressed, Belle took him to lunch, and they remained friends for many years afterward. His name was Walter Lippmann, and he would later claim that it was Belle Gardner's inspiration and encouragement that made him decide to become a writer.

Back home in Boston, Belle continued to correspond with Berenson by letter and cable, and more paintings were acquired—a Titian, a Raphael, Van Dykes, Vermeers, Zorns, a Rembrandt self-portrait, a second Botticelli. The collection was now outgrowing the Beacon Street house, and the Gardners began giving serious consideration to the idea of building a museum. As usual, they could not agree. Belle wanted to build an addition on the back of 152. Jack argued that this would cut off their neighbors' sunlight. Belle said she didn't care. Jack proposed building a separate structure on newly reclaimed land on the Fenway, but Belle thought this was too far from the center of town. Then, on December 9, 1898, Jack Gardner was stricken with a heart attack at his club. He was brought home, doctors were called, but he died early that evening. He was sixty-one years old.

Belle, once again, was devastated. After his funeral she went into deep seclusion, and it was assumed that she was suffering from another of her nervous breakdowns. Actually, the plans for her museum were proceeding. Now that she had no one to argue with, she decided that her late husband had been right after all, and she purchased the property he had wanted on the Fenway. Before her husband's death she had hired an architect, Willard T. Sears of Boston, and told him what she had in mind. To further her endeavor she now had additional financial support in her inheritance from her husband, in the form of two trust funds totaling $2,300,000.

With her husband's death, however, she became notoriously tightfisted with her money. Everything was to be spent on her art collection and her museum, and it was said that each time Isabella Gardner bought a painting she put her servants on short rations. This may have been true, because even her friends complained of the meager fare and tiny servings at her dinner table. The custodian of her collection, Morris Carter, had a daily errand which was to go down to a corner store and buy a fresh orange for his mistress. One day, thinking to save himself a trip the following day, Carter ordered two oranges. The sales clerk at the grocery store was astonished. "The old lady going to have a party?" she wanted to know.

To help pay for the museum, the house on Beacon Street would be sold, but with characteristic stubbornness she refused to sell until the new purchaser had agreed not to use the number 152. Number 152 belonged to Belle, and the new owner could use 150 instead. And she continued to bicker with Bernard Berenson back and forth across the Atlantic. A friend, she told him, had advised her that she had paid too much for a certain picture. She complained about his commissions, even though, out of gratitude for her early sponsorship of his studies, he charged her only five percent instead of the ten that was customary. She would delay paying him, and then react angrily when he sent her "dunning letters." His letters to her were full of pleas of "Dear lady, *do* please be reasonable!" She never realized, of course, how fortunate she was to be paying the kind of prices Berenson was obtaining for her, since she was assembling her collection a few years before much wealthier collectors such as Eva Stotesbury and J. P. Morgan, who also worked through Duveen, would drive European art prices to the skies.

But Berenson's travails with Belle were as nothing compared with those of her architect. What Belle had in mind was an Italian palazzo in Back Bay. To begin with, everything had to be kept a deep secret. No news of the proposed palace was to be released to the press because Belle wanted her museum to be sprung on the public as a glorious surprise. The façade of the house was to be kept simple, almost stark. The idea was that the structure should be turned inward, about a huge center courtyard, covered with glass, which was to contain a fountain and sculpture and flowers and tropical foliage that would bloom year-round. Sketches were submitted and rejected, revised and resubmitted. Doorways were relocated, rooms shifted from place to place. If Sears pointed out to Belle that a room was too large to carry a ceiling without supporting columns, Belle would merely reply that she wanted no columns, and Mr. Sears would simply have to figure out a way. Even as the ground for the great house was being broken, the plans were still in a state of flux.

The house was to be called Fenway Court, and its design belongs to

Isabella Gardner as much as to Willard Sears. She insisted, for example, on having windows from the façades of Venetian palaces line the indoor courtyard, and capitals that should have gone on the tops of pilasters placed at their bases instead. She also wanted her new house to remind her of 152 Beacon Street in little ways, and walls and chimney pieces were imported from the old house. An unfounded rumor circulated to the effect that one wall covering was to be done in fabric from one of Belle's old ball gowns. Repeatedly Mr. Sears warned her of the danger of creating a hodgepodge of eclecticism, but Belle assured him that it would all work. The rooms of the palazzo would reflect the art they would eventually display. There would be a Titian Room, a Dutch Room, a Gothic Room, a Raphael Room. As the building began to rise, daily changes in the plans and specifications were made, and Belle found it practical to spend her days at the construction site, eating out of a lunch pail, chattering excitedly with her Italian laborers in their language. At one point, rebelling against Belle's excessive demands and instructions that changed from one moment to the next, her laborers struck. Belle responded by firing them all. Within a few days they were back at the job.

When it came to the interiors, she was equally hard to please. In one particular room the painters seemed unable to get the color right. Belle wanted a yellowish pink that was not too pink and not too yellow. Finally she seized a paint bucket and a brush and climbed a tall ladder to show the painters what she wanted—a tiny lady, nearly sixty, in an ankle-length skirt. Miraculously, the color that she achieved was perfect.

Meanwhile, all of Boston speculated about what was going on in the Fenway. Sears had been engaged in 1898, and by late 1900 the building was still far from finished. But Boston began to get a clue when a huge marble plaque was installed over the front entrance of the building. It read:

THE ISABELLA STEWART GARDNER MUSEUM IN THE FENWAY

MDCCCC

The date marked the incorporation of the museum, but it would not be until January of 1903 that Belle Gardner pronounced herself satisfied with the house, the collection was installed, and Fenway Court was ready for its official *vernissage*. This took place at a formal, invitation-only gathering for two hundred guests. Guests had been told to arrive at "nine o'clock, punctually," which created congestion on the street outside and a long line up the walk to Belle's front door, where the cream of Boston society in all its finery waited for the clockstroke. At nine, the door swung open, and there stood Mrs. Gardner's major-domo, resplendent in green knee britches, black patent-leather boots with gold buckles, and a crimson swallow-tail coat splashed with gold epaulettes and much gold braiding. Guests were ushered up one flight of the curved double staircase to where, in a balcony at the top, their hostess—all in black, roped with her pearls, a ruby at her throat and the two huge diamonds in her hair—stood waiting to receive them. They then proceeded down the other branch of the staircase into the Music Room, there to be entertained with a concert by the Boston Symphony Orchestra. Throughout the musical portion of the evening, Mrs. Gardner sat regally alone on her balcony above.

Then it was time to explore the magnificent house and the art treasures it contained. The entire palazzo was lit by thousands of candles, and wood fires burned in the huge fireplaces as guests moved through room after room of Titian, Rembrandt, Vermeer, Botticelli, and tapestries, gasping at the wonder of it all. But the most thrilling moment came as they entered the central, glass-roofed courtyard, where champagne was being served. The courtyard, too, was lighted with candles, torches, and braziers. Though it was the middle of a New England winter, the effect was of entering the Alhambra Gardens in southern Spain. Fountains splashed, and from the balconies of the tall tiered windows that rose above, crimson nasturtiums cascaded down like brilliant waterfalls. In the garden itself, monumental pieces of Greek and Roman sculpture reposed among tall palms and ficus trees, fiddle-leaf figs, showy hibiscus, and purple, red, and orange bougainvillaea. The house itself was beautiful, but the courtyard garden was breathtaking. There was no question that Fenway Court was a work of art on its own. Throughout the winter of 1903, Boston talked of little else but Fenway Court and Belle Gardner's periodic evening entertainments.

As a museum, of course, the Isabella Stewart Gardner was from the outset something of an anomaly. There was the annoying problem, for example, of exactly what it was. From the large marble plaque above the entrance, it had first appeared to be a public institution. Then the plaque was mysteriously covered with a blank marble slab, as though to remind visitors that this was also Belle Gardner's house, and her only one. Many art collectors wait until their death before offering their collections for public view. But Belle wanted the fun of seeing the public admire and enjoy her art. At the same time, she quite understandably felt that she was entitled to a certain amount of privacy in her home, but from the outset she discovered that it would be difficult to have her cake and eat it, too.

When she first opened Fenway Court to the public during the daytime, she had somewhat naïvely assumed that her visitors would be a genteel and gentle group of serious art lovers and connoisseurs. Instead, there was a pushing, crushing, elbowing mob of tourists, sightseers, and merely curious Bostonians. The building codes and fire laws permitted no more than two hundred visitors to the museum at a time, and during the first days of its opening hundreds of angry people had to be turned away. Clearly, some form of ticketing seemed to be indicated, and Belle decided to charge a dollar a ticket. There was more outcry over this, and complaints that other local institutions of art and learning—the Boston Museum of Art, the Public Library—charged no admission. Why should the Gardner Museum? Why did Mrs. Gardner consider herself so special? There was angry talk of boycotts.

Belle also quickly discovered that the museum-going public was not the breed of gentlefolk she had imagined. People came with their lunches and spread out picnics in the courtyard. They brought small children, whose muddy boots soiled her rugs and whose sticky fingers smudged her silk brocade upholstery and wall coverings. Visitors constantly tried to invade Belle's private apartments on the upper floor and to wrench open locked closets and storage rooms to see what might be inside. There was also outright theft and vandalism. Belle had never believed in the banality of keeping the smaller *objets d'art* of her collection locked in vitrines or glass cases. These objects were openly displayed on tables and shelves, and during the first few days of public viewing a number of precious pieces disappeared. Chips appeared in marble statues. At one point Belle noticed a woman visitor fingering the corner of a Gobelin tapestry and stepped over to her, starting to explain the subtlety of the Gobelin's texture and design, only to discover that in the woman's other hand was a pair of scissors. She had been about to snip off a corner of the tapestry for a souvenir.

One of Belle's rules was that there could be no photographing, no sketching, and no note taking in her museum. This irritated the members of the press, who seemed to feel that their First Amendment rights were being infringed. She was attacked in the newspapers, where dark hints were dropped that Belle had been permitted to bring her art into the country duty-free on the ground that it was to be displayed for the public weal, but here was a museum that was not public at all. Belle, the newspapers claimed, was guilty of defrauding the citizens of Boston and the United States taxpayers. Belle quickly made a new rule: No members of the press to be admitted to her museum under any circumstances. Now, of course, the grumbling in the papers was even nastier.

Exasperated with what appeared to be happening to her innocent dream, Belle Gardner decided to adopt a policy that was really no policy at all: She would open her museum when she felt like it, and keep it closed when she didn't. Now there was no way of telling from one day to the next whether a hopeful visitor would find Fenway Court open or closed, and, of course, this fact created more public anger and resentment. It was a damned-if-she-did, damned-if-she-didn't situation which might have defeated a less doughty woman. Though she occasionally expressed bitterness over the way her gift to the public was being received, she did her best to ignore it. "I never expected gratitude," she once said airily. She was happy, she said, if only a handful of the public could obtain some delight from seeing her art collection. As for the rest of them, they could go straight to hell.

On days when her museum was open, meanwhile, she usually succeeded in rewarding visitors with one thing they wanted. Many came not so much to see the art collection at Fenway Court as to get a glimpse of the legendary lady behind it, and they were seldom disappointed. On open days there she would be, a tiny, imperious figure hovering about and keeping a watchful eye on things. In this endeavor, of course, she needed help, and a variety of paid and volunteer docents was tried with varying degrees of success. Finally she hit on a perfect solution: she would use Harvard students, but of course not just any Harvard students. The young men selected to work for Mrs. Gardner's museum had to have certain qualifications. They must be clean, well-groomed, and well-mannered. It helped if they were studying Art, and it helped even more if they were good-looking. It was essential, however, that they all be earning good marks. For the next twenty years, until her death in 1924, the succession of bright, young, and attractive men who served her as guards and ushers in her capriciously run museum, and amused her with their company and conversation in their spare time, would be known as "Mrs. Jack's Museum Boys." Collectively they began to think of themselves as members of a select fraternity.

It struck many people as ironic that Belle, who had lost her seemingly robust husband when he was only sixty-one, should have survived him, despite her own record of delicate health, to the ripe old age of eighty-four in the middle of the Roaring Twenties. During her later years she nearly always wore white. Black, she decided, was an old woman's color, and in white she felt youthful. In 1894 Anders Zorn had painted her in a white dress, her bare white arms outflung against an open French door with the city of Venice shimmering in the background. Many years later a series of small strokes left her without the full use of the hands and arms she was so proud of, and so she concealed them beneath huge white shawls and scarves of white silk and net. Sometimes she wound a white shawl about her head, turban-fashion, and let the rest of the fabric fall over her shoulders, arms and hands. John Singer Sargent painted her that way in 1922, wrapped in yards and yards of white fabric like a mummy, everything concealed except her white face with its stern and piercing eyes looking straight out of the canvas, inscrutable and Sphinx-like.

Even at the very end, Belle enjoyed a good time. She celebrated her eighty-fourth birthday in 1924 in her usual fashion, with a large party at Fenway Court. Just a few days before her death, she was driven into Boston in her old Pierce-Arrow to watch the street parade for a local Elks convention.

Everyone in Boston who remembers her has a favorite Isabella Stewart Gardner story. Edward Weeks, the retired editor of *The Atlantic Monthly*, remembers being invited to her house for tea in the early 1920s when he was a Harvard student. She lay on a Récamier sofa, swathed in white under an ermine rug. It was an occasion, like most, of some drama, for Belle announced to young Weeks that she was destroying all her correspondence. Mounds of it lay about her on the Récamier, and as Weeks watched, appalled, she tore it up and tossed letter after letter into a blazing Indian brazier at her side. Weeks could only imagine what a loss to future scholarship might be involved as the letters went up in flames. They might have been letters from the great Bernard Berenson, or from any of the other protégés and friends whom she had entertained and with whom she had corresponded over the years: Pablo Casals, to whom she left a cello in her will, Sargent, Zorn, Henry James, Ralph Waldo Emerson, John Greenleaf Whittier, and of course the faithless Frank Crawford. Up in flames went all their words to her, while Weeks tried to lift a shaking teacup to his lips. All she wanted to be remembered for, it seemed, was her museum.

Of course the burning-the-letters scene that afternoon would later turn out to be a typical example of Gardner melodramatic stagecraft. Weeks certainly watched her burn *some* letters, but hardly all of them were commended to the flames. Left safely in her museum archives were some six thousand others, including four hundred and sixty-four from Berenson, more than two hundred from Sargent, a hundred from Henry James, and ninety-eight from Crawford. The property that now constitutes the museum was left in her will to seven individual trustees, along with a

$1,200,000 endowment fund to maintain and support it. (The Gardner Museum is now open six days and one evening a week, and though there is no fixed admission charge a voluntary contribution is requested at the door.) In her will, she stipulated that the trustees must not move a single stick of furniture—not a chair, not a table, not a doily—from where she had placed it, and red marks were painted on the floor to indicate precisely where each item went. She also stipulated that if at any time anything was added to the galleries, or if the "general disposition or arrangement" of any articles was changed, the museum and all its contents were to be sold and the proceeds to go to Harvard.

Along with elaborate directions for how the museum must be run was a thick sheaf of papers headed "Directions for My Funeral," which she had prepared some years earlier. It was all very specific—the music that should be played, who should deliver the eulogy, who should be invited, and who should sit where. Her coffin was to be draped with the purple pall—the color of royalty—which had covered Jack Gardner's casket, and on this were to be placed purple violets "if in season." If not, then white roses and heather. (Belle died in mid-July, and so she got white roses.) Tall lighted candles were to stand at either end of the bier. Finally she added, "Carry my coffin high—on the shoulders of the bearers," adding a bit impatiently, "They will have to be told exactly how to do it." She left Fenway Court carried high.

She also left an inheritance, in small but memorable ways, to *grandes dames* who would come after her. Not long after she opened Fenway Court, for example, as the house was being prepared for the debutante party of one of her nieces, word came from the White House in Washington that young Alice Roosevelt would like to be invited to the party. Alice had heard about Fenway Court and Mrs. Gardner and wanted to come to Boston to view these linked phenomena. Absolutely not, said Mrs. Gardner. She would not have the daughter of the President of the United States stealing her niece's thunder.

A few years before that, a beautiful young actress named Eleanor Robson had been walking down Beacon Street, where Belle was still living, and as she passed number 152 there was a sharp rap on the window. It was a parlor maid gesturing Miss Robson to come to the front door. Miss Robson, who had recently scored a critical success in a play in San Francisco, thought she had been recognized as a budding theatrical star and was being asked for an autograph. She walked up the front steps, the door was opened, and there stood the small, commanding presence of Isabella Stewart Gardner. "Walk erect, young woman!" Belle instructed.

Then she closed the door. It was almost as though Belle, with her un-canny ability to recognize talent, was passing her torch of civic leadership on to the younger woman, because Eleanor Robson would go on to be-come Mrs. August Belmont, one of America's great patronesses of the arts.

According to the Gardner Museum staff today, Belle Gardner still runs things there and keeps everyone walking erect, chin held high. She re-turns to Fenway Court, a guard told Louise Tharp, on the third Tuesday of every month at two o'clock in the morning, "to see if everything is all right. If not, there's hell to pay at the office."

PART THREE

Jewish Princess of the Old South

1   Eva and her first husband, Oliver Cromwell, with their three children in 1898. As the wife of a descendant of *the* Oliver Cromwell, Eva rose straight to the heart of New York's prominent Four Hundred.

Eva Roberts Stotesbury

After Cromwell's death in 1910, Eva married Philadelphia's Edward T. Stotesbury, a banking genius and partner of J. P. Morgan. Though an outsider in the snobbish world of proper Philadelphia, Eva soon became a hostess without peer; her personal Versailles was Whitemarsh Hall.

2

3

"He taught me how to live," Eva said of the art dealer Joseph Duveen who was the *grand monsieur* behind so many American art-buying *grandes dames* between 1886 and 1939. "My dear woman," he told his clients, "when you are buying something that is priceless, no price is too high!"

4

Eva's name appeared regularly on "best dressed" lists. Her jewels were worthy of an empress, and enemies falsely claimed she paraded guests past her entire collection displayed in glass cases.

The Stotesburys' El Mirasol was the largest villa in Palm Beach, where they ruled as the winter colony's acknowledged social leaders.

5

Eva's favorite charity was what she called "the personal kind." At Christmas in 1930, she and Ned gave presents to the poor children at Staff Garden Recreation Center.

6

Eva Roberts Stotesbury

Eva and Ned on the lawn at the wedding of Leta Sullivan and Lt. A. T. Barberini of the Italian Military Mission to the U.S.A. Eva was considered eminently gracious in an era when graciousness meant a great deal.

7

John Lowell Gardner of Boston, whom Isabella Stewart married in 1860.

Belle Gardner so admired John Singer Sargent's portrait of Mme. Gautreau, *Madame X*, that she commissioned the artist, shown here, to paint her own portrait in 1887.

Bernard Berenson, the renowned specialist in the Italian Renaissance, taught Belle to buy art selectively and carefully. She in turn financed his travels and study in Europe; meeting her exacting standards was part of his training. Her other protégés included George Santayana and T. S. Eliot.

Isabella Stewart Gardner

10

Marion Crawford, another of her "finds," renounced a career as an opera singer on Belle's advice and became a successful novelist and a fixture at her salon. Belle fell head over heels in love with him.

11

12

13

Portrait of Isabella by Sargent (12). When originally shown to the public, it caused comments that Sargent had portrayed more of Belle's *poitrine* than was entirely proper, and her outraged husband withdrew it from exhibition. The work is now one of the centerpieces of her museum in Boston. The center courtyard, north, of Fenway Court (13), designed by Willard Sears and Isabella. In Back Bay, Boston, she created an Italian *palazzo* and filled it with great works of art. It became The Isabella Stewart Gardner Museum, her gift to the city.

The Tragedy of Lucretia, which Berenson acquired for Belle at the astonishingly low price of $16,000, was the first Botticelli ever to hang in an American collection.

15

Isabella soon after the opening of Fenway Court in 1930. Though far from beautiful, Belle was considered one of the most brilliant, charming, and attractive women on earth.

16

Julius Rosenwald quickly rose from meager means to enormous riches as one-quarter owner of Sears, Roebuck & Co. The older children, Lessing, Adele, and Edith, remembered poverty; the two younger, Marion and Bill, knew nothing but luxury.

17

Of all the children, Edith was temperamentally most like her father—she got things done. Effie was her nickname; it stood, her family said, for Efficiency.

Edith Rosenwald married Edgar Bloom Stern of New Orleans. They had three children, Edgar, Jr., Audrey, and Philip; but she still found time to tackle the city's power structure and was the prime force in organizing voter registration for black people.

18

19

Longue Vue was designed by William Platt for Edith in the Classical tradition, drawing on examples of Greek Revival buildings in Louisiana. Edith donated the house and its magnificent gardens to New Orleans, and every detail has been preserved as it was when Edith lived there.

Edith Rosenwald Stern

21

20

Edith's greatest pride was in being honored by her adopted city. In 1965, she was awarded the New Orleans *Times-Picayune* Loving Cup, presented annually to the citizen deemed to have done the most for the city. The cup's image is embossed on her tombstone.

22

23

Edith Rockefeller McCormick's parents, John D. Rockefeller, the founder of the fortune, and Laura Spelman Rockefeller. The Rockefeller family was German, but Edith preferred to believe herself descended from the noble de La Rochefoucauld family of France. She occasionally signed her letters "Edith de la Rockefeller."

24

25

Edith believed herself the reincarnation of the child bride of King Tutankhamun.

It was to Carl Jung in Switzerland that Edith—unhappy in her marriage, no doubt bored and depressed by her life—decided to commit herself for eight years of therapy.

26

The four Rockefeller children: Bessie, Edith, Alta, and John. A demure, shy child, Edith showed few signs of becoming a future *grande dame*. Her marriage to Chicago's Harold McCormick of the reaper fortune merged two great American families.

In the years after the death of her elder son, Edith seemed increasingly eccentric. She built a huge forty-room mansion called Villa Turicum in suburban Lake Forest but never moved in.

Edith Rockefeller McCormick

Harold McCormick was usually referred to as "the rich playboy" in the newspapers. He divorced Edith in 1922, underwent a rejuvenative gland transplant, and married the Polish soprano Ganna Walska, whose career, sponsored by her new husband, was an unmitigated disaster (28).

29

28

Edith with Edwin Kren (29). She supported him, but their relationship was entirely chaste. His duties were to help her realize her dream of awakening Chicago to the wonders of psychoanalysis. They planned to convert Villa Turicum into a clinic.

30   31

Few women in American history have managed to conceal their pasts as successfully as Arabella (30). While passing as his "niece," she was the mistress of C. P. Huntington for nearly fifteen years. Collis Potter Huntington (31) was the mastermind behind the enormous Central Pacific and Southern Pacific Railroads. He was a man of stupendous wealth who kept his first wife so totally in the background that most people did not know he was married.

32

33

The Moorish salon in Arabella's first "important" house, at 4 West 54th Street in New York City. Huntington paid for it in cash, and she, though self-educated, decorated it so successfully that her rooms are currently on display at the Museum of the City of New York and the Brooklyn Museum.

On July 12, 1884, nine months after the death of his wife, C. P. made Arabella Yarrington Worsham the second Mrs. Collis Potter Huntington. It was a smallish ceremony, and the next morning the newspapers put their formal imprimatur on her utter respectability.

34

Henry Huntington (35) nephew of the late C. P., built Rancho San Marino (34) in the foothills of the San Gabriel Mountains east of Los Angeles to lure his beloved Arabella to the West Coast. When they eventually married, they assembled at San Marino one of the most important private collections of rare books and art in the world. Its contents, including Gainsborough's *Blue Boy* (36), were to become the Huntington Art Museum. They lived in the house only a month or so every year. Where Arabella (37) led, her adoring Henry followed.

Arabella Worsham Huntington

35

6

37

38

40

39

Eleanor Robson (38), the third generation of a minor theatrical family, was an overnight star at 17. At 25, she captivated G. B. Shaw (39) when she starred in *Merely Mary Ann* in London (40). "I am forever yours devotedly," he wrote, and created *Major Barbara* for her. Also captivated was the socially prominent multimillionaire August Belmont, Jr., recently widowed (41). Twenty-seven years her senior, he obviously adored her.

41

43

"It was another world," Eleanor wrote of her new life as a budding *grande dame*. She shared her husband's enthusiasm for racehorses, naming the Belmont horse Man o' War, and she frequently held trophies while victorious team captains drank (42). During World War I, she traveled extensively both in the United States and abroad for the Red Cross. In 1934 she was given the Gold Medal, its highest honor (43).

Eleanor Robson Belmont

Her husband died in 1924, leaving her a beautiful widow at 45, but not a breath of scandal ever touched her name. Cecil Beaton perfectly captured her in her greatest role of *grande dame* (44).

DECEMBER 9 1978 $1.50

OPERA NEWS

Eleanor Robson Belmont
100th BIRTHDAY CELEBRATION

Known as "the woman who single-handedly saved the Met," she created the Metropolitan Opera Guild to guide the company through the Great Depression. Her photo appeared on the cover of *Opera News*, the official publication of the Guild, in celebration of her 100th birthday, although she in fact died two months short of that date (45).

Ima, named after the heroine in an uncle's epic poem, bore her name proudly, even defiantly. Her brothers, Tom and Mike, each had at one time or another to fight people who ridiculed her name. When she became the acknowledged "First Lady of Texas," she was known throughout the state as "Miss Ima," or "Mizima."

47

48

The lovely Ima never married. "I am fatally attracted to handsome men," she would say, "and I know if I had married, I would have picked a handsome husband who was worthless." She took herself to New York to study music, then traveled unchaperoned to Germany. Rolled up in her bag on her return were the canvases, still cheap at that time, of the Post-Impressionists that she bought in Europe.

Her father, James Stephen Hogg, was elected Governor of Texas when she was eight. The death of her mother forced little Ima to serve as his hostess, presiding over formal dinners, teas, and receptions. As Governor, "Big Jim" set a strong example for Ima by fulfilling his campaign promises for economic reform.

49 Miss Ima's home, Bayou Bend, in Houston housed her great art collection. In her youth, she developed an interest in American antiques and decorative pieces at a time when the affluent bought French, English, and Italian collectibles. Bayou Bend was the scene of her famous dinner parties where much that "needs correcting," as she put it, was set to rights. In 1966 she turned Bayou Bend over to the Houston Museum of Fine Arts and its Director Emeritus, James Chillman (50). Her 90th birthday was celebrated with a special concert by the Houston Symphony Orchestra, which she founded in 1913, and sustained with her Symphony Society until her death at 93 in 1975. At her party, she downed her customary quota of man-sized bourbon old-fashioneds, and sang and played the piano (51).

Ima Hogg

51

50

52

53

54

Charles J. Livingood's uncanny resemblance to Mary's dead son, his Harvard classmate, won him the job of right-hand man. He managed her business affairs and civic projects for the rest of her life, and theirs was a perfect working relationship.

Mary Emery was soft-spoken, gentle, domestic, and retiring, more than a little shy. As the richest woman in Cincinnati, she embarked upon an extraordinary 31-year career in philanthropy.

Annie Sinton Taft exchanged daily "breakfast letters" with Mary, her best friend, to decide that day's benefactions. Gossips believed them enemies because if one supported a project, the other withdrew (54).

Mary Hopkins Emery

55

56

In 1923, Mary broke ground for her most ambitious project. Attempting to rid Cincinnati of slums, she built Mariemont, a model community, to provide a good life for the poor. The homes and apartments were leased for low rents with an option to buy. During the Depression, the middle class took possession. Mary Emery died in 1927 at age 83, but the town was not completed until 1965.

9

J.R.'S MONEY

IT USED TO SEEM to the Rosenwald children that they belonged to two different families, that they had two different sets of parents, even though they had only one. This was partly because of the difference in their ages. The first three children born to Julius and Augusta Nusbaum Rosenwald were Lessing, Adele, and Edith. There followed a hiatus of seven years. Then came two more, Marion and Bill. When the two younger ones were growing up, the older three were all in their teens or beyond, and seemed more like aunts and an uncle than sisters and a brother.

But more important than the generation gap between the two sets of children was the fact that in the space of those seven years, their father had become an enormously rich man. The older children had grown up in an unpretentious house at 4239 Grand Boulevard in Chicago. The younger ones, on the other hand, knew nothing but the luxury of the great family mansion at Forty-ninth Street and Ellis Avenue and the huge wooded country estate at Ravinia, where there were servants, governesses, private tutors, tennis courts, bodyguards, and chauffeur-driven limousines.

Augusta Rosenwald, a simple woman from Plattsburg, New York, could never quite adjust to the changes that her husband's sudden change of fortune had brought, to all that had happened to her in those seven years. The idea of being invited to dinners at the Teddy Roosevelt White House terrified her, and she was always "nervous" when, as she was required to do, she entertained captains of industry and their poised, bejeweled wives in her suddenly enormous Chicago house. The idea of employing an English butler frightened her too—the English were so condescending and intimidating. She hired a Japanese butler. Who, after all, could be intimidated by a diminutive Japanese? Years later, Marion Rosenwald's son would come home from a visit with his Aunt Edith. "Aunt Edith talks about your mother a lot," he said. "Why don't you ever talk about her?" "We didn't have the same mother," was Marion's reply. The older children had had a mother who fixed dinner for the family and a father who came home at six o'clock to tell the children stories. The younger children had a mother and father who were hardly ever there, so caught up were they in the exigencies of money—millions and millions of dollars, perhaps as much as $250,000,000, and it all happened in those seven years.

The Rosenwald children could have provided a clinical psychologist with a case study of how two sets of children fared with the same parents under dramatically different circumstances, and the hypothetical doctor would no doubt have concluded that the older children, who had had a taste of simple living, emerged the better for it. "We inherited, in addition to a lot of money, an enormous sense of guilt," says Marion of the younger "generation." Her younger brother, William, was both miserable and sexually impotent by the time he was twenty-seven. It was then that he began psychoanalysis, which continued for the next fifty years of his life. He was convinced, among other things, that he had been given his commonplace first name because his parents had been too busy to think of anything else (his older brother had the distinctive name of Lessing), and was sure he had been named after an old vaudeville routine called "Hello, Bill." Both younger children were embarrassed by their socially insecure mother, and by her maiden name, Nusbaum, German for "nut tree"—there was a comic character on the old Fred Allen radio show called Mrs. Nusbaum. So, apparently, were a number of Gussie Nusbaum Rosenwald's relatives, who changed the name to Norman. Both younger children were married more than once, and psychoanalysis figured importantly in Marion's life, too.

Julius Rosenwald's rise from meager means to enormous riches reads like a Horatio Alger tale, with its full share of funny coincidences and unlikely twists of fate and luck. In 1891 the United States Post Office had begun work on a system called Rural Free Delivery. Up to that point, rural farmers had had to hitch up a horse and wagon and drive to the nearest village post office to collect their mail, often to be disappointed when they found there wasn't any. Now the mail came directly to their houses. Coincidentally, the Post Office had declared that advertising circulars and catalogues fell into the category of "educational materials," along with books, newspapers, and magazines, and could be mailed at a cheaper rate. One of the first to see the money-making possibilities inherent in this twin set of developments was a Chicagoan named Aaron Montgomery Ward. Soon Ward was followed in the mail-order business by two other midwesterners, Richard Sears, a former watch salesman, and Alvah Curtis Roebuck, who repaired watches.

The mail-order catalogues were an immediate shopping boon to rural farmers and their wives, who were cut off from big-city department stores and who, up to then, had relied on itinerant peddlers—often Jewish immigrants—who toured remote communities with horse-drawn carts or with heavy packs of merchandise on their backs. The catalogues would spell the end to that sort of enterprise. Now the peddler came to the door via Rural Free Delivery.

Of the two big catalogues, Ward's and Sears's, the Sears, Roebuck catalogue was easily the fatter, the more colorful, the more daring and the more outrageous. One of the secrets of the Sears catalogue's allure was its surprising sexiness. Countless rural youths enlivened their masturbatory fantasies by thumbing through the illustrations of the ads for ladies' undergarments, and young women could also obtain a sex education of sorts from the ads for union suits, which revealed the general outlines of the male anatomy. The Sears catalogue also opened up a world of consumer goods such as most country folk had never dreamed existed. Never would so much merchandise be displayed through a single medium until the advent of television. The catalogues provided hours of happy reading, viewing, and dreaming, and in themselves they were considered works of art. The work of a popular illustrator usually adorned the cover of a Sears catalogue, or sometimes the lines of a popular poet such as Edgar Guest.

Richard Sears—Roebuck dropped out of the partnership fairly early —was clearly some sort of advertising genius. It was he who wrote all the copy for the catalogues and, like many an advertising genius after him, he was only marginally concerned with telling the truth. An "upholstered parlor set" for the incredible price of 95 cents, which looked like a sofa and two chairs in the picture, might turn out to be a set of doll furniture. His favorite words were "astonishing" and "amazing." His "amazing bust developer" machine, for instance, looked, in the illustration, suspiciously like an ordinary plumber's helper. His catalogue was full of amazing and astonishing potions and elixirs and lixiviums. He offered cures and remedies for baldness, drunkenness, sterility, frigidity, indigestion, bed-wetting, headache, backache, general indisposition, constipation, "female complaint," cancer, and the common cold. He also advertised a great many things he didn't have. A "fine men's suit of black wool" might be advertised for $11. Then, when the orders came in, he would scurry around town to try to find a manufacturer who would run up garments, more or less like the article described, overnight. Also, one had to read the very small print in a Sears ad to learn that the luxurious ladies' fur coats of "Baltic Seal" or "Electric Seal" were actually made of rabbit.

Mr. Sears's motto, "Satisfaction Guaranteed or Your Money Returned," seemed almost too good to be true, and Sears operated on the theory that most not-fully-satisfied customers would not go to the trouble and expense of rewrapping their purchases and mailing them back. This was probably true. But many dissatisfied customers, whose bald spots had not disappeared or whose bosoms had not increased in size, did return their merchandise and ask for refunds. This meant that, though Mr. Sears's business was booming, he was perennially short of cash.

It was at this point that a young man named Aaron Nusbaum entered Richard Sears's life. Nusbaum was a poor peddler from upstate New York who made his way to Chicago, where he tried his hand at various endeavors with little success. Then one day in the early 1890s, Nusbaum read in the newspaper that Marshall Field, the city's largest department store, had somehow managed to lose, or misplace, an entire trainload of merchandise. A train struck Nusbaum as an easy thing to find, and find it he did, parked on a siding, and reported his discovery to the store. He was called into Mr. Field's office and personally thanked by the great merchant, who asked Nusbaum what he could do for him in return. Nusbaum replied that he would think about it and let Field know if anything came to mind.

This did not occur until a few years later, when Chicago was preparing for its 1893 Columbian Exposition, of which Marshall Field was one of the sponsors. Going back to collect his favor, Nusbaum asked if he could have the ice-cream concession at the fair. Field was as good as his word, and in a few months of selling ice cream, Aaron Nusbaum cleared a profit of $150,000, a princely sum in those days.

Nusbaum now looked for a way to invest his windfall. He had heard about Richard Sears's expanding mail-order business, and also about his cash-flow problem. He approached Sears and, in 1895, the deal was struck. In return for $75,000, Sears gave Nusbaum a half-interest in the business. Next, Nusbaum tried to recoup some of his Sears investment, and offered Sears shares to various relatives, who, to their later deep regret, turned him down. Five years earlier, Aaron Nusbaum's sister Gussie had married Julius Rosenwald. When Nusbaum came to his brother-in-law, Rosenwald agreed to purchase half of Nusbaum's one-half interest in Sears, Roebuck & Company. Though no one realized it at the time, Julius Rosenwald was on his way.

Julius Rosenwald's father was not wealthy, but Julius did have rich uncles, the Hammersloughs, who were men's-clothing retailers and manufacturers in New York, and who were well connected—through marriage, through business, and through common worship at Temple Emanu-El—with New York's retailing and investment-banking German Jewish upper crust. The Hammersloughs had tried, at various times, to set young Julius up in the clothing business in New York, but he had been a disappointment. He appeared to have little business acumen and had become that familiar family problem, the young man who couldn't seem to "find himself." As much to be rid of him as anything else, the Hammersloughs had lent him some more money and sent him to Chicago for another stab at the menswear business. In Chicago, he had prospered modestly.

At Sears, Roebuck, however, it quickly began to seem that if Julius's talent was not merchandising it was organization. He looked around at the Sears organization and saw that it was a model of inefficiency. Orders were sloppily taken and sloppily filled. Among other things, Julius installed a letter-opening system, whereby envelopes containing orders were slit open by machines, sorted, and passed along on conveyor belts to the clerks whose job it was to fill them. Sears's service was now much speedier. (When the young Henry Ford was experimenting with assembly-line production of automobiles in Detroit, he visited the Sears operation in Chicago and took home a number of Sears ideas.) Rosenwald was also able to curb Mr. Sears's strong streak of charlatanism, and insisted that merchandise be actually in the warehouse before it was advertised in the catalogue. The advertisements for amazing cure-alls were also discontinued, along with other misleading or deceptive practices. All this meant many more satisfied customers, and far fewer returns of merchandise for cash refunds.

One thing that wisely was not changed about the Sears catalogue was its sexiness. In fact, as photography gradually replaced drawing—with live male and female models posing in the underwear—the catalogue got even sexier.

The Rosenwald approach was so successful that, by 1901, Julius Rosenwald was able to buy out his brother-in-law for $1,250,000—not a bad return, in six years' time, on Nusbaum's original investment. A few years later, to be sure, realizing that what he had sold to Rosenwald was now worth perhaps thirty times that price, Aaron Nusbaum reappeared with a claim that he and Julius had entered into some sort of buy-back agreement, and that Julius had cheated him. But since Nusbaum could never produce any evidence to document this claim, the result was simply an unhappy family money feud in which Gussie Rosenwald became permanently estranged from her only brother.

In 1908, Richard Sears wanted to increase the company's sales promotion budget—sales promotion, after all, was his forte. Rosenwald and the other directors were opposed, but Sears would not budge. To break the deadlock, a vote was taken, and Sears was unanimously voted down. He submitted his resignation. Now Julius Rosenwald—J.R., as he was called—controlled Sears, Roebuck, one of the largest corporations in the world.

Edith Rosenwald, the younger of J.R.'s daughters from the first—or "poor"—set of his children, would display many of her father's characteristics. Effie was her nickname. It stood, they said, for Efficiency.

One remarkable thing about J.R. as he became a rich man was his personal penuriousness. Though Ravinia, his big wooded estate on the shore of Lake Michigan, had tennis courts, he refused to buy tennis balls for his children. Their weekly allowances were the meagerest of any of their friends'. When they complained of a lack of spending money, J.R. suggested that they open a lemonade stand in front of the house. The lemonade stand was a brief success, as far as the children were concerned, but high overhead forced it out of business. A table was set up at the foot of the drive and spread with a white damask cloth. Crystal goblets were set out, along with silver pitchers filled with fresh lemonade. The white-coated Japanese butler was deployed to the roadside to help serve cars coming down the opposite lane, because the children were not permitted to cross the highway. The high-overhead problem ruined the business when J.R. learned that most of the motorists, after paying a nickel for their lemonade, simply drove off with the goblets.

Gussie Rosenwald was just as penny-pinching as her husband. She kept trunkfuls of rags and old clothes, and from these her children's wardrobes were painstakingly pieced together. The raggedly dressed Rosenwald children were the butt of all their classmates' jokes. J.R. was equally stingy when it came to paying his Sears, Roebuck employees. Some of his shipping clerks, most of whom were young women, earned as little as $5 a week, though if they "worked out," and lasted three months, the wage was raised to $5.50. In the early 1900s Chicago was smarting under its growing reputation as America's capital of crime, and the newspapers were trying to do something about it. Prostitution, the papers decided, was the root of the problem. Prostitution supported the pimps, and bought them their guns, with which they committed their armed robberies and murders. And the cause of prostitution was the shockingly low wage paid to clerks in the big retailing operations like Sears. The *Chicago Tribune* published a blistering exposé, full of alarming statistics and all the elements of a story that would sell thousands of newspapers—sex, the exploitation of the innocent by the greedy, the slavery of the poor to the wealthy. How could a girl survive on $5 a week, the paper asked, if she did not turn to prostitution in her spare time? The newspaper's stories led, in 1913, to an investigation of crime and prostitution in Chicago by the Illinois State Senate, and one of the first witnesses called was Julius Rosenwald. He admitted that some of his clerks got as little as $5 a week, though some were paid $6 and $7. He also admitted that Sears, Roebuck had had a profit of over $8,000,000 that year, but he refused to disclose his own income. As in the case of most Senate investigations, nothing much in the way of reform came from this one. Several years later, though, Sears did institute a profit-sharing plan for employees that was fairly generous.

Oddly, although J.R. hated spending money, he loved giving it away, and ironically, the recipients of his philanthropy were the poor. His particular concern was the plight of black schoolchildren in the South who were being educated under the "separate but equal" system, and he began building what became known as Rosenwald Schools. All told, 5,357 schools, shops, and teachers' houses were built with Rosenwald money in 883 counties of fifteen southern states. In these black schoolhouses two portraits hung side by side, Abraham Lincoln's and Julius Rosenwald's. He established the Rosenwald Fellowships to aid blacks in higher education, and both Ralph Bunche and Marian Anderson were Rosenwald beneficiaries. All told, in his lifetime, J.R. gave away $65,000,000, but he still would not buy his children tennis balls.

His philanthropies, of course, fed his expanding ego. Unlike other Jewish philanthropists such as Jacob Schiff, Felix Warburg, and Otto Kahn, J.R. did not adhere to the Talmudic principle that "twice blessed is he who gives in secret." He loved to see his name attached to his gifts. He argued that, if he were going to achieve some sort of immortality on earth, he wanted to be immortal for the right reasons. Too many famous and successful individuals went down in history with their names attached to objects unworthy of them. Count Karl Nesselrode, for example, was not known as a great statesman and diplomat but as a fruit custard pie. The singer Nellie Melba was immortalized as a peach dessert, and the coloratura soprano Luisa Tetrazzini ended up on a menu as a chicken casserole. The only thing J.R. refused to have his name attached to was an art museum. This was because he knew that other wealthy collectors were never eager to donate to a museum which already wore the name of an original benefactor—a Carnegie Museum, a Frick Museum, an Isabella Stewart Gardner Museum.

His daughter Edith, born in 1895 when her father was still a man of simple tastes and modest means—the year Uncle Aaron Nusbaum first drew the family into Sears, Roebuck—was now a young woman and had watched her father's progress from the bottom of the ladder to the top, from a men's clothier to a national philanthropist and tycoon. Of his five children Edith was temperamentally the most like him. She had certainly learned a lot from him, from the good side and the bad. When her little sister Marion complained to Edith that all the children in her school were teasing her and laughing at her because of her hand-me-down, patched-together clothes, Edith simply marched Marion off to Marshall Field's and bought her a new wardrobe, charging everything to their father. For all her father's tightfistedness, she knew that all Rosenwald bills were paid by one of the staff of secretaries, and that J.R. never even saw them. Edith was like that. She got things done in a quick, high-handed way. But it would not be until Edith Rosenwald married Edgar Bloom Stern of New Orleans that little Effie would begin to come into her own as her father's daughter, and start to show her husband's city a thing or two.

10

J.R.'S DAUGHTER—R.A.U.

JULIUS ROSENWALD, it might be gathered, did not support causes simply because they were fashionable or trendy. Building schools for blacks in the rural South was an unheard-of preoccupation in the early 1900s—so unfashionable that J.R.'s contributions went virtually unnoticed for a number of years, except, of course, by the recipients of his gifts. (At the time, his German Jewish counterparts in New York, such as Schiff, Warburg, and Louis Marshall, were toiling in a totally different direction: establishing hospitals, settlement houses, and loan societies to aid the great wave of Jewish immigrants that had arrived in America from the pogroms of Tsarist Russia and Poland.)

J.R. explained his interest in "the Negro," as he put it, this way: As a Jew, he considered himself a member of a race that had endured discrimination and persecution for centuries; he identified with the plight of southern blacks, he said, and just as education had provided the Jew with an avenue out of the ghetto, the same would hold true for the blacks. Also, he had read and been deeply impressed by Booker T. Washington's *Up from Slavery*. Later, he had met Washington and been impressed with the man. He had invited Washington to Chicago, and honored him at a large fund-raising luncheon at the Blackstone Hotel—the first time the hotel had ever entertained a black guest. In return, Washington placed Julius Rosenwald on the board of trustees of his Tuskegee Institute.

To be sure, Booker T. Washington's views would later be denounced as simplistic by many blacks. Washington stressed schools for blacks that taught manual arts and trades, designed to lift blacks out of poverty and into the ranks of the blue-collar working class. J.R. very much approved of all this. It might be pointed out that Sears, Roebuck & Company was also a working-man's store. If there was a somewhat more commercial motive behind the Rosenwald philanthropy—to create a whole new market of blue-collar customers—he was wise enough not to make a point of it. Suffice it to say that Sears today has a large and loyal black clientele.

J.R. also differed from his German Jewish counterparts in New York in that he did not insist that his daughters make dynastic marriages within "the crowd." His son William might argue that J.R. was too busy running Sears to care whom his children married, but J.R. did say that all he asked of his sons-in-law was that they be hard-working and honest and able to support their wives. Edgar Bloom Stern of New Orleans, when he married Edith Rosenwald, was by no means rich on the Rosenwald scale, but he was respectably prosperous.* His family had started in the cotton business in the South with the original Lehman brothers, who later came to New York to found the famous investment banking house, and Edgar was a cotton broker, a member of the family firm, and on the Cotton Exchange. He was a pleasant, mild-mannered man, some ten years older than his wife and clearly fascinated by her energy, enthusiasm, and determination. Determination was a quality which he himself lacked. During their courtship she had extracted a promise from him: when he reached age fifty, he would take a year off from his business, and they would spend that year traveling all over the world. He made the promise and promptly forgot about it, only to be reminded of it years later—a little, it seemed, to his regret.

Edith was a small, trim woman with a thin, handsome face, bright eyes, and an attractively crooked smile. She had vivid red hair and the temperament that is often associated with redheads. Her education, in the tradition of moneyed young ladies of the era, was minimal but genteel—the social graces: how to preside at a tea table, how to dance, play the piano, a smattering of French and Italian, tennis, horsewomanship. She had never actually graduated from high school, but she had been brought up in the tradition that with wealth went civic responsibility. Like her father, she was a very organized person, and it was said of her that if Edith were ever stranded on a desert island the first thing she would do would be to organize the grains of sand on the beach according to size, shape, and color.

When Edith Stern arrived in New Orleans as a bride just before the

* Edith had earlier been briefly and unhappily married, at age eighteen, to a man named Germon Sulzberger—no kin to the New York Sulzberger family. Her father bitterly opposed her getting a divorce, but she did it anyway.

First World War, she found a very different sort of world from the one she had left behind in bustling, no-nonsense Chicago. New Orleans was —and is—a dreaming city, full of secrets and rites and arcane rituals, a city of hidden courtyards and fountains behind high bougainvillaea-covered walls and filigreed iron gates. It was a city of mysteries guarded from outsiders—who will the Queen of Carnival be?—a girlish city of whispers and giggles and gossip. Sultry in summer, damp in winter, it was a city that seemed to have been frozen in time somewhere in another century. It was also a city so entrenched in prejudice that prejudice had become a social art—not so much against Jews or blacks as against anyone you didn't really know. It was a city of the dainty, flirtatious, lazy southern belle, whose pose, at least, was helplessness and a weakness for Coca-Cola laced with a tot of Bourbon. When Edith Stern first arrived in New Orleans, she was not entirely pleased with what she saw.

What she saw was a community pleasantly congealed in a state of civic lethargy. Public philanthropy was virtually nonexistent. In general, the Jews of New Orleans were more charitable and public-spirited than the Christian majority, but even the Jews were not contributing to the extent that they were in other cities. The total preoccupation of New Orleans appeared to be its annual Mardi Gras, and no sooner had the curtain been rung down on one year's Carnival revels than the city's leaders sat down to begin another year-long planning for the next. The various Krewes— the Krewe of Comus, the Krewe of Rex—that ran the Carnival were, Edith quickly realized, based not only on snobbery but on fantasy and myth. The identity of Rex, for example, the King of the Carnival, was supposed to be a closely guarded secret. Everybody in town knew who he was. And the Queen—"Princess Summer-Spring-Winter-Fall"—was supposed to be the lucky debutante who found the gold coin in her piece of cake after it had been cut. No one wondered how it could be that, immediately after she had found her coin with a cry of gay surprise, the girl and her parents would drive home to host a gala catered dinner dance for six hundred guests under a tent, to celebrate the lucky accident.

The Carnival balls, meanwhile, excluded Jews. Early on in her New Orleans career, Edith Stern made it a conspicuous point to leave the city with her husband during Mardi Gras as an expression of disapproval. Soon other prominent Jewish families would follow the Sterns' example.

Obviously, Edith decided, if one were going to change the ways of an inbred and ingrown city, one needed an imposing platform from which to do it—a stage, such as Eva Stotesbury and Isabella Gardner created for themselves at Whitemarsh Hall and Fenway Court. The architects

William and Jeffrey Platt were summoned from New York, and plans for a great estate in suburban Metairie were laid out, an estate that would include a grand Greek Revival house and acres of formal gardens. "We'll do the house," her husband told her, "on one condition—that you never look at a single bill." This was a little odd, of course, because the house would be built entirely with Edith's money, but it was like Edgar—supportive, making her feel that whatever she did was perfectly all right with him.

Interestingly enough, J.R.—the man who had raged at his children when a light bulb was left burning—was delighted with the idea of Edith's building a splendid house. Had he mellowed in his older age, or was it just, as his children suspected, that he was happy to see them married so that they would not come home and be a burden to him? In any case, J.R. contributed generously to the construction of the house; when he visited, Edgar Stern would often find a bookmark in a book he was reading replaced by a check from J.R. for many thousands of dollars.

The estate was called Longue Vue, and when it was finished in the early 1920s it was considered one of the most beautiful houses in the South, and the view was long indeed—clear to the shores of Lake Pontchartrain. It was a place designed for grand entertainments, and it was not long before Edith's parties were the talk of the city. Wisely, for her formal bow to New Orleans society Edith chose not to appear as a haughty northerner bent on changing an old-fashioned city's backward ways (though this was exactly what she had in mind). Instead, she made a display of embracing local customs—giving her estate a French name was part of this campaign—and cuisine. For her parties Edith always offered favorite local dishes and in lavish amounts: whole oyster bars set up with hundreds of raw and fried oysters, gumbo, *grillards*—a regional dish of veal with grits—and, finally, *café brûlot*, over whose flaming bowl she presided. As a hostess, she simply set out to out–New Orleans New Orleans. Over her lifetime she would earn many nicknames in addition to Effie, but one of her husband's pet names for her was "Angèle, my Yankee Creole."

"If she had wanted to," her son Philip said in 1981, "she could have organized General Motors. We used to say that if Mother couldn't get a seat on an airplane, she'd buy the airline." One of her favorite retorts, when told that something she wanted done would be difficult if not out of the question, was "Don't be ridiculous!" "Don't be ridiculous!" she would cry if told that ten thousand Japanese lanterns, which she wanted to decorate her gardens for a party, were not available in the entire South.

Hours later, they would be flown in from somewhere. For her parties she kept elaborate lists, everything referenced and cross-referenced, of guests, menus, flowers, table settings, wines, indoor and outdoor décor, the waiters' uniforms, what the musicians would wear and what the musical selections would be. As she moved through her day she carried a thick sheaf of papers, checking off chores that had been completed against those that remained to be done. Through entertaining, Edith and Edgar Stern established themselves as members of New Orleans society—parties were what New Orleans was really all about, anyway—and when the New Orleans Country Club was organized, the Sterns were among the very few Jewish families invited to be charter members.

As the children—Edgar, Jr., Audrey, and Philip—came along, their birthday parties became a part of Edith's repertoire of entertainments and were always lavish affairs. One children's party, for example, was a full-scale circus held under a striped tent, complete with dancing bears and performing seals. The children were supplied with play money to admit them to the sideshows. At the same time, in the tradition of J.R., the Stern children's allowances were smaller than any of their friends'. It was supposed to be their father's chore to pass out these weekly sums, but he inevitably forgot to do so and on Saturdays, when the allowances were due, Edith took to wearing a dress that had nickels for buttons, to remind him. "And," Philip Stern recalls, "a nickel a week was about all we got."

The Stern children were born into an era when "progressive" education had become the fashion, and, reading every book and article she could find on this subject, Edith Stern quickly made herself an expert. The New Orleans school system, she discovered, was as casually organized as the rest of the city. The public schools were hopelessly inadequate and out of date, and the few private schools, where the "best" families sent their children, were not much better. It was in the area of education that she first decided to reform New Orleans; when she approached other mothers, however, she found interest but no real enthusiasm or willingness to work. The women of New Orleans, she once said, "gave nothing at all. Southern women are brought up to be decorative not forceful, modest not vital. I must have seemed a monster to them." Monster or not, her oldest child was approaching nursery-school age, and so Edith simply built a nursery school of her own. It stands today as the Newcomb Nursery School. That done, she next began building the Metairie Country Day School, hiring the headmaster and teaching staff, and opened its door to a first-grade class in 1929, the autumn of the Great Crash. Crash or no, she continued to add a grade a year until she had the customary eight. Like its forerunner, Metairie Country Day still operates and is considered the preeminent elementary school in the city.

In the course of her school building, Edith found herself sparring with the city's bureaucracy over zoning variances, building codes, and fire codes. In the process of dealing with building inspectors and other local politicians, she learned what everyone else in town had merely taken for granted—that political corruption in New Orleans was as much a genteel tradition as Mardi Gras, that bribery and graft had been elevated almost to the level of an art form. All the best people were involved in it in one way or another. This led Edith Stern to investigate the means by which some of these politicians were elected to office. She found, among other things, that many voters who could read and write were listed as "illiterate," which meant that a voting commissioner could accompany them into the voting booth and instruct them how to vote. Perfectly able-bodied men and women were listed as "disabled," and were given the same assistance. She unearthed voters who were registered under a variety of names, thus permitting them to vote dozens of times apiece. She also found voters whose actual whereabouts were in the local cemeteries. It was the New Orleans blacks, of course, who were the most victimized in these schemes, and blacks who were unwilling to go along with them were afraid to vote at all. After getting permission to examine the city's voter rolls, she announced that she had found at least 10,000 illegally registered voters, and that this was only the tip of the iceberg.

If J.R.'s work with black causes had not been particularly fashionable in Chicago and the Northeast, his daughter's crusade for black enfranchisement and an honest voter-registration system in an old, tradition-ridden southern city was even less so. Nor did her announcements about voter fraud in the local papers endear her to the politicians. There were threatening letters. There were anonymous telephone calls. Edith Stern paid them no heed. In a modest office she set up the Voters Registration Service, which had a twofold purpose: to get the phony registrations off the rolls and, at the same time, to educate the black population in the importance of what she was trying to do.

Obviously, she was helped in her enormous and unpopular task by the fact that she was very rich. But Edith's power was more than the power of her purse. There was also the power of her don't-be-ridiculous personality. A tiny woman, she charged into situations with such force that lethargy and indifference gave way before her like the waters of the Red Sea. Seeing how effective she could be, other New Orleans women now began to go along with her. (And who would want to be left out of the best parties in New Orleans?) Soon she had marshaled a small army of women for her Voters Service, and she organized a "broom parade" of socially prominent women who, brooms in hand, marched on City Hall, the message, of course, being that it was time to sweep the rascals out. Within a year, a mayor was out of office and Edith's Voters Service was supervising registrations. It has done so ever since.

"Edith operated on one rule," says her sister, Marion Rosenwald Ascoli, the widow of Max Ascoli, founder and editor of the *Reporter* magazine. "If you didn't agree with her, you were *wrong.*" Another of Edgar Stern's pet names for his wife was "R.A.U.," which stood for "Right, as usual." "Right, as usual," he would say to her whenever she ventured an opinion, to which her usual reply was simply, "Of course." (At their huge summer camp in the Adirondacks, Edgar Stern had christened the family motor launch the *Rau*.) She could be more than a little autocratic. Once, after a large dinner at the Royal Orleans Hotel, Edith Stern decided to leave through a side door. Going out the front door would have meant an additional walk of perhaps a hundred feet to her car. But the side door was locked. "Don't be ridiculous!" cried Edith Stern, and she waited impatiently while a janitor who had the key was summoned and the door she wanted to use was unlocked for her. Her success at revamping New Orleans politics may have owed a lot to the fact that New Orleans politicians had no experience in dealing with such imperious autocracy—and from a woman, at that.

Who but Edith Stern, for instance, would have had the audacity to give a huge buffet supper honoring a black woman, even though the black woman was Marian Anderson? Now she had gone too far, they said in New Orleans when the invitations were received. New Orleans would just not stand for that. But stand it they did, and turned out, albeit perhaps a bit warily, in droves. Soon it was announced that Edith Stern had been made a trustee of a black college, Dillard University. It was, she explained, merely an extension of her father's crusade for black education in the South.

One reason why Edith Stern was so effective was that she employed a kind of tyranny of temper. Her rages, when not everyone immediately agreed that she was right, as usual, were becoming legendary. Powerful businessmen and politicians in New Orleans often did her bidding simply because it was easier than enduring one of her excoriating tirades. Her father had used this technique effectively, too, having discovered that if a polite request did not get him what he wanted right away, a thundering command, coupled with an insult or two, usually worked wonders.* His daughter tackled the New Orleans power structure the way he had run Sears—as a benevolent despot—and her bailiwick soon extended to include, in addition to the Voter Registration Service and Dillard University, the New Orleans repertory theatre, the Symphony Society, the Isaac Delgado Museum of Art, and the New Orleans chapter of the Garden Clubs of America. "Don't worry, I am at the helm," she would say when confronted with any problem, and it was certainly true that, in her demanding way, she was able to cut through all sorts of confusion and red tape and get things done.

She ran her household and her family the same way. Her children were always a little afraid of her, and without question her soft-mannered husband was. Whenever Edgar Stern saw a new storm brewing in his wife's eyes, he made himself scarce, and spent the rest of his time mollifying and cajoling her and assuring her that, as usual, she was *right*. And yet he adored her, and the Stern children today feel that their parents' was a particularly happy marriage, a successful partnership, and, despite the tirades, they worshiped her, too, and remember a generally happy childhood with her. (So did her older and younger brothers and sisters.) A lot of it had to do with the fact that her tempers were short-lived. Once a storm had passed, she would flash her enormously bright and winning smile and toss her mane of red hair, as though to say, "Well, now that I've got that out of my system, let's have some fun." Her love of fun— and wonderful parties—more than balanced her fits of anger. "The thing I remember most about growing up," her son Philip says, "is Mother clapping her hands and saying, 'Let's have a party!' Then she'd get out her files and notebooks and start organizing it. What she was, really, was an impresario."

* Only once was J.R. known to have lost his magisterial self-confidence and air of ruling all he surveyed. That occurred one Sunday in 1924. J.R. was in Boston, lunching with his son Bill, then a student at Harvard, in the dining room of the Copley-Plaza. J.R. was in a courtly, paternal mood, and Bill Rosenwald had brought along a young friend from Wellesley named Gladys Fleischman. Lunch was proceeding pleasantly until J.R. was called from the table to answer a telephone call. He returned to the table a few minutes later looking shaken and pale, and Miss Fleischman would never forget the awful change that seemed to have come over him. He looked as though he was about to become violently ill. He had just learned that two Chicago youths, Nathan Leopold and Richard Loeb, had confessed to the "thrill killing" of fourteen-year-old Bobby Franks. Loeb's father was a Sears, Roebuck vice-president. Something had finally happened within J.R.'s domain over which he had no control.

But like any great impresario, or diva, she was unpredictable. One never knew quite how Edith would react to any given idea. None of the Rosenwalds, for instance, was devout, and neither were the Sterns. Edgar Stern was a *pro forma* member of the Reform congregation of Temple Sinai, but never went to temple or became involved in any of the congregation's activities. Edith and her husband were on-and-off Jews. That is, when it was necessary to stand up and be counted, they were Jewish; otherwise they never talked or seemed to think about it. They gave routinely, but not magnificently, to Jewish causes, but their main philanthropic interests lay elsewhere, and the Stern children were raised in a completely a-religious household. Therefore, when Edith's daughter Audrey was making plans to marry a young New York writer and editor named Tom Hess, Audrey Stern was totally unprepared for her mother's rage at learning that a rabbi was not going to perform the service. A rabbi was summoned. Then, when the rabbi mentioned that he planned to include in the service the ritual shattering of the wineglass beneath the bridegroom's foot, with its symbolic meaning of the bride's loss of her virginity, Edith flew into another rage. She was not going to include *that* barbaric practice in her daughter's wedding. She wanted, in other words, a wedding that would be Jewish, but not too Jewish. And, as usual, she got what she wanted.

She treated her servants in the same high-handed manner, and they too were expected to swallow their mistress's torrents of abuse whenever some detail in the smooth running of Longue Vue seemed short of the mark she demanded. Also, for all their travail, she followed her father's example at the store and paid very low wages, though she did regularly present her help with bonuses in the form of shares of Sears stock—with, perhaps, an exaggerated notion of how wealthy these gifts were making them. And yet, again, mysteriously, the servants appeared to worship the imperious lady of the house. At least they were remarkably loyal. They were Johanna and Minnie, Emma and Amanda and Lily and Rita; Philip Bradbury, Adam and Isaac, Vilma, Nancy, and Eloise. These people would serve Edith Stern for twenty, thirty, and, in at least two cases, more than fifty years. It all had to do with her mercurial personality—laughing one minute, screaming the next—and with whatever extraordinary ingredient it was that gave her such power over people.

Once, when she was involved in litigation with the United States Government over taxes, her son Edgar noticed a sheaf of legal documents on her desk under the heading *Edith R. Stern* v. *The United States of America*. Edgar commented, "Hell, that's not an even contest. The United States of America doesn't stand a chance!" And it didn't. Edith, right as usual, won the case. And once, commenting casually to her sister Marion that when she and her husband first moved to Metairie, none of the streets in the town had been paved, Marion exclaimed, "Good God, Edith, don't tell me you did that *too!*"

One afternoon late in 1935, when Edgar Stern was approaching fifty, he came home from his cotton-brokerage office to find the floor of his drawing room at Longue Vue covered with maps, and Edith marching up and down among them, with file folders and notebooks, making notes. What was R.A.U. doing? he wanted to know. Had he forgotten his courtship promise? His fiftieth birthday was at hand, Edith reminded him, and this was the year they would devote to travel, splendid travel, circumnavigating the globe. Edith was working on their itinerary now. The children would be placed in Swiss schools. Reservations had been made for a suite of cabins on the *Kungsholm* for the first leg of the journey. Edith was organizing everything.

Edgar had forgotten the promise, but she was right, as usual.

"My father's only role in that grand tour," Philip Stern recalls, "was to grasp Mother's arm at the last minute and say, 'My God, have you got the tickets?' "

It would indeed be a grand tour, with every last detail organized at every stop—the tickets, the hotels, the restaurants, the sightseeing, the theatres, the museums, the contacts with local banks, everything. It would also be the end of Edgar Stern's business career. From that moment on, the rest of his life would be run by his wife's capable executive hand.

11

"THE EXAMPLE WE SET"

LIKE BELLE GARDNER, Effie Stern made a great to-do over birthdays, her own especially, and at intervals of not more than five years she saw to it that an especially spectacular gala was given in her honor in some exotic place. For her sixtieth birthday she flew her entire family to Bermuda, where she insisted on taking scuba-diving lessons. For her seventieth, all the relatives were flown to Paris, and for her seventy-fifth it was to Venice. At this point the Rosenwald-Stern clan had grown to such proportions—what with grandchildren, nieces, nephews, and in-laws, ranging in age from eight or nine to almost ninety—that an entire floor of the Gritti Palace Hotel was required to house the week-long party.

As always, every detail of the adventure was organized by the hostess. During the day, the guests were permitted to come and go as they chose, though printed lists suggesting a visit to this or that church, monument, palace, or museum were distributed daily. And throughout the day the door to the suite belonging to the matriarch—who had seen all the sights of Venice long before—was kept open to receive members of her family while she held court. At six o'clock, everyone was expected to gather in the principal suite for cocktails. Reservations for the entire group would have been made well in advance at a number of the city's top restaurants, and Edith would read off the list of choices, along with a few words about the atmosphere, setting, and menu specialties of each. Then a vote would be taken, the reservations at the rejected restaurants canceled, and the party would repair to a fleet of gondolas which would carry them all to the elected eating place.

For her eightieth birthday, in 1975, Edith Stern announced to her family—now grown even larger—that the locale would be Walt Disney

World, which had recently opened in Florida. Her sister Marion Ascoli was apprehensive about this choice, and told her so when Edith first mentioned the notion on the phone. Marion was certain that, at the Disney World Hotel, her sister would not find food, service and accommodations at the level she was accustomed to in such places as the Gritti Palace and the Paris Ritz. "But it will be so much fun for the children," Edith said, determined, as usual, to have her way. At first Marion declined the invitation. But as the date approached, and as Marion sensed her sister's increasing tension and irritation over little details that kept going wrong—reservations were misplaced, the hotel did not have the number of suites Edith wanted, no limousines were available, only buses —Marion decided at the last minute to fly to Florida and help Edith through what was becoming a sizable ordeal.

Arriving at the hotel, Marion Ascoli asked for Mrs. Stern's room, only to be told, "She hasn't come through the computer yet." Then, offered no further assistance, Marion set off through the hotel, starting on the top floor and working down, to find her sister's room by trial and error, knowing that her clue would be the open door. At last she found it and stepped inside. Edith was standing outside on a balcony, furiously flipping through her file folders on the trip—the schedules, the itineraries, the suggestions, the lists of restaurants, all carefully typed, collated, organized. Sensing someone's presence, Edith turned and, seeing her sister, ran into the room, fell in her arms, and burst into tears. It had taken the huge Disney World organization to defeat Edith Stern.

Of course, there were still many enormously successful parties—parties at Longue Vue, where luncheons for eighteen were the general rule, and where tables set up in the garden were always matched by identically set tables in the house as insurance in case of rain. There were huge house parties, with guests invited for weeks at a time, at White Pine Camp in the Adirondacks, which during the Coolidge years was lent to the President as a Summer White House. Later Edith acquired a second summer place, outside Lenox, Massachusetts, so her family could enjoy the Tanglewood and Jacob's Pillow music and dance festivals. Edith christened this house Austerity Castle. It was hardly austere, but she liked to point out that she had furnished it entirely from the Sears catalogue. During all these house parties her loyal and underpaid servants could not even look forward to the bounty of tips. Tipping any of her staff, Edith explained, was against the rules. This, she said, was because she also entertained a goodly share of struggling young artists as well as ill-paid teachers and university people who could not afford to tip. In the same breath she usually mentioned her Sears stock bonus system, implying that the servants were becoming almost as rich as she.

Edith hated missing parties as much as she loved giving them. Her husband was proposed for membership in the elite Jewish Century Country Club in New York's Westchester County, and, not long after joining, he managed to win the club's golf tournament, along with a $1,500 purse. Edgar Stern was gently reminded that it was a club tradition for the purse winner to use his winnings to throw a party, which he proceeded to do. At the time, his wife was giving birth to their second son, Philip. She was furious because she couldn't be there.

Edith and Edgar Stern's full year of foreign travel was an extended party, and during the course of it Edgar Stern would invent a new pet name for his wife, "The hostess with the mostes' on the bill." Edith could never quite grasp the fact, for instance, that her favorite fresh oysters, which she ordered many dozens at a time, were much more expensive in the great restaurants of Rome, Paris, and Madrid than at the fishmongers' in New Orleans, or understand why they were completely unavailable in Nepal. "Don't be ridiculous!" she would cry, and the next day a shipment of oysters would be flown in to Katmandu. When she tired of the location of Longue Vue, which had been built on Metairie Lane, it was her iron whim to have the entire house moved to Garden Lane, a few blocks away. While the big Georgian house was being transplanted, which took several days, Edgar Stern would climb aboard the moving house each evening to collect clothes to wear to the office the next morning.

The Sterns returned to New Orleans from their year of travel in 1936, and it soon appeared that, from the experience, Edgar Stern had lost his taste for business. Though he had risen to the position of president of the Cotton Exchange, cotton trading no longer seemed to interest him. Perhaps a solid year as his wife's factotum had convinced him that this was the career he was best cut out for. He had become, in a sense, her assistant, and in that role he seemed happy enough. She might be the hostess with the mostes' on the bill, but she was the one who paid the bills, and there was no clear reason for him to work at all. He sold his business, disposed of his seat on the Exchange, and retired at the age of fifty-one.

Now he continued as her assistant full-time. The Rosenwald fortune had managed to weather the Depression virtually intact, and Edgar Stern helped Edith set aside some of her money to establish the Edgar B. Stern Family Fund—later renamed the Stern Fund—a foundation to support worthy philanthropic and civic causes. For the next twenty years the Sterns' principal activities were philanthropic, and, in the process, they endeavored to instill a sense of philanthropic mission in their children.

Edgar Stern died, at seventy-four, in 1959, and with his death the first rift appeared in the Stern family. (Edith's daughter Audrey died soon afterward, of that mysterious illness called *anorexia nervosa*, or prolonged loss of appetite.) The directors of the Stern Family Fund were now sons Edgar, Jr., and Philip, their respective wives, and, of course, Edith.

There had never been much question that Edith's favorite son was her younger, Philip. Edgar, Jr., was very much a businessman, and he was good at it. He was on the Sears board of directors, had headed the New Orleans United Fund, was active in the promotion and development of Aspen, Colorado, and had invested in other profitable enterprises. But Philip had both literary and political talent. He had written many magazine articles and published several books, including the controversial *The Rape of the Taxpayer*. He had graduated with honors from Harvard, studied law, and served as campaign manager and chief speech writer for Adlai E. Stevenson. (Like his mother, in the southern tradition of her adopted state, he was an ardent Democrat.) He had written for *The Washington Post*, edited scholarly journals, and served on the boards of many charitable institutions. The only enthusiasm he didn't share with his mother was her fondness for high society. "I keep trying to launch Phil socially," she often said, "and he keeps sinking." For every fraction of an inch that Edgar B. Stern, Jr., managed to add to this biographical sketch in *Who's Who in America*, his younger brother managed to add just a bit more. That the boys were a mite competitive was a fact that Edith didn't mind at all, but when she looked for advice she turned to Philip.

Not long after Edgar Stern, Sr.,'s death, the five-member board of the Stern Family Fund was asked to consider a proposal involving funding for research on corporate responsibility. In particular, the study proposed to investigate certain antisocial activities of the General Motors Corporation. Earlier, Edgar, Jr., had been acutely embarrassed by a Stern Fund grant that paid for a critical study of the broadcasting industry. Among young Edgar's business interests was his ownership of WDSU Broadcasting in New Orleans. Now, from his position on the Sears, Roebuck board, Edgar felt certain that he would be severely criticized if his family's fund offered to finance a study that would be anti–big corporation. Sears, after all, was very much in the big-corporation category; it would not look right. Also, Edgar argued, such a move could open him up to stockholder lawsuits. He announced to his mother and to his brother and sister-in-law, "If this grant passes, I will have no choice but to resign." A family meeting was held to discuss this touchy matter.

Philip and his wife voted in favor of the grant. Edgar and his wife, as expected, voted against it. The pivotal vote was then Edith's. She voted for it, and Edgar promptly did as he had threatened—and resigned from the Edgar B. Stern Family Fund.

To say that Edgar Stern, Jr., never forgave his mother for siding with his brother would be putting it a little strongly, but it was noticed that after this episode Edgar, who had always lived near her in New Orleans, more or less permanently removed himself to Aspen.

In the years following her eightieth-birthday party at Walt Disney World, Edith Stern—who had always seemed slight and frail despite her enormous energy—became increasingly ill. Like her daughter, she seemed to lose her appetite for food, even for her favorite oysters, and her weight dropped alarmingly. She had to be forced to eat, and, in the late 1970s, she entered a hospital. From far and wide the family gathered— children, grandchildren, great-grandchildren, nieces, nephews, grand-nephews and grandnieces, her devoted sister Marion and her brother Bill. The end, it seemed, was at hand. An intravenous device was placed directly in her heart. It failed. Sadly, the doctor informed her assembled family, "There's nothing more we can do. She might as well go home and die there." She was carried by ambulance back to Longue Vue, where it was assumed to be only a matter of hours.

Once home, the family resumed its vigil at her bedside to bid her good-bye, while Edith surveyed their concerned and anxious faces mutely from her pillow, her hair still dyed a vibrant red—a queen saying a last farewell to her loyal court and courtiers.

Then, as though satisfied that her deathbed scene had been a success, with all the desired effects and fuss, and with the proper attendance figures, Edith began to improve. She began to eat again. She gained weight. Soon she was up and about, rummaging through the trunks of costumes she kept upstairs for fancy dress, talking about another party. The family, suspecting that she had staged her departure from this life as effectively as she had orchestrated her famous entertainments, dispersed, feeling somehow a little cheated. When the end finally came, in the late summer of 1980 when she was eighty-five, it came quietly, in her sleep. There was no need for another scene.

In New Orleans, flags flew at half-staff. At her memorial service, held in her lovely Longue Vue, the weather was oppressively hot and humid.

Just before the service, the air-conditioning system broke down, and the hundreds of perspiring guests fanned themselves with paper fans. Her son Philip remarked, "If she were still around, she would have had it fixed immediately."

"She turned New Orleans around," one of her old friends says. "From a sleepy, corrupt little Mississippi River town, she brought it into the twentieth century." There were other legacies—a small but elegant collection of modern art, including a Kandinsky, a Victor Vasarely, a gallery of Barbara Hepworth works, and an exquisite collection of miniature Alexander Calder mobiles. There were her two schools, her Voter Registration Service, and innumerable lesser benefactions. Not long after her death, Philip and his wife were traveling in Israel and visited the Billy Rose Sculpture Garden. There they were surprised to find a Vasarely sculpture commissioned and donated by Edith Rosenwald Stern. Philip has no idea how many other such random gifts may turn up around the world.

One of her more important presents to New Orleans was Longue Vue itself—donated to the city, along with its magnificent gardens, and accompanied by a $5,000,000 endowment to maintain it for the public. At Longue Vue, every detail of the house and its furnishings is preserved as it was when Edith lived there. It is a museum, as it were, of a certain way of life.

She once told the writer Leon Harris, "I think that one thing we children each learned from our parents was the importance of the example we set. And I don't mean a snobbish sort of fashion . . . just the opposite in fact. My mother never ceased telling us with pride about the calluses she wore on her hands as a child scrubbing floors and helping to raise her sisters and brother. And after my father made so much money and they went East, where they were entertained at the feudal estates of the Schiffs and the Strauses outside New York, my mother was more than ever resolved never to become like that, never if she had a country place to have statues or anything else she considered pompous or stiff. Mother was very naïve, but she was a very great lady—very sensitive, in the good sense of being sensitive to the feelings of others and not just her own. And when she built Ravinia, she insisted that it be kept natural, using the ravines and local flowers and only tanbark and gravel roads—nothing forbidding."

In a rare moment of modesty, she added, "We tried to set a pattern here, Edgar and I. We hoped to change the local way of life, but I think we failed." She was referring, of course, to Mardi Gras, whose force in New Orleans has become as inexorable and immutable as the tides. Each year the flashy face of Carnival appears, puts on a wig and paper mask, dances drunkenly in the streets and scatters cheap trinkets and fake doubloons to the "poor."

Edith had lived to see the Sears Tower in Chicago rise to become the tallest building in the world, but of course she could take no personal credit for that. Her greatest pride was being honored in her adopted city. Each year the New Orleans *Times-Picayune* presents a loving cup to the citizen deemed to have done the most for the city during the previous year; it is considered the highest honor the city can bestow. Edgar B. Stern won his loving cup in 1931, and Edith herself was given the annual award thirty-four years later. The two of them were the only his-and-hers recipients of the awards in the city's history. The twin cups reposed on a mantel, side by side, in the drawing room at Longue Vue, and their images are embossed on Edith's and Edgar's respective headstones.

It must have amused Edith, in a grim way, when her son Edgar was invited, in a gesture of gratitude for his various civic services and philanthropies in New Orleans, to join the Carnival Krewe of Comus, and accepted the invitation. It was not the elite Krewe of Rex, to be sure, to which such Old Guard Christian families as the Williamses and LeGendres belonged; Comus was the next step down the ladder. It was not just that Edith despised Carnival, and all the cavorting and silliness and snobbery that the yearly rite of Fat Tuesday entails. It was simply that she would never have accepted anything second-best.

PART FOUR

The Queen
of Gomorrah

12

1000 LAKE SHORE DRIVE

"ALL THE ROCKEFELLERS ARE PECULIAR." This was the sentiment expressed, in the summer of 1978, by a former Rockefeller-by-marriage, Mrs. Barbara Sears Rockefeller—born Jievute Paulekiute—the famous "Bobo." The ex–Mrs. Winthrop Rockefeller was referring specifically to such members of the family as her husband's aunt Alta Rockefeller Prentice, who lived reclusively on a vast Massachusetts farm surrounded by a collection of ancient automobiles; to a cousin, Ethel Rockefeller, who changed her name to Geraldine, married Marcellus Huntley Dodge and shared a New Jersey estate with him, though in separate houses, and collected dogs; to William G. Rockefeller, a chronic alcoholic; even to her former brother-in-law Nelson Rockefeller, who had a curious fondness for fires and firemen, and coincidentally managed to be on the scene at the time of two major conflagrations, where he was able to put on a fireman's helmet and help man the hoses—at the Museum of Modern Art in New York, and at his Governor's Mansion in Albany. But the oddest Rockefeller of all was certainly Edith Rockefeller.

Edith was the second-oldest daughter of John D. Rockefeller, Sr., the founder of the fortune. In her youth, Edith displayed few signs of becoming a future *grande dame* and social force. On the contrary, she was a demure, shy child, with pale hair done up in modest ringlets, gray eyes, a high forehead—not really pretty, but not bad-looking, either. Her favorite pastime was riding her bicycle, and her principal social activity was teaching a Sunday-school class. She was considered bookish. All this changed, however, on November 26, 1895, when she married Harold Fowler McCormick, the son of Cyrus Hall McCormick, Chicago's "Reaper King."

Edith's older sister Alta had also married a Chicagoan, Ezra Parmalee Prentice, but the Prentices had moved East. The new Mr. and Mrs. McCormick, however, announced that they would make Chicago their home, and moved into a huge, turreted stone mansion on Lake Michigan at 1000 Lake Shore Drive. Chicago was still a very young city, a creation of the railroad-building boom that had followed the Civil War, and just two years before Edith Rockefeller's arrival it had made its first bid for greatness, and to be taken seriously as an important metropolis, with its World's Columbian Exposition of 1893, the same Exposition that started Julius Rosenwald on the road to riches when his brother-in-law got the ice-cream concession. Chicago was proud of its muscular newness, and even of its growing reputation as a capital of vice and crime. Guidebooks were actually printed to direct out-of-towners to the local dens of sin—to one street where every building consisted of a saloon, and to a number of other areas devoted exclusively to prostitution.

Chicago boasted of being the home of the "world's richest street-walker," who called herself Waterford Jack (her real name was Frances Warren) and who claimed to have worked the streets without missing a night for ten solid years until she was able to open an establishment of her own, where, after deducting her commission, she invested the earnings of her girls and helped them to become rich as well. The banks Waterford Jack used were proud to have her patronage. Down the street from Waterford Jack's place was another celebrity in this "Gomorrah of the West," a barkeep named Mickey Finn, whose specialty was a concoction made from raw alcohol that had been soaked in snuff, plus a secret ingredient he claimed to have obtained from a voodoo witch doctor. So powerful was his potion that, after downing it, its victims remained comatose for days, and Finn kept drugged gentlemen in stacks in his back room until they came to—usually with no recollection of what had happened to them—having been relieved meanwhile of their wallets and other valuables.

Coincidentally, the World's Columbian Exposition also marked one of the last public functions of the great Chicago dowager Mrs. Potter Palmer, the jewel-encrusted belle of an old Kentucky family who had married one of Chicago's richest men. Potter Palmer had started out as a dry-goods merchant, and had made himself wealthy—and popular—by initiating the uncommon practice of letting his customers take goods home from his store on approval. From laces and pinafores he had gone on into real estate, and had built the Palmer House, the city's most luxurious hotel, which he presented to his bride as a wedding gift. For more than twenty years before Edith Rockefeller's arrival, Bertha Palmer had been the unquestioned ruler of Chicago's social seas. When royalty visited, a reception at Mrs. Palmer's was a required part of the schedule. Her annual New Year's Day party provided the only barometer in town as to who was who. Every year her guest list was scrutinized with care and some anxiety since, unlike Mrs. Astor, whose list was rigidly predictable, Bertha Palmer's was not, and she had a way of dropping people she felt had fallen from fashion. She also ran the city's annual Charity Ball, the principal fund-raiser for worthy causes and the "deserving" poor. Her taste in art, for its time, was *avant-garde*. She was among the first Americans to appreciate the Barbizon and Impressionist painters, and her collections of Monet, Degas, and Corot became the nucleus of the Chicago Institute of Art. She was also an early feminist, and at the Columbian Exposition her domain was the Woman's Building, which she saw to it was designed by a woman architect, and which was devoted to exhibits heralding the strides of American women in science, politics, the professions, education, and the arts, as well as displays of model kitchens, nurseries, and more traditional female endeavors. After finishing her work with the Exposition, Mrs. Palmer more or less retired from the Chicago scene, and began spending more and more time at her house in Newport and in Europe. The post of Chicago's *grande dame* lay open. Edith Rockefeller McCormick would step forward to fill it.

Twenty-odd years earlier, Bertha Palmer had established her social leadership by orchestrating, in Chicago, the wedding and reception of her sister Ida to Frederick Dent Grant, the son of the President of the United States. Both the President and Mrs. Grant had come out for the festivities, and were almost if not quite outshone by the beautiful hostess and her emeralds and diamonds. Edith McCormick would launch herself in Chicago in an equally dramatic fashion. The McCormicks had had, in short order, four children—John Rockefeller, Fowler, Muriel, and Mathilde—but Muriel was her mother's clear favorite. Kindergartens and nursery schools were not common in the United States in the early 1900s —they were a European upper-crust convention--and when little Muriel McCormick reached the age of five, her mother decided to start her own school for toddlers. Edith McCormick's kindergarten, however, was drawn along far less egalitarian lines than Edith Stern's some two dozen years later. The McCormick classes were designed exclusively for little girls of Chicago's upper crust, including the various McCormick relatives. (One young pupil was Felicia Gizycka, the daughter of Count Josef Gizycki and Eleanor Medill "Cissy" Patterson, a cousin by marriage.) Edith

McCormick appropriated her mother-in-law's ballroom for a classroom, hired a small staff of French teachers, and all the classes, as well as the games, were conducted in French.

Now, having established *"mon lycée,"* as she understandably called it, she began to make a series of spectacular public appearances. Though Edith McCormick's collection of jewels was not as large as Mrs. Potter Palmer's, it included certain single pieces that were considered beyond price. There was, for example, one necklace, specially assembled by Cartier, which was composed of ten large emeralds spaced along a rope of 1,657 diamonds. Another necklace was fabricated, reportedly, from the Russian crown jewels—twenty-three large pearls, twenty-one large diamonds of various sizes and shapes, plus a hundred "lesser" diamonds. One long rope of perfectly matched pearls had cost $2,000,000. Though she had taught Sunday school as a young woman, she detested hymns; she had, she said, been forced to sing them so often as a child by her pious Baptist father. But she loved opera, and selected the Chicago Opera Company for her special patronage. She would arrive at the opera in her plum-colored Rolls Royce driven by a chauffeur in a plum-colored uniform, in her jewels, and wearing her famous ermine cape composed of 275 skins which fell like a tent around her. News that Mrs. McCormick was planning to attend the opera was enough to guarantee a sold-out performance. A small woman, she was particularly proud of her little feet and slender ankles. When she was helped from her car, she was always careful to flash a glimpse of ankle, around one of which she often wore a gold bracelet—a fashion touch previously unheard of in Chicago.

The McCormick dinners at 1000 Lake Shore Drive were more like state occasions than parties. And no wonder. Mrs. McCormick demanded that menus and place cards be printed in French for every meal, including breakfast. For formal dinners, the menus and place cards were engraved in gold. Seated dinners for two hundred or more were commonplace, with a footman stationed behind every other chair. Four butlers were required to serve a simple luncheon for two. For large gatherings, guests might be served on the golden service which Napoleon had given his sister Pauline. It consisted of over a thousand pieces containing over 11,000 ounces of gold.* It was said of Edith McCormick that "she taught Chicago how to wear and to own a dress suit." Still, for all their opulence, there was not much merriment at Edith McCormick's parties, and at her

---

* At 1980s gold prices of $500 an ounce and more, that would work out to at least five and a half million dollars' worth of flatware.

first formal dinner in Chicago she noticed this, recalling later, "My party was not very well under way before I noticed a certain lack of spontaneity that had marked the other dinners I had attended. The gaiety seemed forced and formal." She asked her husband why this might have been, and he told her, "My dear, don't you realize that these red-blooded young Chicagoans are used to having their liquor? They simply must have their cocktails, their wine, their highballs and cordials." But this was too much for Edith. She might have rebelled against her teetotaling father in hymn singing, but she would not break her girlhood pledge to him never to drink or serve alcohol in her home. Though her husband and (privately) her guests continued to complain, evenings at the McCormicks' remained relentlessly sober.

There was intoxication of sorts, of course, to be gained from viewing the furnishings of 1000 Lake Shore Drive itself, which Edith had assembled to recall the days of the French royal court. This was due in part to the fact that one of Edith's odd beliefs was that she was descended from the noble de La Rochefoucauld family of France. Though the Rockefellers had originally come from Germany, Edith saw the name Rockefeller as a kind of corruption of Rochefoucauld, and occasionally signed her letters "Edith de La Rockefeller." (Edith also believed that she was the reincarnation of the child bride of King Tutankhamun.)

Certainly the house contained many splendid things. One rug had been the gift of the Shah of Persia to the Winter Palace of the Tsars of Russia at St. Petersburg during the reign of Peter the Great. Later, it had been presented to the Emperor of Austria in gratitude for the Austrians' aid to Russia. When it eventually made its way to a London auction house, Edith bought it for $185,000. In the large room which Edith called the Empire Room, there were four of Napoleon's royal chairs, two marked with the crest and initial "N" and two marked with "B" for Bonaparte. On the fourth floor of the house was a 15,000-volume library of rare books. One book alone was valued at $30,000. There was an *Histoire Héliodore* worth $6,000, a *Pâtissier François* dated 1655, and an illuminated Byzantine manuscript of the New Testament in Greek valued at $14,000. And there was much, much more. In her Aubusson-carpeted bedroom, Edith McCormick slept in an oversized gilded Louis XVI bed, and on her dressing table reposed a long gold box with the initials "M.L." emblazoned on its top in diamonds, said to have been a gift from Napoleon to the Empress Marie Louise. The various halls and sitting rooms were filled with Buddhas from Chinese temples, tapestries from Brussels, and old English silver pieces dating back to the time of Oliver Cromwell.

To care for the acreage of her house and its contents, Edith had her staff—among them a first and second butler, two parlor maids, a coachman, footman, houseman, and no fewer than six detectives. One man's daily duty was simply to polish the silver. Another's was to wind the clocks. Edith's personal maid had an assistant, called the sewing woman, and the sewing woman had her own assistant, called the mending woman. Another woman only arranged the flowers. In the kitchen were a chef and a sous-chef to work at the big coal stoves—Edith would not permit the use of gas—and any number of scullery helpers. Perhaps because of the sheer logistics of the problem, Edith McCormick refused to learn any of her servants' names. Nor would she speak to any of them, nor were they permitted to speak to her. In fact, she would speak to only two members of her staff—her chief steward and her personal secretary. All instructions were then channeled down through the chain of command. When she ventured out in her car, the full schedule of stops, times, and pick-up points would be typed out for the chauffeur in advance, thus eliminating the need for any communication between Mrs. McCormick and her driver.

Only once was the unalterable rule, that no member of the staff should ever interrupt Mrs. McCormick during dinner, broken. This was when her oldest child, John Rockefeller McCormick, was ailing with scarlet fever at the family's country place in Lake Forest. After much discussion in the servants' quarters, it was decided to whisper to Mrs. McCormick during dinner that the little boy had died. Mrs. McCormick, appearing more annoyed by the interruption than by the news, merely nodded and the dinner party continued.

Though Edith Rockefeller McCormick may often have seemed an extraordinarily cold—if not totally unfeeling—woman, there was no doubt about her devotion to the opera, and to uplifting the musical tastes of her adopted city. (To be sure, it might be argued that, on the evening of her son's death, she felt that her first obligation was to her dinner guests, who were still living, rather than to her child, who was past help—but still, one wonders.) Her pre-opera dinner parties were particularly harrowing. For these occasions the hostess kept a small jeweled clock beside her place at the head of the table, along with a printed card listing the number of minutes she expected each course of the meal to take—"Soup: six minutes; fish: seven and one half minutes," and so on. The purpose of this was to ensure that the McCormicks and their guests would be in their seats at the opera house punctually for the opening curtain. Guests on opera nights had to be on their toes, or half-eaten plates of food would be snatched away from them by the efficient servants because Mrs. Mc-Cormick had signaled that the allotted time for the course was up. She got away with it because—well, because she was a very rich woman who was used to getting her way, and because there was no one of sufficient audacity around to challenge her.

She hated anything that smacked of scandal, and was exceptionally sensitive to public criticism of anything in which a whiff of immorality was involved. But her tastes in opera were quite modern, and she was influential in bringing Mary Garden to Chicago to sing the title role of *Salomé*, the relatively new Richard Strauss opera based on a verse play by Oscar Wilde.

Mary Garden, to begin with, was herself controversial. By all accounts she was as much a performer as a singer—a kind of early-day Maria Callas. One went to see Mary Garden more than to hear her. She was a genius at generating publicity about herself, and cared little whether the publicity was good or bad, as long as Mary Garden's name was mentioned. She was a legendary beauty, and was said to have scattered broken hearts across the map of the United States and Europe. It was said that she had lovers by the score. It was said that she had once given birth to an illegitimate child. Whenever a new rumor about Mary Garden's free-wheeling private life appeared, she called a press conference to deny it, thereby creating more columns of print. She had become, in the process, an enormous box-office draw, and she translated her flamboyant living style into flamboyant performances on the operatic stage. For all of this, there were some people in Chicago who felt that Mary Garden was stuff too strong even for the tastes of "red-blooded Chicagoans."

Then there was the problem of *Salomé*. Richard Strauss was a hugely popular composer, but the name of Oscar Wilde had fallen under a definite cloud. Wilde had come to Chicago in the early 1880s, and Chicago had not been impressed with the fey young man who lolled about on sofas swathed in fur lap robes and silk scarves and who sniffed a nosegay of fresh lilies while he talked incomprehensibly about "the new aesthetics" and "art for art's sake." Wilde's timing for his Chicago visit was also unfortunate, in that he arrived at the same moment as John L. Sullivan, who had just won the world's heavyweight title. The newspapers made much of the contrasting styles of the two visiting celebrities—Sullivan, the shining example of American manhood, and Wilde, the epitome of European decadence. One paper called Wilde an "ass-thete."

Then, in 1895, Oscar Wilde had unwisely chosen to sue the Marquis of Queensberry over allegations concerning Wilde's relationship with the

Marquis's son Lord Alfred Douglas. The papers of the day had been very dainty about reporting the exact nature of this untidy matter—so dainty, in fact, that most American readers had no clear idea what it was that Oscar Wilde had been accused of doing. Even the word "pederasty" was considered too strong for print, and so readers were required to use their imaginations about what had been going on. All that was clear was that it was something "unnatural" and vile, that Wilde had been carried off to Reading Gaol for his part in the nastiness, and that Wilde was a degenerate and an enemy of decency and morals.

Thus it was an incendiary mixture that Edith McCormick was planning to bring to the stage of the Chicago Opera Company, but, needless to say, tickets for the opening-night performance sold extremely well. Mary Garden had made a special study of the dance in preparation for her *Salomé* because, as she said at the time, "I want the Dance of the Seven Veils to be drama and not Folies Bergère." And her opening night was nothing if not dramatic. She threw herself into the role with as much histrionics and frank sensuality as she could muster, and red-blooded Chicago, which published its "Sporting and Club House Directory," was scandalized. Of Miss Garden's fiery Salomé, the music critic Percy Hammond, calling Miss Garden "the feminine colossus who doth bestride our operatic world," wrote that her performance was "florid, excessive, unhampered tour de force, lawless and inhuman."

The reaction of Police Chief LeRoy T. Steward, who had also been in the opening-night audience, was more specific. "Miss Garden wallowed around like a cat in a bed of catnip," he announced. "There was no art in her dance that I could see. If the same show were produced on Halsted Street the people would call it cheap but over at the auditorium they say it is art. Black art, if art at all. I would not call it immoral. I would say it was disgusting." Chief Steward then announced that he was sending his head censor, Detective Sergeant Charles O'Donnell, to see the second evening's performance and deliver an opinion. Still another custodian of public morality was Arthur Farwell, who, though he had not seen *Salomé*, denounced it generally. Miss Garden, Mr. Farwell said, was a "great degenerator" of public morals, and he would not see the opera lest his own morals undergo degeneration. "I am a normal man," he said, "but I could not trust myself to see a performance of *Salomé*."

Miss Garden was outraged, and shot off one of her famous ripostes. "I always bow down to the ignorant and try to make them understand," she said, "but I ignore the illiterate."

The controversy drew long lines at the box office, and the second performance quickly sold out.

Detective O'Donnell's report was also negative. The show was an affront to decency. Though Chief Steward was willing to compromise if Miss Garden would "tone down the head business"—in which Salomé dances with the severed head of the prophet—Miss Garden refused to alter a single gesture or bit of business. Inevitably, the opera's great patroness, Edith McCormick, was drawn into the fray, and in her memoirs Mary Garden directly blames an uncharacteristic attack of spinelessness on Edith's part for the closing notice of *Salomé* that was posted the following day. According to Miss Garden, Mrs. McCormick sent for her and said, "The truth came to me after your third performance . . . I said to myself, Edith, your vibrations are all wrong." And so the opera that had promised to be the most successful of the season was closed. Edith's "vibrations," of course, came from her intense dislike of any scandal. But the closing of *Salomé* was also, as Emmett Dedmon put it in *Fabulous Chicago*, "a recurrence of Chicago's unpredictable puritanism—which tolerated the nation's largest vice area on the edge of its business district but rose up in horror over a sensuous work of art."

In the years after the death of her elder son, Edith McCormick seemed to grow odder. She became more interested in the occult and the supernatural, and in reincarnation. She paid $25,000 to have her horoscope charts written. She became even more autocratic and demanding. Now even her three surviving children had to make appointments through her private secretary in order to see her. She built a huge forty-four-room mansion in suburban Lake Forest called Villa Turicum, but never moved in. Barrels full of French china were shipped to Villa Turicum but never unpacked. Antique French and Italian pieces of furniture were arranged in the principal rooms, but were never taken out of their packing crates. Thirteen master bedrooms of identical size and shape were completely furnished with identical pieces—only the colors of the walls were different—but no one ever spent a night in any of them. Gardens were filled with topiary and hothouses with flowering plants, but their only use seemed to be to supply fresh flowers for 1000 Lake Shore Drive, and these were delivered daily in a lavender truck.

At about the same time, in New York, Edith's cousin Geraldine Rockefeller Dodge was beginning to do similarly strange things. She built a large and exceptionally ugly house on the corner of Fifth Avenue and

Sixty-first Street in Manhattan, filled it with dark, heavy furniture and hangings, and, like Edith, never moved in, though she bought adjacent pieces of property as soon as they became available until she owned most of the north side of the block between Sixty-first Street and the Knicker-bocker Club on the Sixty-second Street corner, and between Fifth and Madison Avenues. This acreage she let become overgrown with weeds and scrubby trees. The purpose of this, she explained, was to provide a "woods" for her dogs, even though, like her, the dogs never came. For years the Rockefeller-Dodge mansion remained New York's mystery house—shuttered and dark and forbidding, illuminated only by a faint light from behind a barred caretaker's window. People wondered espe-cially about the erratic and helter-skelter placement of the exterior win-dows: the reason was that the upper floors of the house had been designed as a giant kennel—a kennel that was never inhabited by man or beast. Geraldine Rockefeller Dodge's peculiarities were also blamed on the death of a son, her only child, who was killed in an automobile accident just after his graduation from Princeton.

In Chicago meanwhile, Edith McCormick continued to preside over the Chicago Opera Company and her grand, stiffly regimented dinners. She was becoming a creature of habit. She would invariably open a conversation at dinner by asking the gentleman on her right, "What has been interesting you lately?" Then, when it was time to "turn the table," her right-hand partner would hear her ask the identical question of the gentleman on her left. Her other interests included walking, and she took the same walk, carrying the same muff, every day. She established a zoo, and pronounced herself particularly partial to the giraffes. Her astrologist had told her that she had her own Christmas, which she celebrated "by the stars" on December 15. She studied philosophy. "My object in the world," she once said, "is to think new thoughts." And in the Beyond she communicated with Ankn-es-en-pa-Aten, Tutankhamun's bride, her pre-vious incarnation. She also took up song writing, and at least six of her sentimental love songs—including "Love," "Between," "Thou," and "It Is Spoken"—were published.

But close friends—and she actually had a few—had begun to suspect that, for all her wealth and social power, Edith Rockefeller McCormick was a seriously unhappy woman. A scandal in her own family life was brewing, and she knew it. Already there were whispers. It involved her husband, Harold McCormick, a short, balding, bespectacled man with the figure of a pouter pigeon. It appeared that though he seemed genu-inely to love Edith, and that though she seemed almost passionately to love him—all the love songs, she said, were written to him—Harold McCormick had, as they put it in the delicate language of the day, "an unfaithful nature."

Today we would no doubt diagnose it as satyriasis, combined with a taste for easy women.

13

MRS. McCORMICK DEPARTS

IN A WAY, the tragedy of the McCormick marriage was that both Edith and Harold McCormick had too much money. The legendary "joining of two great American fortunes" has not happened all that often in American history, but it had happened in the McCormicks' case, and the result was that there was no way one partner in the union could bring financial pressure to bear upon the other to bring the other into line. Edith, enormously rich, could do what she wanted to. Harold, enormously rich, could do the same. Edith was nowhere near as pious a person as her churchgoing, Bible-spouting father, but she did, she often said, see marriage as a sacred commitment, and the idea of divorce appalled her. At the same time, though she was too much of a *grande dame* ever to speak of it, the awareness of her husband's increasing infidelities must have been both painful and embarrassing for her.

Edith, furthermore, was not the kind of woman who could easily confide her troubles to another. Even the women in Chicago whom she considered her friends were hardly intimates. The friendships were always very formal and polite, and the ladies addressed each other as "Mrs. Pullman," "Mrs. Armour," and "Mrs. Swift," hardly ever relaxing to the point of first names. For one of these dowagers to have touched a luncheon companion's arm and said, "My husband is having an affair— what should I do?" would have been an unheard-of breach of etiquette, a shocking lapse of taste.

In Europe, however, two men were beginning to be talked about in the United States for the new kind of help they were trying to offer people. They were Sigmund Freud and his sometime colleague Carl Jung, and what they were practicing and theorizing about was psychoanalysis, or, as it was called at the time, "synthetic psychology." Freud's special baili-wick seemed to be sexual psychotherapy, and some of his theories about Oedipus and Electra complexes and phrases such as "penis envy"—were regarded as very startling. Dr. Jung seemed less sexually oriented, more focused on problems above the waist, on the entire individual. Jung seemed to many people more rational, less revolutionary, more liberal and practical in his approach. It was to Carl Jung in Switzerland that Edith McCormick—unhappy in her marriage, no doubt bored and de-pressed by her surroundings—decided to commit herself. When she de-parted from Chicago, it was assumed that she would be gone only a few months. Her stay under Dr. Jung's auspices would last eight years.

Before leaving, Edith assured Chicago that her husband would be "in charge" of the Chicago Opera Company in her absence. Unfortunately, he quickly turned out to be a poor choice as her deputy. Whether Harold McCormick actually had an affair with Mary Garden is unknown, but one of the things he did was to install Miss Garden as director of the Chicago Opera Company, which she agreed to be provided her title on the program be listed as "directa," the proper feminine form of director, as she saw it. McCormick had said something to her about this being his last season connected with the opera, and had indicated to his new directa that he wished to depart in "a blaze of glory." Miss Garden decided to take him at his word, and in the process she very nearly succeeded in scuttling the entire company. She engaged more artists than there were evenings for them to perform, and ran up enormous bills for elaborate costumes, props, and scenery. When Miss Garden had completed her year of directaship, the Chicago Opera Company was a million dollars in the red, but this fazed the glamorous directa not at all. In her book, *Mary Garden's Story*, she wrote of the whole experience: "The newspapers said that the company lost one million dollars during the season I was director. I don't know because I had nothing to do with the business end of it. It was news to me. I do know we finished the way Mr. McCormick wanted us to finish—in a blaze of glory. That's what he asked for and that's what he got. If it cost a million dollars, I'm sure it was worth it."

Harold McCormick, meanwhile, was busily pursuing other interests. He was nothing if not fun loving. He was also very much a dandy, fond of jeweled cuff links and stickpins and rings, bright striped shirts with contrasting collars, embroidered waistcoats and gray mohair spats. The newspapers usually referred to Harold McCormick as "the rich playboy," a term he rather resented. After all, he pointed out, hadn't he done all the right things? He had graduated from Princeton, married John D. Rockefeller's daughter, fathered children, gone to work for his father's company, toiled in behalf of such respectable causes as the Chicago Opera. Still, he admitted that he was justly regarded as something of a nonpareil with the ladies, and when he spoke of himself it was often in the innocent manner of Shall-I-compare-me-to-a-summer's-day? *

When his brothers and sisters complained to Harold about his extramarital dalliances, he was also resentful. After all, he reminded them, when a man's wife had departed his bed and company for an indefinite stay with a Swiss analyst, was the red-blooded husband expected to live like a monk until such time as the strong-willed wife saw fit to return? Of course, it was an argument that put the cart before the horse, since it was Harold's dalliances that had sent Edith abroad to seek counseling in the first place.

In any case, long before Mary Garden had completed her term as directa of the Chicago Opera, Harold McCormick had become heavily involved with a Polish soprano named Ganna Walska, a flamboyant, full-bodied creature whose singing talent was regarded as inconsiderable, but who did have a knack for attracting rich older men who then had the sense to die and leave her their money. Her first husband, Baron Arcadie d'Engor, was killed in the First World War. She next married Dr. Joseph Fraenkel, a wealthy New York throat specialist she had consulted about a throat problem. Much older than she, he had been so smitten by her that he proposed during their second appointment. When he died, Dr. Fraenkel left her half a million dollars.

Dr. Fraenkel was still living, however, when Mme. Walska, as she called herself professionally, first met Harold McCormick. Her ambition was to sing with the Chicago Opera, and, learning that McCormick was in New York on business, she telephoned him in his suite at the Plaza and requested a meeting. McCormick tried to put her off, explaining that he was just on his way out the door to catch a train. With this information, Walska stationed herself in the lobby and waylaid him there. McCormick was evidently sufficiently impressed. Within a few months, Dr. Fraenkel had died and Ganna Walska and Harold McCormick were sailing to Europe together aboard the *Aquitania*.

The story at this point becomes as complicated as the most improbable opera plot. Also sailing on the *Aquitania* was one Alexander Smith Coch-

---

* Writing to his sister Anita from the Adirondacks in 1925, he marveled at how he had learned "so much about *simple living* . . . If you could have seen me washing the dishes after the meal . . . going to the market and ordering only what was needed . . . you would have said, 'Can this be Harold?'—but it *was* him!"

ran, whom the newspapers of the day called "the world's richest bachelor." Cochran was said to be worth $80,000,000, and reportedly proposed marriage to Ganna the first night they met. Now Ganna obviously felt she could have her pick of millionaires. McCormick possessed a couple of advantages: he was probably richer than Cochran, and could also get Ganna on the Chicago Opera stage. The disadvantage, however, was that McCormick was already married and Cochran was not. Clearly, Ganna Walska spent the ocean crossing doing some heavy weighing of the odds.

The purpose of McCormick's European trip, aside from the pleasure of Ganna's company on shipboard, was to go to Switzerland and try to persuade Edith to give him a divorce. This took him several weeks of argument, and in the meantime Ganna languished in Paris. So did Mr. Cochran. Finally, reluctantly, Edith McCormick agreed to the divorce, and Harold hurried eagerly back to Paris to give Ganna the good news. He arrived only to learn that she had married Cochran the day before.

He immediately presented himself at the newlyweds' suite and, as Ganna later wrote in her memoir, tellingly titled *Always Room at the Top*, "While Mr. Cochran was still sleeping in the next room in his first day of married life, I was pouring coffee for Mr. McCormick . . . After my sudden marriage I was more preoccupied with Mr. McCormick's helpless state than with my own thoughts." She was not too preoccupied, however, to embark upon the next phase of a remarkable double game in which she would successfully refute the theory that one cannot have one's cake and eat it too. Her career, she explained to McCormick, still came first, and her ambition was still to perform with the Chicago Opera. This Mr. McCormick assured her she could do. But meantime certain perquisites were required from Mr. Cochran—among them a house in Paris on the rue de Lübeck; a Rolls Royce; a sable coat that cost a million francs; a wedding gift, which was to pick out anything she wanted at Cartier's; "eight or nine" bracelets from the same store; an annual allowance of $100,000 for pin money; and an immediate long holiday at the Carlton Hotel in Cannes, where she took an entire floor for herself and six servants. Still, she confessed that Cochran failed to satisfy her "inner being."

Rested from her Riviera vacation, the new Mrs. Cochran now proclaimed herself ready to resume her operatic career and headed for Chicago, where, it was announced, she would sing the title role in Leoncavallo's *Zaza*, a little-performed work that was not considered particularly demanding. The debut was scheduled for December 21, 1920, and, since the broad outlines of the Walska-Cochran-McCormick triangle were now a matter of public knowledge, the production promised to be a *succès de scandale*. Seats for the event quickly sold out. Then, just a few days before the performance, Ganna Walska suddenly departed for Europe again.

Publicly, the reason given for the opera's cancellation was that it was "not ready." But from behind the scenes came other stories. The temperamental star, it seemed, refused to take direction. The musical director complained that her singing voice could not achieve sufficient volume to be heard beyond the first row. The New York conductor and composer Walter Damrosch, a McCormick family friend and relative by marriage,* was called upon for assistance and advice. In view of the situation, Damrosch tried to be as tactful as possible. While conceding that Ganna was "very pretty," he wrote that, unfortunately, from the "absolutely unanimous accounts of my musician friends who have heard her, her voice is absolutely devoid of charm . . . What a tragedy, if only she would leave art alone, she would be much happier."

Ganna Walska herself blamed the opera's cancellation on her husband. Mr. Cochran had objected, she said, to certain scanty costumes she would be required to wear, as well as to a couple of lengthy stage kisses which, being the great actress that she was, she had naturally tried to make realistic. Cochran, meanwhile, had hastily left Chicago just a few hours ahead of his wife, angered, it was said, because she had registered at her hotel as Mme. Ganna Walska, not Mrs. Alexander Cochran. Cochran promptly sued for divorce, and, after briefly considering a countersuit, Ganna decided to grant him one, in return for a cash settlement of $200,000.

Now, by the early spring of 1922, Mme. Ganna Walska and Mr. Harold McCormick were both legally rid of their respective spouses, and were free to marry each other. He was fifty and she about forty—Ganna was always a little vague about her birth date—but before the marriage could take place, McCormick had a bit of business which he felt required to undertake.

In Chicago there was an eminent surgeon named Victor Lespinasse, whose specialty was urology, and who had been hailed by the American Medical Association for his pioneering work on spermatogenesis and sterility. He had been described by *The New York Times* as the dean of gland transplantation and the "author of the saying that 'a man is as old as his glands.'" Through Dr. Lespinasse's technique, it was claimed, an aging

---

* Harold McCormick's older sister, Anita, had married Emmons Blaine, whose sister Margaret was married to Damrosch.

man's flagging sexuality could be restored to the full buoyancy of a teen-
ager's. On June 12, 1922, Harold McCormick entered a Chicago hospital
to undergo one of Dr. Lespinasse's rejuvenative gland transplants.

It was all supposed to be a closely guarded secret, of course. But
somehow the newspapers got hold of it, and Harold McCormick managed
to make it all the worse by threatening to sue for libel a paper which
reported that he had been implanted with the glands of a monkey. If it
had not been a monkey, the papers speculated, then it had to have been a
human, and a rumor began to spread that the donor of the glands in
question had been a young blacksmith. A parody of Longfellow was soon
circulating through the perfumed drawing rooms of the North Shore as
well as the saloons of Rush Street:

> *Under the spreading chestnut tree,*
> *The village smithy stands;*
> *The smith a gloomy man is he;*
> *McCormick has his glands.*

Poor Harold. Edith Rockefeller McCormick would never have permitted herself to become a laughingstock. Now her former husband was one.
From her Alpine retreat in Switzerland with Dr. Jung, Edith had no
comment.

Harold, to celebrate his new-found youthfulness and his freedom from
Edith, now ordered Ganna's birthday present. It consisted of an example
of every piece of farm equipment which International Harvester manufactured, and the lot was shipped to her château outside Versailles, where
she woke on her birthday morning to find, as she later wrote, "to my
great surprise . . . a whole regiment of robot soldiers." Two months after
the operation, Harold joined Ganna in France, and married her there. At
the time, the newspapers suggested that the marriage was probably not
legal, since Illinois law required a one-year waiting period between divorce and remarriage. But Harold's lawyers assured him that the law
stated merely that the couple could not be married in Illinois. (To tie up
the legal loose ends, the couple were married a second time, in February
1923, at Harold's mother's house outside Chicago.) After this ceremony
the bridegroom greeted reporters with "Hello boys, this seems like old
times. You know, I've been in the newspaper so much, I feel like a
newspaperman myself."

Alas, the musical comedy was far from over. Not until a generation
later, when Winthrop Rockefeller married "Bobo" Sears—or, still later,

in 1959, when Steven Rockefeller married Anne Marie Rasmussen, a Norwegian maid who worked for his mother—would the press have such sport with a marital alliance of two persons from widely different backgrounds. Ganna's parents, it was pointed out, were Polish peasants. She was described as an "aging diva," and a "prima donna past her prime," who had an "impossible voice," and who had never sung in an important role.

Ganna, of course, was outraged. She still thirsted for—and intended to have—an operatic career, and viewed herself as the victim of sinister forces, cruel fate, a malevolent press, ignorant and jealous critics, and a hostile, uneducated and unappreciative public. "People made about me quite wrong impression," she wrote to her new sister-in-law in her fractured English with its erratic spellings, "and they imagine that I am foolish, vane, consited personne who imagines that she can sing because she is pretty and through her husband's money tried to push herself. As I a matter of fact I am entirely, not consited, but wrongly or rightly (to be seen some day!) quite sure that something is in me that I should deliver a message and leave something behind me as an example. I want other people to know that Harold did not marry a foolish woman, but a person who wants to give at cost of terrible suffering and undiscrable misery."

Undaunted, she forged on. An American concert tour, sponsored by her husband, was an unmitigated disaster, both critically and at the box office. She was becoming a public embarrassment not only to her husband but to the entire McCormick family. The family did its best to keep stiff upper lips, but Harold was asked to step down from Harvester's board. In Ganna's bitterness at what she considered her unfair treatment, she began to say outrageous things. She stated publicly that she only tolerated Harold because of his money. He had promised her that his money could buy her success and fame, but he had let her down.

Then came the publication of her *Always Room at the Top*, the "message" she felt she had been put on earth to deliver. In it she revealed that if Harold had disappointed her, she had also disappointed him. Harold, with his freshly transplanted lustiness, had wanted a bed partner. She had expected a Platonic union, a marriage of the minds. Harold, she wrote, tended "to idolize the physical expression of love. Nature in her wisdom having fulfilled him by giving him four children had chosen for his second wife an idealist who was able to put so much value on the richness of his soul that she could not even imagine the possibility of his preferring to seek further for a gross and limited pleasure rather than being satisfied with the divine companionship of the spiritual love she was willing to share with him." She added, unkindly, that Harold had become "insatiable in his search for the realization of the physical demands— insatiable because they were unattainable for him anymore." * She hinted that there were other details of her husband's sexual appetites which she might reveal if and when she so chose.

All this was too much for the McCormicks, including Harold. He and Ganna separated in 1931, and were divorced not long afterward. To be rid of her cost him $6,000,000, roughly one quarter of his Harvester holdings. But at least he silenced her.

"I have my life, he has his," she told the press. "Every artist must have her rights."

---

* Considering Ganna's shaky command of English, it is clear that her "auto-biography" was heavily ghostwritten.

14

MRS. McCORMICK RETURNS

WHILE HAROLD McCORMICK was trying manfully to cope with his second wife, his first wife returned to Chicago, ready to pick up the sceptre of social leadership that she had laid down eight years earlier. There had been speculation that, after the divorce, Edith McCormick might abandon Chicago and move to New York, where most of her relatives lived, but she made it clear that this was not to be. The big house at 1000 Lake Shore Drive was reopened, its furniture uncovered, its chandeliers removed from their bags, the rugs rolled out, the paintings, silver, and china brought up from their vaults. The gold service would once more be brought out.

The years with Dr. Jung, however, had changed Edith in certain ways. For one thing, she appeared less interested in the welfare of the Chicago Opera, and less interested in displaying her furs and jewels, although she still turned out in them from time to time. Her new crusade, not surprisingly, was for psychoanalysis, and one of her notions was to turn her long-unused Villa Turicum into a psychoanalytic center, staffed with Jungians who would provide psychiatric care and counseling for the entire city of Chicago. She also had a new man—of sorts.

His name was Edwin Krenn, and Edith described him as an "architect," though he did not appear to practice at his profession and had no visible means of support, and as "the son of a famous European painter," though the painter was never identified. She had met Krenn at Dr. Jung's clinic and, naturally, she described him as brilliant. She had selected him to help her reorient Chicago toward psychology and psychoanalysis. "It was pointed out to me," she said on her arrival, "that psychologically Chicago will be the greatest center in the world. That is why I have come back here to live. That is why I have planted my roots in the soil, hoping they will grow deeper and deeper. I am vitally interested in psychology." For psychology, she would be Chicago's standard bearer. Krenn's duties would be to help her carry her dreams to fruition.

Chicago did not care much for young Mr. Krenn. Short, plump, baby-faced and dandified, he seemed mainly interested in his collection of custom-tailored suits, which soon numbered more than two hundred. One Chicagoan described him as "small and blond, with pudgy, dimpled fingers," and another was reminded of a "newly hatched duckling." It was perfectly clear that Krenn was being kept by Mrs. McCormick, but it was also obvious to everyone that their relationship was entirely chaste.

Edith McCormick continued to be a woman of punctuality and ritual, but with Krenn she devised a somewhat new routine. He had been given a large suite of rooms at the Drake Hotel, just across the street from 1000 Lake Shore Drive, and at precisely 9:15 every morning Edith would telephone him there, and they would plan their day. At 1:00 P.M. on the dot, Krenn would arrive at Edith's door bearing a small floral nosegay for his patroness. Then they would lunch. Usually they would lunch at home, but occasionally they would be driven to a nearby hotel or restaurant. Whenever they were observed together, it was noticed that their conversations were stiff and formal—even sedate—and that they never addressed each other by first names. If there were no other guests, they spoke in formal German. Their afternoons were devoted to language lessons, which they took in separate rooms, and then, around four, Krenn would reappear. The Rolls Royce would be waiting and, with the chauffeur and footman and at least one but sometimes two detectives, they would go to the movies. Sometimes they would manage to take in as many as four movies in an afternoon and evening, and the driver and footman always parked outside the theatre, even when the film happened to be showing in one of Chicago's seedier neighborhoods. Then they would be driven home, where two butlers, stationed on either side of the front door, waited to usher Mrs. McCormick in. Unless it was an exceptionally early evening, Krenn did not enter Mrs. McCormick's house. Everything was rigidly circumspect; that way, there could be no talk, no scandal. Edith explained why she had lost her taste for travel. She could see as much of the world as she wanted in the movies.

Usually, after her movie-going evenings, Edith went straight to bed. But sometimes she would summon her staff and spend an hour or so rearranging the furniture. This was definitely post-Jungian behavior, the sort of thing she had never done before.

Some people suggested that Edwin Krenn was an emotional substitute for Edith's dead son. Certainly he was a more reliable person than any of her remaining three children, all of whom had gone on from structured childhood to lead variously disordered lives. Her son Fowler, who would later become president of International Harvester, had, in 1921, married Mrs. Anne "Fifi" Stillman. A considerable difference in their ages could not be ignored. In fact, Mrs. Stillman was the mother of Fowler's Princeton roommate. Furthermore, Mrs. Stillman and her ex-husband had been principals in a well-publicized divorce fight, in which adultery had been charged on both sides. Fifi Stillman had claimed that her husband was keeping a Follies girl. Her husband countercharged that she had exchanged favors with an Indian guide in the backwoods of Canada.

Of the two girls, Mathilde—"the pretty one"—had run off at seventeen and married a Swiss riding instructor named Max Oser. He was forty-seven. Muriel—"the plain one"—had the strangest marital history of all. Her first marriage had been a "spiritual" one, to the ghost of Lieutenant G. Alexander McKinlock, Jr., a soldier who had been killed in World War I and whom she had never met. Then she "divorced" her ghost, went on the stage briefly under the name of Naranna Micor, tried her hand at singing, tried running a fashionable dress shop—none of these endeavors was successful—and then married a man named Elisha Dyer Hubbard who was also of her parents' generation. A wounded First World War veteran, Hubbard was virtually bedridden, but he managed to survive five years of marriage to Muriel before expiring, during the course of which Muriel became a chronic alcoholic. She insisted on having her husband's dog attend his funeral. Her brother Fowler tried unsuccessfully to have his sister declared insane.

If Edith McCormick had perhaps not been the perfect mother, she certainly found the perfect pet in Edwin Krenn. He doted on her, and except at bedtime they were inseparable. She would make no move without Krenn's advice. This, alas, would be her downfall, because, if Edith had one fatal flaw, it was her belief that she possessed a financial genius equal to her famous father's. Though she had all the money she could possibly need, she began to be obsessed with the idea of creating an entire new fortune of her own. It may have been a notion Dr. Jung had instilled in her—that she needed an "independence" of her Rockefeller inheritance.

Though nothing much had come of the idea to turn Villa Turicum into a psychological center—the house remained empty and unused—her interest in Jungian analysis remained strong. She boasted that, through analysis, she had cured herself of tuberculosis on three separate occasions. Soon she began taking on patients of her own—one of whom, she said proudly, was herself, and many of whom no doubt consulted her out of curiosity to meet the celebrated Edith Rockefeller McCormick. Soon their number reached a hundred. Still, she was choosy about those she would treat. One Chicago woman had come bubbling up to her, saying, "Oh, Mrs. McCormick, I would adore having you give me some lessons in psychoanalysis!" Edith's icy reply was, "I could do nothing for you, and you could do nothing for me." At the same time, other plans—which had nothing to do with treating the mentally or emotionally disoriented— were brewing in her mind and that of Edwin Krenn.

She wanted to build a city. Not a city for the poor, the ill, or the deranged, but a city for the grandly affluent. This was, after all, still the 1920s; affluence seemed everywhere, and limitlessly on the rise. Her city would be built along the luxurious lines of Palm Beach or Beverly Hills, but it would be built on the shore of Lake Michigan. She would call her city Edithton and, naturally, her architect would be Edwin Krenn.

To carry out this project, she formed the Edith Rockefeller McCormick Trust, initially financed with $5,000,000 worth of her Standard Oil stocks. In charge of the trust she place Krenn and a boarding-school classmate of his named Edward Dato, who had followed Krenn to Chicago. Edith proudly sent a copy of the trust prospectus to her aging father in New York, along with a detailed description of the Edithton development. John D. Rockefeller was less than sanguine about the project. He wrote to his daughter, "While you are a brilliant and mature woman of great mental capacity, I cannot forget you are my own flesh and blood. Therefore, it seems to be my duty to warn you of the pitfalls and vagaries of life. I would urge you to select an honest, courageous and capable man to advise you in these affairs."

Obviously Edith believed that she had found two such men in Krenn and Dato, and plans for Edithton continued. Offices were established in downtown Chicago. Over fifteen hundred acres of lakeshore property south of Kenosha, Wisconsin, were purchased for more than $1,000 an acre. Naturally, when sellers learned that the person buying all this land was Edith McCormick, prices went up. Four million dollars was spent in dredging and landscaping a marina capable of berthing large yachts. Krenn had been much impressed by the Spanish-style architecture of such cities as Palm Beach, Coral Gables, and Santa Barbara, and had decreed that the castles which would be built for this millionaires' paradise must follow that example. Red-tiled roofs, bell towers, courtyards, and Moorish arches abounded—at least on the drawing boards—and every mansion's design had to have Krenn's approval.

As the building of Edithton began to consume more and more of her time—not to mention her money—there were fewer of her grand entertainments, but Edith had not forgotten how to give them. One such was her seated luncheon for eighty honoring the visit to Chicago of Queen Marie of Rumania. For one New Year's Eve, she shifted the venue of her party across the street to Krenn's hotel, the Drake, and in *Chicago with Love* Arthur Meeker recalled, "The room was full of balloons. There was Edith, stiff as a poker, gravely batting them back and forth across our table, because that was expected of her."

That there is no glittering city of Edithton on the Michigan shore today is to a large extent Edith's own fault. There is absolutely no evidence to suggest that Krenn or Dato was cheating her, but Edith's approach to the project was so unbusinesslike that the young men's business methods suffered as a result. She refused, for example, to leave Chicago to visit the building site. (In fact, from the time of her return from Switzerland until her death, she never set foot outside the city limits.) She would not look at the company's books. She rarely even visited the downtown offices, and on one of these occasions her only instruction was to tell Krenn to tell one of the employees to stop smoking. When Krenn tried to give her a receipt for several million dollars' worth of bonds she was turning over to him, she waved him away. Everything, she said, should be based on mutual respect and trust; she did not believe in legal documentation. As a result, enormous sums of money passed into and out of the Edith Rockefeller McCormick Trust unrecorded.

Then came the shattering events on Wall Street in the autumn of 1929, and the death knell of Edithton was struck. Incredible as it seemed, Edith had lost everything—everything, that is, except some unwieldy and unsalable pieces of real estate, for which the tax collector wanted taxes. Everyone had assumed that Edith's fortune was locked in iron-clad family trusts, but everyone had been wrong. The fortune, quite simply, was gone.

Her brother, John D. Rockefeller, Jr., was summoned from New York to try to make some sense of Edith's affairs. Her relatives chipped in, and Edith was moved from 1000 Lake Shore Drive to a suite at the Drake, where she was placed on a rigid, though quite generous, family allowance of $1,000 a day.

To make her situation more dolorous, she had discovered that she had cancer. Vainly, she tried to cure herself by psychology, but finally even she admitted that she had failed. Arthur Meeker recalls her toward the end: "Her eyes, my mother said—when the latter called to say good-bye before leaving for the summer, and they both knew it meant good-bye for good—were like a frightened child's."

She died in the summer of 1932. She was only sixty.

After her death, it was revealed that, in the years since their divorce, Harold McCormick had sent Edith a red rose every year on her birthday. It was also revealed that, during those same years, Edith had kept Harold's room at 1000 Lake Shore Drive exactly as he had left it—not a stick of furniture changed or moved, his suits still hanging in the closets—in hopes that he might some day return.

Even Edith's father survived her. So did Harold, who was the same age—they had been childhood friends first, sweethearts later—and of course her ungrateful children, who would now have to wait for their father's death before receiving any significant inheritance. Harold McCormick took up whistling. He even went on the radio to offer a whistling program. In 1938, he took up marriage again. Recovering in southern California from a series of heart attacks, he married his nurse, Adah Wilson, who was thirty years younger than he. It was his only really tranquil marriage, unsettled only briefly by a breach-of-promise suit for $2,000,000 instituted by a Mrs. Olive Colby. She settled out of court for $12,500, and Adah Wilson McCormick nursed her husband through his final years until his death in 1941.

Later, Adah remarried, had a son, and died bizarrely in a fall from the lip of the Grand Canyon.

If there were any justice in the world, we would have to report that the faithless Ganna Walska squandered her ill-gotten gains on drugs and gigolos, took to the streets, died of a lingering and painful ailment, and is buried in a pauper's grave somewhere outside Paris.

Actually, nothing of the sort happened. She invested her money very shrewdly, and bought, among other things, the Théâtre des Champs Elysées in Paris. Here the frustrated performer could work off her histrionic energies as the proprietor of a successful and fashionable theatre. Her new Paris house in the rue du Bac became a sort of salon for visiting artists and intellectuals, and one wall of her drawing room was covered with the exquisite sketches of Erté, the famous theatrical costume designer, including a number of designs he had done for Ganna. She also maintained a handsome winter home in Santa Barbara, where she entertained visitors with fanciful tales of her operatic career, and how this career, of such great promise, had been blocked and sabotaged by mischievous others.

She laid the blame for most of her career misfortunes at the feet of the perfidious McCormicks.

Among the stories she liked to tell were these:

The producer of the Ravinia Summer Opera outside Chicago had pursued her for weeks, begging her to perform for him, offering her the then-unheard-of sum of $1,000 a performance. Finally, she agreed to accept his offer. But mysteriously the promised contract was never delivered. She learned later what had happened. Edith McCormick had heard about the offer, and had bribed the producer, offering him enough money for a whole season of operas, provided Ganna Walska never be permitted to set foot in Ravinia.

She had sung the lead soprano role in *The Mikado* one summer in Nice. (She actually had done this, at least for one performance.) Critics from all over the world had been ecstatic—all, that is, except the reviewer from the *Chicago Tribune*, a McCormick-owned paper. Later she found out why. Bribery again. The critic has been paid by a rival soprano to write an unfavorable review. (In the files of the *Chicago Tribune* is a cablegram dated February 22, 1925, saying that the mayor of Nice had banned Ganna Walska from giving another performance in his city; the audience's reaction to the first performance had been so vociferously unfriendly that the mayor feared that any further appearances would erupt into a riot, in which the beautiful star might suffer bodily harm. The cable added: "M. Audier, the director of the opera, concurs with the Mayor's opinion.")

There had always been some question about Ganna Walska's age. Most published accounts of her gave her birth date as "about 1893." But in September of 1967, in an interview for *Opera* magazine, M. Erté, who knew her well, told the interviewer that she was then "about eighty-five," which would place her actual birth date some ten years earlier.

In the spring of 1971 she appeared briefly in the news when some items from her jewelry collection—including one large diamond which she had named The Mogul—went on the block at Sotheby–Parke Bernet and fetched a tidy $916,185. It was not that she needed the money. It was just that she didn't wear any of the big pieces any more.

Living quietly in the semitropic loveliness of her Santa Barbara estate, called Lotus Land, she became known as a gently dignified, sweet-faced little old lady, always interested in the arts. By the early 1980s, though age had slowed down her activities somewhat, she was still willing to open her beautiful home and spectacular gardens for charity benefits, particularly when the beneficiary had something to do with music or the theatre.

And, as this is written—in the early summer of 1981—that is where Ganna Walska is: alive and well at Lotus Land, every inch a *grande dame*.

PART FIVE

The Loneliest Millionairess

15

"GUPPY"

CINCINNATIANS LIKE TO POINT OUT to newcomers that Cincinnati was a city when Chicago was still an open prairie and Cleveland no more than a wide place in the Erie Canal System. Cincinnati reckons its existence from 1788, the year a Kentuckian named John Filson and a couple of partners purchased 740 acres in a natural amphitheatre beside the Ohio River surrounded by a handsome semicircle of hills and bluffs. Filson, an amateur surveyor, began laying out plans for his new city. He was also something of a scholar, and appears to have been fond of word games. He christened his city Losantiville, which sounds French but is actually a kind of reverse acronym. The basin of land that Filson and the others bought lay on the shore opposite the point where the Licking River enters the Ohio. The "L" in Losantiville therefore stood for Licking. *Os* is the Latin word for mouth; *anti*, of course, means opposite, and *ville* is French for city. Thus, read backward, Losantiville meant "the city opposite the mouth of the Licking." The name, however, did not last long. John Cleves Symmes, another early settler, thought the name ridiculous, and allegedly bellowed, "Losantiville! What an awful name! God damn it, call it Cincinnati!"—honoring the Society of the Cincinnati, a veterans' society of Revolutionary officers to which Symmes happened to belong. Symmes's choice won, and outsiders have never since been quite sure how to spell it.

First-time visitors to Cincinnati, expecting to find a rawboned midwestern town on the order of, say, Omaha, are usually surprised to find a city of fine old houses, stately squares and parks, gas-lit streets and hills where, as in San Francisco, homes with the finest views command the highest prices. Even in 1819, Cincinnati startled visitors with its subtle mixture of Old World elegance and southern charm. Graham A. Worth, who came to Cincinnati around that time to direct the Branch Bank of the United States, exclaimed later, "Talk to me of the backwoods—these people live in the style of princes! The costly dinner service—the splendid cut glass—the rich wines—the sumptuous dinner itself." Even Boston was impressed with the degree of culture achieved by Cincinnati; a correspondent from the *Boston Courier* in 1816 was moved to comment on "Pianofortes by the dozen in Cincinnati."

Cincinnati used to be able to boast that there was no real poverty in the city. Everyone was hard-working, and everyone was reasonably prosperous. Some people, of course, had become very rich. Two world wars, and subsequent migrations of blacks from the rural South and whites from Appalachia, would change all that, and Cincinnati now has its share of poverty proportionate to that of any other American city, but the fact that the city was so stable for so long is reflected in a certain complacent, *nil admirari* urban attitude. The people who became very rich in the early days, furthermore, tend still to be very rich.

Among the "first-cabin" families are the Tafts—still very much around —who produced both a United States President and a United States Senator. For years the *grande dame* of the Taft family was Mrs. Charles P. Taft, Sr., who reigned over, among other things, the Cincinnati Symphony Orchestra. Nor can one overlook the Longworths. It was said of the first Nicholas Longworth that he owned more land than anyone west of the Allegheny Mountains, and one of his descendants, Nicholas Longworth III, would become a congressman, Speaker of the House of Representatives, and the husband of Alice Roosevelt. In the Longworth family, one of the more remarkable ladies was Maria Longworth, an early feminist and artist who founded the Rookwood Pottery, which produced ceramic ware famous for its unusual designs and glazes.

All the prominent families knew one another, and society was very close-knit. Mrs. Charles P. Taft's best friend, for instance, was Mrs. Thomas J. Emery, and the two ladies regularly sent "breakfast letters" back and forth to each other via their coachmen, even though their houses were very close. The Emerys are an altogether extraordinary family. The first Emery, Thomas, was born in England and came to America in 1832, bringing his wife and a young son, Thomas Josephus Emery, Jr. Soon a second son, John Josiah Emery, was born, and the groundwork for a small but important family dynasty was laid.

There has always been a pleasant logic to Cincinnati's prosperity. The rich farmland around the city meant corn, and corn meant fodder for pigs. (At one point Cincinnati cheerfully earned the nickname "Porkop-olis" because it had become such an important pork center.) Pigs provided bristles for brushes, hides for shoes and gloves, sausage for the city's early German-immigrant population, and lard for candles and illumination. When John D. Rockefeller came out with kerosene as a substitute for lard oil, it was discovered that lard could also be used in soap making, and two Cincinnatians, William Cooper Procter and James Gamble, managed to make a very nice thing out of that. Procter & Gamble is still one of the city's flagship industries. Even in hard times, it is pointed out in Cincin-nati, people still need soap, and from the soap business Cincinnati has earned a reputation as a "depression-proof" city.

Thomas Emery, however, started out as an "estate and money agent," with a specialty of selling "country seats, situated from one-half a mile to eight miles from the city, not surpassed for elegance of buildings, gardens and orchards in Hamilton County." Later he branched out into the lard business, and by 1845 his Emery Candle Company was one of the most successful in the country. "In the candle business we had a new process of distilling cheap greases," he said later of his success. "Our competitors were using costly tallow and lard. Candles were high and our profits large for a number of years."

Thomas Emery died in 1851, after falling through a hatchway in his factory, but his two young sons were ready to carry on. (There were also two girls, Kezia and Julia, who inherited large shares of their father's fortune, but Kezia died and left everything to Julia, and then Julia died and left everything to the Salvation Army of England.) This was a long time before kerosene, and John D. Rockefeller was still an owlish school-boy, but the Emery brothers shrewdly decided that, though they would keep the candle business, they would devote their principal energies to what had been their father's first love: real estate. They formed Thomas Emery's Sons, Incorporated, "Builders of Hearths and Homes." One of their first big projects was the Hotel Emery, opened in 1877. Borrowing from the Piccadilly and Burlington arcades in London, the Hotel Emery had a block-long heated arcade of shops running through it, and office space above, which was unique in America at the time.

The Emerys also built one of the city's first luxury apartment houses, again a very daring and foresighted move. At the time, apartments, or "flats," as they were called, were considered fit habitations only for the poor; the affluent lived in private houses. But the Emerys' first apartment house was found to be so convenient and comfortable that the young William Howard Tafts became tenants for a while. Spurred by this success, the boys built more, giving their apartment houses romantic, European-sounding names—the Lorraine, the Lombardy, the Brittany, the Saxony, the Normandy, the Warwick, Somerset, Cumberland, Essex, Clermont, Navarre, Verona, Madrid, Suffolk, Granada, Seville, Garonne, Aragon, and Castile—to name only a few. They built the Carew Tower, a forty-five-story office skyscraper, which is still Cincinnati's tallest building. Like the Hotel Emery, the Carew Tower featured an enclosed shopping arcade, and it also included another hotel, the Netherland Plaza.

Two competing hotels were the Grand and the Gibson, which, young Thomas J. Emery believed, were profiteering by charging $3.50 a day for a room with meals. A good hotel, he claimed, could offer the same accommodations and service for $2 a day. The result was his Palace Hotel, opened in 1882. "As long as the sun shines," Thomas Emery promised, "the Palace will be a two-dollar hotel." To be sure, there was only one public bathroom and toilet to a floor, but that was standard for hotels of the time.

The Emerys began expanding their real estate operations beyond Cincinnati, and soon they were developing and building projects in such widely scattered places as San Francisco, Denver, Kansas City, Toledo, Indianapolis, Chicago, New York, Trinidad, and Puerto Rico. The brothers had more than two thousand tenants in Cincinnati alone, not counting, of course, the stream of transient guests in their hotels. By 1930 it was estimated that the only family in America which controlled more real estate than the Emerys of Cincinnati was the Astors of New York.

The Emery Candle Company, in the meantime, had weathered the age of kerosene, of gaslight and, eventually, electricity, and was turning out stearic acid, oleine, and glycerine products sold all over the world. Two other Emery companies had spun off from this—the American Oil Treating and Hardening Company, specializing in the hardening of oils, and the Twitchell Process Company, which supplied a reagent for splitting fats.

In 1866, Thomas J. Emery married twenty-two-year-old Mary Hopkins of Brooklyn. (His younger brother would remain a bachelor until fairly late in life, when a wife became necessary for dynastic reasons.) Mary's background and upbringing were genteel. Her father, a New York clergyman named Francis Swaine Muhlenberg, was the son of General Peter Muhlenberg, a soldier-clergyman who had been a companion-at-arms of General George Washington in the Revolution, and a member of the family after whom Muhlenberg College is named. But Mr. Muhlen-

berg had died when Mary was quite young, and, when her mother remarried a well-to-do dry-goods merchant named Richard H. Hopkins,
Mary began using her stepfather's surname.

But her nickname was "Guppy." No one knew where that came from,
but she clearly liked it because she often signed her letters that way. And
in appearance she did rather call to mind a little fish. She was small and
plump, and not really pretty, though she had big, deep-set eyes and was
proud of her flawless white skin and her tiny, delicate hands. She was
also bookish. She spent the equivalent of her high-school years, from
1857 to 1862, studying at the Packer Collegiate Institute in Brooklyn
Heights. Packer was, in those days, a school for well-born young ladies
—tuition was $12 a quarter, plus 50 cents each for "books in ink," which
made it, for its time, an expensive place. It was also unusual in that it was
then the only school in New York City where a woman could receive the
equivalent of a higher education—indeed, it was the only school of its
sort for miles around. Vassar did not come into existence in Poughkeep-
sie, New York, until 1861, and Barnard was established some years after
that. While others of her generation were learning to work petit point and
pour tea, Mary was studying science, mathematics, Latin, German,
French, and art history. Before meeting Thomas Emery, she had planned
to become a schoolteacher.

When Emery brought his bride home to sober, solid Cincinnati—Serene Cincinnati, it has been called—she fitted right in. The population
base of Cincinnati was largely English and German, two nationalities not
known for extravagance and show. On Mary Emery's father's side, her
ancestors were German Lutherans; on her mother's, they were English
Episcopalians. Cincinnati has never been accused of being trend-setting
or *avant-garde*, and neither was the new Mrs. Emery. Though she was
married to one of the city's richest men, Mary Emery's bearing was
modest. Her simple coiffure was tucked carefully under a net made of her
own fine hair. Instead of hats, she favored bonnets. Her dresses were
high-collared, long-sleeved, long-skirted, and nearly always of black or
dark purple, though she occasionally appeared in a white mohair outfit.
When she ventured out, she was always black-gloved and carried a black
parasol.

Edgecliffe, the house the Thomas J. Emerys built for themselves in
Cincinnati, was large, but not overpowering in the sense of a Whitemarsh
Hall. It contained only sixteen principal rooms, plus a kitchen, service
area, and basement. Mary Emery had chosen the site—high on a bluff
overlooking a wide bend in the Ohio and the Kentucky hills beyond—

because of its literary overtones. Both Henry Wadsworth Longfellow and Charles Dickens had visited Cincinnati, and had declared this particular hilltop view the most beautiful in the city. Edgecliffe was built of gray stone in the style of a castle on the Rhine, and a round third-floor tower faced the river and overlooked a series of balconies and terraces. From the rooftop widow's walk a panoramic view extended for miles in all directions.

Edgecliffe was decorated and furnished with Victorian exuberance, and yet with a certain amount of Victorian restraint. The wide wrought-iron doors of the entrance led into a marble-floored central atrium with a fountain at its center, lit by a coffered skylight ceiling three stories high. In this hall stood two marble lamps of learning imported from Italy, and a statue representing the youthful Michelangelo. Up from the atrium led a wide marble staircase, culminating in a balcony which connected the rooms on the second floor. Just off the entrance hall was the music room, its walls covered in pale green silk brocade, its windows hung with green velour drapes, the room itself furnished with Louis XV and XVI pieces. Opposite was the dining room, with an elaborate, tapestry-hung fireplace, carved-plaster walls and ceiling, and four Moorish-style hanging sanctuary lamps. The furniture in this room was all hand-carved by local artisans in the Jacobean Renaissance style. Also on the main floor were a library with an Italian marble fireplace, with walls covered in red brocade, lighted by brass chandeliers and twin nine-foot-high French Renaissance torchères; a morning room, containing a Louis XVI desk, a copy of the one used at the signing of the Treaty of Versailles; and a river-facing solarium with French doors leading into the terraces and gardens. Outbuildings included a carriage house and two hothouses, for Mary Emery was very fond of flowers.

Though the Emery house was certainly a grand one, it was by no means the grandest—or largest—house in Cincinnati. (That distinction probably belonged to the Wurlitzers, who manufactured organs.) Nor was it really designed for huge entertainments. There was no ballroom, and the dining room could accommodate sixteen at most. Mary Emery did not like to give large teas or receptions and, in fact, had little interest in becoming a great hostess. Her entertaining was limited to her long and formal Sunday dinners, served in the middle of the day, and the guests were usually close friends and family.

Because Mary missed the East and the fresh sea breezes off Brooklyn Heights, the Emerys built a second home in Newport, called Mariemont (pronounced, in the English fashion, Mary-mont.) But here again, Mariemont was austere compared with the castles which Vanderbilts, Astors, and Belmonts were building in Newport at the time. Mariemont, built in the Victorian shingle style, was far from the fashionable reaches of Bellevue Avenue, and it was not even on the waterfront—nor did the Emerys, who could certainly have afforded to do so, care to mingle or compete with the other families of the summer colony. The gardens, not the house, made Mariemont a showplace, and fourteen Portuguese gardeners were required full-time to maintain them. And so a pattern was established. For the six cold months of the year, the Emerys lived at Edgecliffe in Cincinnati, where Mary was quietly beginning to assemble her art collection. For the six warm months, the family stayed in Newport under the supervision of Sophie, Mrs. Emery's personal maid. Travel was usually by private railroad car, but even here there was a prudent Cincinnati difference. Though the Emerys could have afforded to buy their own private car, as other rich Americans were doing, the Emerys leased theirs for the trip. It made sense, considering the size of the staff that traveled with them. A private railroad car rented for the same price as a carful of Pullman accommodations, plus a surcharge of 15 percent—and was cheaper than the cost of ownership and maintenance.

Mary Emery was to demonstrate that, to be a *grande dame*, it was not always necessary to be haughty, despotic, arrogant, eccentric, demanding, vain, or outrageous. As the wife of a very rich man, she was none of these things. On the contrary, she was soft-spoken, gentle, domestic and retiring, and more than a little shy—plain little Guppy. In addition to art, she loved music. She seemed to have a dread of becoming a public figure, and she set aside every Wednesday as her private day. On Wednesdays she would receive no callers, and, instead, would work in her gardens, or meditate, or read, or listen to Bach and Beethoven on her wind-up Victrola with its painted morning-glory amplifying horn.

Like so many *grandes dames* of the era, Mary Emery was not immune to personal tragedy. The Emerys had two children, both boys, Sheldon and Albert. Albert, the younger, was an athlete and an outdoorsman. Sheldon was scholarly, like his mother something of a bookworm, and a brilliant student. Like many introverted youths, he was also sickly, but Mary Emery loved both her sons unqualifiedly. Albert Emery was killed in 1886 at the age of eighteen in a sledding accident at St. Paul's School in New Hampshire. Sheldon died in 1890, at twenty-three, from pneumonia, while a student at Harvard.

Sheldon's funeral in Cincinnati was attended by a Harvard classmate and friend named Charles J. Livingood, and Mary Emery was immediately struck by what she saw as Livingood's uncanny resemblance to his dead classmate. Subsequently she asked him if he would consider coming to work for her, and from then on, and for the rest of her life, Charles Livingood would be Mary Emery's right-hand man, managing her business affairs and civic projects.

In 1906, Thomas J. Emery died while on a business trip in Egypt, and Livingood—now married and a father himself—became a sort of surrogate husband as well as son. Livingood's daughter Elizabeth recalled in 1981 that, as a little girl, she had owned a coral necklace with a gold clasp fashioned in the shape of two angels' heads. Mrs. Emery had admired the necklace and asked to see it. Fingering the clasp, she said to Elizabeth Livingood, "The names of these two angels are Albert and Sheldon."

Elizabeth Livingood recalled that she was not particularly pleased to hear that her two gold angels had boys' names. Later, of course, she realized that the death of Mrs. Emery's two sons, followed by the death of her husband, had a lot to do with the sort of woman Mary Emery would become.

Because it was at this point, with all the menfolk in her family dead and easily the richest woman in Cincinnati, that sixty-two-year-old Mary Emery quietly—almost secretively—embarked upon her extraordinary career in philanthropy.

"I think now," said Elizabeth Livingood, "that she may have been one of the saddest, loneliest women I've ever known. Though she was by nature extremely shy, she felt that somehow she had to reach out and touch the world."

16

A LITANY OF GOOD WORKS

MARY EMERY'S FIRST IMPORTANT PHILANTHROPY came not long after her husband's death, when she donated $250,000 to build a YMCA in Newport, specifically for the Army and Navy enlisted personnel who were stationed there. She had noted, she wrote in a letter outlining her plan, that Newport offered the military men little in the way of entertainment or recreation except "bar rooms and picture shows." Her YMCA, she hoped, would provide "a better rallying place than you now have for your leisure hours . . . preferring it as a resort." As would become typical of her giving, however, she was secretive about it. She was not present at the cornerstone laying, and the identity of the donor was not made public until half an hour before the event. The plaque placed on the building did not even include her name, but merely read:

A MOTHER'S MEMORIAL TO HER SONS
SHELDON AND ALBERT EMERY

To her alma mater, Packer Institute, Mary shipped off $50,000 Brooklyn Union Gas Company bonds to establish a teachers' pension fund, directing that the fund be named in memory of a favorite mathematics teacher, Miss Adeline L. Jones. In her home town, another $250,000 was presented to the University of Cincinnati Medical School to endow a professorial chair named in honor of her pediatrician, Dr. Benjamin K. Rachford. Another large gift went to the Cincinnati Children's Hospital, and a grand total of $20,000,000 was set aside to establish the Thomas J. Emery Memorial Fund in memory of her husband. Because her husband "had a kindly and sympathetic interest in the welfare of the Negro race," she built a 250-bed "Negro orphan asylum" in Cincinnati, as well as a black YMCA. Clearly, as the widow of a builder, she had acquired a taste for building things.

In Cincinnati, meanwhile, the gossips said that Mary Emery and Mrs. Charles P. Taft were not, as they appeared to be, best friends at all, but were actually bitter philanthropic rivals. It was noted that whenever Mrs. Emery stepped forward to support a project, Mrs. Taft withdrew her support from that particular endeavor. Annie Sinton Taft was also very rich. Her father, David Sinton—though the fact was politely overlooked by the time of the second generation—had been a Civil War profiteer. Sensing, with the South talking of Secession, that a war was in the offing, and having a good hunch that war would mean a demand for pig iron, Sinton had cornered the prewar iron market. From the fortune he made selling iron for cannon balls to both the Union and the Confederacy, Sinton had built, among other things, Cincinnati's Sinton Hotel, which rivaled the Emerys' Netherland Plaza in both size and luxury. Annie was David Sinton's only child.

Actually, what Mary Emery and Annie Taft did in Cincinnati—it was often the subject of their daily "breakfast letters"—was to divide things up. When Annie Taft's interest in the Cincinnati Symphony began to wane, and she became more interested in the Cincinnati Opera, Mary Emery took over the Symphony and built the 2,200-seat Emery Auditorium, where, for years, the Symphony performed. Considered acoustically perfect, the auditorium contained—and still contains—a giant Wurlitzer theatre organ, one of two or three of its kind in the world. The Emery Auditorium, which was completed in 1914, was designed along the lines of the great opera houses of Europe, with a "Diamond Horseshoe" first balcony. For reasons of fashion as much as anything else, the arms of the horseshoe sweep down to the edges of the proscenium in grand curves, embracing the audience as it were, so that the gowns and jewels of the gentry in the boxes are on full display for the lesser folk downstairs in the stalls.

To assure that Culture, or at least a bird's-eye view of it, would also be available to the least affluent, the architects also included a steep and lofty second balcony, which offered narrower and harder seats in more closely packed rows. The theory in theatre architecture at the time seemed to hold that, though the rich and poor might be permitted to attend cultural events under the same roof, it should not be necessary for them to rub shoulders with one another, and, to that end, admission to this steerage section of the great hall was possible only through a single rather narrow stairway and a separate entrance from the street. (Because this arrangement failed to satisfy later fire-law requirements, the second balcony is no longer used.)

Hard by the auditorium, to fill up the block, perhaps, Mary Emery built the Ohio Mechanics' Institute, a school devoted to the teaching of trades, which later became part of the University of Cincinnati system. Its capacity was 4,000 students, and an industrial museum adjoined it. Though the Emery name appears on the auditorium's marquee, Mary's name is nowhere affixed to either of the two other buildings.

Putting the lie to tales of a philanthropic rivalry, Mary Emery and Annie Taft did sometimes cooperate on the same civic projects. Both women were animal lovers, and at one point each pledged $125,000 for the Cincinnati Zoo, provided other citizens would do the same. Others did. But the Sinton-Taft fortune was never a match for Mary Emery's. Her annual $40,000 contribution to the Cincinnati Community Chest, plus another $25,000 from the Emery Memorial Fund, made her for twenty years the city's largest individual donor.

Reciting a list of Mary Emery's benefactions in Cincinnati and elsewhere very quickly becomes a litany of good works, but among the more important were the building of the Parish House for Christ Church in Cincinnati; a farm for the Fresh Air Society; the Ohio-Miami Medical College for Cincinnati's General Hospital; The Vacation House, a farm and home for children on the Ohio River; the Central Building of the Cincinnati YMCA (in addition to the "colored" YMCA); the Reception & Medical Building at Trudeau Sanitarium in Saranac, New York; memorial buildings at Tuskegee Institute, Berea College, Lincoln University of Kentucky, Miss Berry's Schools in Rome, Georgia, Sewanee University, and Hobart College of San Juan, Puerto Rico; the Administration Building of the Children's Home in Cincinnati; the Salvation Army Rescue Home for Colored in Cincinnati; the waterworks for the Pine Mountain Settlement School in Kentucky; "cathedral houses"—children's shelters, in memory of Sheldon Emery—in such far-flung places as Salt Lake City, Phoenix, Sacramento, and Circleville, Ohio.

The list goes on. She endowed free beds in St. Luke's Hospital, Denver; in St. Luke's Hospital, Phoenix; at Children's Hospital, Denver; at Esmeralda Hospital, Sewanee, Tennessee; at St. Luke's Hospital, McAlester, Oklahoma; at St. Margaret's Hospital, Boise, Idaho; and at Good Samaritan Hospital, in Cincinnati. She also endowed Emery Free Day (free admissions on Saturdays) at the Cincinnati Art Museum, and the Mary M. Emery Chair of Pathology at Ohio-Miami Medical School. She established the Emery Foundation of San Francisco, the Emery Arboretum "for the study of trees and shrubs in the Ohio Valley," and the Mary M. Emery Bird Reserve, a plan to "bring back the birds to the city."

Among the social institutions she actively supported were the Ohio Institute for Public Efficiency, a foundation with headquarters in Columbus, Ohio, whose goals were to improve state and municipal administration; and the Council of Social Agencies, a centralizing bureau of some eighty benevolent and corrective agencies in Cincinnati. She presided over the Cincinnati Model Homes Company, which supplied "ideal housing to over 200 families, mostly negroes." (In this latter endeavor, she skated on thin ice. Since the "ideal housing" was rented out to the tenants, she was accused of "commercialized philanthropy.")

For years, the identity of a mysterious "Madame X," who had given $250,000 to build a "working girls' home" for young Frenchwomen of slender means called Cercle Concordia, at 19 rue Tournefort near the Bon Marché business district of Paris, was a secret. The home, built in 1907, accommodated 120 young ladies. It was not until Mary Emery's death twenty years later that it was revealed she had been Madame X.

Like Isabella Gardner, Mary Emery had young protégés, though she never uncovered a talent comparable to that of Bernard Berenson and there was never the suggestion of a romantic involvement with any of them. There was a young man named Chalmers Clifton, whom she helped as a conductor and composer, and Charles Hackett, an opera singer. Marion Green, an actor who once toured with a road company in the title role of *Monsieur Beaucaire*, was another. Though none of these young talents was ever to become exactly a household word, she helped with their schooling and they were frequent house guests at Mariemont.

Through all this, Mary Emery was exceptionally fortunate in having at her side, as her right-hand man in every decision, Charles Livingood. A New England aristocrat and *cum laude* graduate of Harvard—where he majored in English literature, history, and philosophy—Livingood was not only a man of the utmost probity but also a man of intelligence, taste, and sophistication. He was a gentleman and scholar of the Old School, and his personal enthusiasms were the life of Petrarch, prehistoric man, and the history of Provence—"anything that begins with P," he used to say. But he was also a shrewd, tough-minded businessman. Every morning Livingood met with Mrs. Emery in her library at Edgecliffe, and when it was time to go to Newport, he and his family followed her to Mariemont, where the Livingoods occupied a comfortable cottage nearby. Livingood would carefully go over her accounts, managing the intricate details of her huge estate, advising her which stocks or properties ought to be bought, which might be sold, and how much might be left over to be given away.

Understandably, Mary Emery endured what is the bane of every philanthropist—the endless stream of requests for money, from individuals as well as from organized charities, that arrived daily at her doorstep. No sooner had an Emery gift been announced than thousands of letters asking for more arrived in the mail. The effect of this on Mary was to make her more reclusive, more secretive. She had to be. If word got around that Mary Emery was buying up land for a bird preserve, real estate prices instantly shot up. The successful philanthropist must be a cynic, and develop a hide of rhinoceros thickness when faced with the pathetic entreaties and tales of woe—some perhaps true, many more probably false —which never cease. Mary Emery, however, was incapable of cynicism, and admitted that softheartedness was her most serious flaw. Fortunately, she had Charles Livingood as her cynic-in-residence. Sometimes, after being moved by a particularly doleful letter and request, she would reach for that piteous communication and say, "Now, Mr. Livingood, don't you think we just might—?" Slowly but firmly he would shake his head and reply, "No, Mrs. Emery, we might not." Screening the letters, sifting the legitimate requests from the shady and suspect, became Charles Livingood's job. Of, perhaps, five hundred mendicant letters in the morning's mail, Livingood might select as many as two or three which he deemed worthy of Mrs. Emery's serious consideration. Then, if she approved of a project which he considered worthwhile, he would review the whereabouts and sizes of the various pieces of her scattered fortune to see from which of the little stacks of figures funds might become available. Theirs was a perfect working partnership. Always addressing each other formally, they never quarreled. In the end, they always agreed.

Though Livingood managed her books and wrote out the checks, there was one area in which he felt he was not qualified to advise her: her growing art collection. He did, however, see to it that she got the best advice possible, in the person of Joseph Guest, the director of the Cincinnati Art Museum. Since her husband's death, Mary had made it a point to buy at least one important painting every year, and soon her collection included Titian, Rubens, Van Dyke, Rembrandt, Tintoretto, Lorenzo di Credi, Mabuse, Bronzino, Murillo, Fouquet, Dirk Bouts, Hals, Nattier, Le Brun, Gainsborough, Romney, Lawrence, Raeburn, Israels, Lhermitte, and a great many masters of the Barbizon School. But she was a safe and cautious buyer, and never purchased anything without Mr. Guest's approval. Though she occasionally bought through Joseph Duveen, who was always on hand when rich people were spending money on art, she did not, like Eva Stotesbury, give Duveen carte blanche. Joseph Guest was always her agent and go-between in the negotiations —much to the displeasure of Duveen, who was always looking for ways to deal with Mrs. Emery directly. She kept herself at arm's length, however, and when she and Guest had decided, say, to buy Velásquez' *Philip IV*, Mrs. Emery would write a note to Guest, saying, "Now be sure to tell Mr. Duveen to place the painting in a suitable frame, and install the right picture-light above it. . . ."

Because, like Livingood, Joseph Guest was a tough trader, there were occasional hackles raised. When Guest purchased Titian's *Philip II* for her, at something over $300,000, there was a great outcry in England at the news that the painting was leaving British shores for the United States. And a few mistakes were made—it was almost inevitable that there should have been. Mary Emery's Rembrandt later turned out not to be a Rembrandt, and had to be redesignated "after Rembrandt." But for the most part Guest's choices were astute ones, and their prices were in line with the market of the day. After all, it behooved Guest to select the pieces of Mrs. Emery's collection carefully. She had made it clear to him that she considered herself only the temporary "guardian" of the collection, and that one day it would all go to his Cincinnati Art Museum, as indeed it has—housed in the Emery Wing, which she also donated. (As Fiske Kimball in Philadelphia often reminded everyone, Eva Stotesbury's collection might have suffered a kinder fate if she had taken his advice instead of Duveen's.)

In 1914, however, a plan even more ambitious than Mary Emery's art collection—by then valued at more than $3,500,000—was under way, and the details of it were consuming more and more of Mrs. Emery's and Mr. Livingood's working days. It was to be Mrs. Emery's ultimate philanthropy to her adopted city, and naturally, considering its size and scope, the utmost secrecy was essential. Aside from herself and Livingood, only a few carefully chosen aides and confidantes had any notion of what was afoot for Cincinnati. Nor would anyone else get wind of it for several years.

17

THE TSARINA AND THE LADY

THE PHRASE "LADY BOUNTIFUL," if used at all in the 1980s, is invariably
used with scorn. But it is important to remember that in the more trust-
ing, more naïve world of America before the First World War, to be a
Lady Bountiful was a very respectable occupation. It was even considered
a high calling, and Ladies Bountiful abounded. Some were ostentatious
and outrageous. Others, like Mary Emery, preferred to remain in the
background, bestowing their bounty through functionaries. But though
their individual styles might vary, their motives were almost never questioned. Gratitude, in those days, was an acceptable response, and a Lady
Bountiful was deemed a valuable asset to her community.

Today, Mary Emery's thirty-year career of giving away money would
doubtless be diagnosed as an extended ego trip. Hers, after all, was a life
spent receiving letters of entreaty, followed by letters of lavish thanks and
praise. And certainly there were earthly pleasures to be gained from
seeing one's name, or one's loved ones' names, chiseled in marble on some
large public building, insuring some sort of immortality on the planet.
But from all the evidence, if Mary Emery was ever tempted to congratu-
late herself on the extent of her benefactions, she did her best to stifle the
temptation. Her motives were somewhat different.

For one thing, as a descendant of at least two Protestant clergymen, she
was a firm believer in such old-fashioned notions as the Golden Rule.
Pious and churchgoing, she was a firm subscriber to the Christian Ethic,
and doubtless also believed that for good works on earth she would be
rewarded in the Protestant Hereafter. She was also an instinctive advocate
of what were then considered American upper-class values, and the concept of *noblesse oblige*.

The curious thing about *noblesse oblige* in America is that it is deemed a subject, like sex, too delicate and too important to talk about. *Noblesse oblige* exists in the same shadowy, but also somehow sacred, area as what goes on behind closed bedroom doors. One would never hear an upper-class American say, "We do such-and-such out of a sense of *noblesse oblige*." Nor would an upper-class American ever say "because we are upper-class."*

Nevertheless, upper-class values—including do-good principles—were taught carefully, subtly, by example, in the homes and classrooms of the well born and well bred of Mary Emery's era. What she might have missed from her minister father was supplied by the Packer Collegiate Institute between 1857 and 1862. When the school was dedicated a few years earlier, in 1846, the Reverend Dr. William B. Sprague of Albany had declared in his address that a Packer education was to be "employed for the formation of human character—for the development and ultimate perfection of human faculties," and that it would offer proper young ladies "such a culture of the faculties as shall constitute that appropriate preparation for an honorable and useful life." This was how Dr. Sprague viewed the role of an aristocratic woman:

> Providence has designated to her, her appropriate sphere, and though it be a retired, quiet, and if you please in some respects a humble sphere, it is a glorious sphere, notwithstanding—glorious, because Heaven has crowned it with the means of honorable usefulness . . . I do not disparage but honor her, when I say that her throne is the nursery, and beside the cradle . . . Think it not hardship, ladies, that public opinion excuses you from appearing in the arena of political conflict, or from saying at the ballot box who shall be our rulers, or from standing forth as God's commissioned ambassadors to treat with a dying world.

* Several years ago, New York socialite Marietta Tree recalled being slapped sharply by her mother when, as a little girl, she remarked that one of her school friends was "rather middle-class." "There are no classes in America!" her mother told her. Then, in a kinder tone, she added, "Of course there are classes. But to use the expression 'middle-class' is very *lower*-class." Mrs. Tree's mother was the late Mary Parkman Peabody, very much of Boston's upper class. It was Mrs. Peabody who in 1964, at the age of seventy-two, led a sit-in by blacks and whites at the racially segregated dining room of a Florida motel. With the local police standing by with tear gas, cattle prods, and attack dogs, the silver-haired mother of the governor of Massachusetts was arrested and taken off to jail. As she was being led away from the demonstration, she expressed upper-class values perfectly when she said calmly, "We are just what they say we are—do-gooders."

Dr. Sprague's version of feminism did concede that a woman would not be a good sovereign of the nursery if "she has an undisciplined and unfurnished mind." These words sound pompous and patronizing today but were startlingly liberal in a day when most members of both sexes thought that educating women at all was a waste of time. A few years later, in 1850, a report to the trustees would stress how successfully the school was instilling upper-class values among its young charges:

> No medals or prizes are offered to stimulate ambition, but the pupil is taught that love of excellence for its own sake, which brings its own recompense. . . .
> In proof of the exemplary conduct of the pupils, the trustees have only to state that among the 650 young ladies attending the academy during the past year, not one unpleasant case of discipline has occurred.
> The love of neatness and good order, so constantly inculcated by the teachers, is mutely taught by the beautiful grounds attached to the institution.
> A habit of forbearance and respect for public property are [sic] fostered here, and as an evidence of the morality in little things, manifested even by the youngest, it may be stated that no one is ever found touching a flower or defacing a grass plot.

In a course called Composition, the young ladies were instructed to write themes which were not only properly spelled and well constructed but which also were marked by "sound moral and religious sentiment." And, in a course called Manual of Morals, came something close to a spelling-out of the notion of *noblesse oblige:* "It is ever the duty of she [sic] whom God has favored with worldly possessions to assume some of the burden of those less fortunate than she."

With such training, and with God's will behind it, how could Mary Emery have done other than she did? With these convictions, Mary, in 1914, embarked upon her most ambitious project. By that year the blight of Cincinnati, as it had long been in other cities, was beginning to be its slums. If anyone could cure this blight, she and Mr. Livingood reasoned, it would be she and Thomas J. Emery's fortune, which, despite her giving, was actually growing larger under Livingood's guiding hand. She and Livingood had both visited the model cities and villages and New Towns that were being built in England. Unlike Edith McCormick, Mary Emery did not plan to build a city of yacht basins for the rich. She wanted to move the slums to the fresh air and green grass of the suburbs

—to provide a good life for the poor. From the beginning, it was to be "an interpretation of modern city planning principles, applied to a small community to produce local happiness—a national example." And it was to be called Mariemont, after Mary Emery's summer home in Newport.

The site she and Livingood selected was a 254-acre tract—later expanded to more than 400 acres—in a sparsely populated, wooded area of low, rolling hills about ten miles northeast of Cincinnati on the banks of the Little Miami River. Quietly, Mary began buying up the land she wanted. Great secrecy had to be observed, of course, to keep prices from skyrocketing, and a real estate agent from as far away as Chicago was hired to oversee these transactions so that no one would suspect a connection with Cincinnati real estate interests. Even the local real estate firm, which made the contacts and completed the purchase of the various parcels, had no idea whom it was working for, and some of the rumors that circulated—that the land was to be the site of a large, noisy, and smelly factory—actually had the effect of driving prices down.

The Mariemont Company was formed, and a prominent city planner, John Nolan of Philadelphia, was hired. Mary Emery then purchased the initial stock in the company for about $2,500,000 to give it some working capital, and presently the plans emerged from Mr. Nolan's drawing board. The streets of Mariemont were designed to radiate from a central square and village green. Along the wide main street, with its landscaped mall which made up the central square, would be buildings for shops and offices and a small inn with a restaurant, with a garden terrace behind it. The new town would have its own elementary school and high school, its own hospital, its own church and cemetery, its own city hall and fire station, its own theatre and museum, and its own central heating plant to serve the entire community. Plenty of space was given over to parks and playgrounds, and near the center of town a tall bell tower with a twenty-three-bell carillon was to stand as Mariemont's symbol. Just to the south of the town an industrial park was laid out, the idea being that residents could live close to where they worked, because Mariemont was envisioned as a town for "the working man" and his family.

The little side streets were laid out in graceful arcs and curves to discourage heavy traffic, and there were plenty of cozy cul-de-sacs. Mrs. Emery asked that two of these—Albert Place and Sheldon Close—be named after her two sons. In general, the housing was to be of three types —small private homes, garden apartments, and "group houses," which were attached town houses. Through the center of each block of housing ran a service alley, so that garbage cans would not have to be placed on the street. The architecture was a loose mixture of English exposed-beam Tudor and New England saltbox, and the result was intended to be almost a storybook version of an English village that would dance perhaps a bit precariously on the edge of cuteness without quite falling over the rim.

The First World War imposed a temporary halt on the construction of Mariemont, but by 1920 the project was able to move forward again and, on April 23, 1923, Mary Emery, in her black bonnet and one of her almost dowdy-looking long black dresses, presided over the groundbreaking with a silver spade in her hand. By 1926 the first families were able to move in; at first most of Mariemont's homes and apartments were leased for low rentals, and renters were given options to buy. And, on March 19 of that year, a small "Greeting" from Mrs. Emery appeared in the first issue of the *Mariemont Messenger*:

Good morning, Is the sun a little brighter, there in Mariemont? Is the air a little fresher? Is your home a little sweeter? Is your housework somewhat easier? And the children—do you feel safer about them? Are their faces a bit ruddier, are their legs a little sturdier? Do they laugh and play a lot louder in Mariemont? Then I am content.

There was one thing, however, about which Mary Emery was not content, and that involved a woman named Marion Devereux. Miss Devereux was a newspaper reporter, but she was somewhat more than that. Commenting on social events for the *Cincinnati Enquirer*, she had gradually made herself what she called "the arbiter of Cincinnati society." She was also irreverently called "the Tsarina," but unfortunately, in her ascent to power, Cincinnati, in its relaxed way, had begun to take her seriously. Though she was of obscure origins herself, her reign over the city had, by the early 1920s, become all but complete. It was a reign of terror and a reign of cruelty. Miss Devereux considered herself *the grande dame* of Cincinnati, and, in Mary Emery's opinion, her influence had become malevolent and destructive.

Miss Devereux had inherited her seat in the Society Editor's chair from her mother, Mrs. Arthur Devereux, who had already turned the job into a harsh dictatorship. Madame Devereux, as Mrs. Devereux was called, had introduced a little book called *Who's Who: A Society Register . . . for Cincinnati*, which listed her highly biased choices of which families were considered "social," as opposed to those who were not. No Jews were included, though there were a number of prominent and wealthy Jewish families in the city, and Roman Catholics were in noticeably short supply. Similarly, Madame Devereux had had little use for the old German families who had made their money in beer, lard, and sausage. Madame Devereux had also arbitrarily reorganized "reception days," those days of the week when ladies were at home to callers, assigning a different day of the week to each part of town. This arrangement, Madame Devereux explained, was only a "suggestion," but her suggestion had very quickly become the rule, and those who had dared to break or bend it soon found their names omitted from the following year's edition of *Who's Who*. . . .

On her death in 1910, Madame Devereux's duties were taken over by her daughter Marion, then a spinster of thirty-seven, who had worked for several years as her mother's assistant. Madame Devereux had already developed a notably florid prose style, to which her daughter proceeded to add elaborate embellishments, swirls, and flourishes. She resurrected long-dead words, and never used an everyday term if an archaic one would do. A woman's gown, for instance, was her "toilet," or sometimes "toilette." She also invented words. Her collective noun for the women at a party was inevitably Femina, always capitalized, as in, "For this supreme occasion, Femina had resplendently arrayed herself in some of the most scintillatingly exquisite creations evoked by the couturier's wand of enchantment." Debutantes were "rosebuds," and two sisters presented at the same time were "twin rosebuds on the parent stem." A table was a mahogany, and a large dining table was "the central mahogany." If a phrase sounded too commonplace in English, she tried French, or at least her version of it. At one party, she noted that tuxedos for the men were "*de rigeuer*," and at the opera one evening, "the Hinkle box was a scene of constant va and vient." On one occasion, writing up a wedding, she penned:

> Into the hush of this ambient twilight came the bridal procession, the feathery green of tender laurel that wreathed choir stalls, pulpit and rood screen, and the curving fronds of a few giant palms massed in the chancel pointing the way to the altar, where the snowy chalices of tall Easter lilies were sentineled by blazing candelabra, seven-branched . . . Very pretty, with lovely light brown hair and gray-blue eyes, the bride's youthfulness suddenly seemed to take on a certain queenliness as she swept from end to end of this line of light. Her gown of soft white, crinkly crepe was the essence of simplicity, and therefore the perfection of chic . . . Held close to her well-poised head, her fair hair visible through its delicate mesh, this airy

unsubstantial fabric drifted in long, broad folds for yards behind her, as fragile as mist, enmeshing her tall figure, concealing her face, and in its upturned brim that circled her shapely head, forming the semblance of a halo, that gave her the air of one of the saints or angels that, in color, looked down from the gorgeous memorial windows on every hand.

At first, Cincinnati was simply amused by Miss Devereux's deep-purple prose. Soon people were collecting favorite Devereux-isms, such as "Mr. and Mrs. Tom Conroy have been the center of many merry moments since their return from their honeymoon." Or "Miss Ruth Harrison whose toilet of black satin was relieved by a touch of ermine." Or "An hour of agreeable intercourse will follow this series of events, the membership being all cocked and primed to stay on to enjoy it." But Miss Devereux was rapidly becoming a force as well. And as her reputation grew, so did the *Enquirer*'s circulation. She sold papers, and, accordingly, her editors gave her more leeway and more space. On and on she trilled and warbled, and it was not long before a single day's social events at the height of a Cincinnati season would be accorded sixteen full columns of Devereux, or two full pages. Soon an unbreakable rule was established at the paper: not a word of Miss Devereux's copy could be altered; not a word could be cut. Thus when Miss Devereux described a group called the Bachelors as "young celibrates," one could never be sure whether there had been a typographical error or whether Miss Devereux had written it that way. Thus there were also times when no one reading her stories had the slightest clue to what she was trying to say, as in:

In nothing to the Philistines are the May Festivals more intriguing than in the boxes and the Audience. Last night these themes of and corridor and foyer were paramount to the carnal-minded devotee of these two yearly events.

Miss Devereux was quick to recognize her growing power, and quick to use it. Though she was not below average height, she ordered the legs of the chairs facing her desk cut down, so that visitors to her office at the newspaper sat before her almost on their knees, like supplicants. At the office she was known to be a holy terror when crossed, and was not above hurling an assistant's copy across the room if it did not come up to her own exacting standards. She would summon a copy boy from a distant part of the building and, when he arrived, order him to stick his head out her window and tell her if it was raining. A copy boy was regularly assigned to walk her home at night.

Her personal vendettas became famous, and, of course, these also made good copy. Her favorite method of revenge upon someone who had offended her was the Fashion Attack. She would write, "Mrs. —— appeared in her customary brown," or "Mrs. —— wore the green toilet in which she always looks so well," or "Mrs. —— appeared in the blue dress which has graced several previous occasions." A recent widow, who had fallen from Miss Devereux's favor, had appeared at a horse show because her son was to be one of the stars. The widow was all in black, but, to show her what she thought of her, Miss Devereux reported that the lady appeared in her box "in a gorgeous red toilette." Jewels of the unfavored were dismissed with faint praise, such as "Mrs. —— wore a string of pearls." And who knew what barb might be intended when Miss Devereux wrote, as she did on several occasions, that a certain woman appeared "in a lovely bead neckless"? Then there were her taunts, which surely had to be tongue in cheek, such as the time a couple of whom she disapproved married rather late in life and departed for a Florida wedding trip, and Miss Devereux wrote that "on their honeymoon [they] will follow the trail of Ponce de Leon in his quest for the Fountain of Youth."

Readers could usually tell when Miss Devereux was out for blood and when she was simply making mischief. She obviously disapproved of a certain woman at a party who "arrived with two or three swains who were constantly in her train. Her frock was white, simply fashioned." And her way of noting that a popular young woman was in a delicate condition was to report her absence at a party, adding, "but of course she is not going out in any large way at present." Her snips and jibes and bitchiness also sold papers, and only when threatened with a libel suit did Miss Devereux turn all dewy-eyed-repentant and apologetic. But there were never any retractions.

Her bailiwick extended far beyond that of any ordinary society editor or, for that matter, any ordinary mortal. Since she controlled absolutely the amount of ink that would be expended on any social event by the city's leading newspaper, it was wise to consult her before planning anything. If it was a wedding, Miss Devereux would not only set the date but would also select the orchestra, the caterer, the florist, and the site of the reception. Any bride who had the temerity to defy her would not have her wedding reported in the *Enquirer*. Marion Devereux also decided who could be a debutante and who could not, and arranged the winter's schedule of coming-out parties. To a hopeful mother Miss Devereux might say, shaking her head sadly, "No, I don't think your daughter is *ready* to come out this year," or "I don't think Doris would be *happy* as a debutante. The crowd this year is so different from hers." One way to court Miss Devereux's favor was with gifts and—some said—money, though whether she ever accepted cash outright is uncertain. From the parade of carriages and limousines that appeared before Miss Devereux's apartment building at Christmastime, bearing brightly wrapped pack-ages, it was clear that she did like presents. But even a gift was no guarantee to someone she had decided was a "social climber."

The Sinton Hotel, which was one of the city's best, hit upon a clever idea. It offered Miss Devereux a suite of rooms, rent-free, and the little gesture paid off handsomely. Thereafter the Sinton was selected for more than its share of wedding receptions and coming-out parties—though it must be said that she did at times pick other places—and the management could be sure that, whenever the Sinton was mentioned in her columns, its décor, appointments, food, and service were elaborately described. "In the long, lofty ballroom of the Hotel Sinton, framed in the replicas of Eighteenth Century panels, gold-bordered, lighted by stately, sparkling chandeliers of faceted crystal placed among the Bourcher [sic] clouds and cupids of the ceiling a la Louis Seize, the second of the Bachelors' Cotil-lions took place with such success as to seem to the guests the ultimate in entertainment. . . ." And on, and on.

Marion Devereux felt, with justification, that Mary Emery belonged to her fiefdom. The Emerys, after all, were very much Old Family. They were very rich, and very civic-minded. The Emerys would even, in time, be elevated to the ranks of European nobility. John J. Emery, the brother of Mary's late husband, had remained unmarried until fairly late in life. Then, in his sixties, realizing that there would be no male Emerys to carry on the family's far-flung enterprises, he married, promptly fathered five children, and died shortly thereafter.* One of his daughters, Audrey, would marry, first, Grand Duke Dmitri Pavlovitch, a cousin of Nicholas II, the last Russian tsar, and, second, the Georgian Prince Dmitri Djor-djadze.

Mary Emery thoroughly disapproved of Marion Devereux, and of the way Cincinnati society bowed and scraped and kissed the hem of Miss Devereux's garments. She found it pitiful that Cincinnati should tolerate

---

* This situation contributed to a certain "coolness of relations" between the John J. Emery children and their Aunt Mary. It was clear that she had her half-share of the original fortune intact; the children's share would have to be split five ways.

Miss Devereux's terrorist tactics, and felt that Miss Devereux, by placing so much emphasis on parties, gowns, and interior décor, was deflecting society's interests from more worthy pursuits. When Mary Emery referred to Miss Devereux at all, it was to "that dangling participle." Miss Devereux, meanwhile, had developed another intimidating technique: the Midnight Tirade. Learning that a party had taken place without her imprimatur, Miss Devereux thought nothing of telephoning the errant hostess in the small hours of the morning and shouting, "How *dare* you give a party without consulting me? Don't you know that *I* am the social arbiter of Cincinnati?" For further punishment, the offender might find herself labeled in print a "climber" or, another Devereux favorite, "a social highway robber." Or she might discover that she had been banished from the society pages forever, along with all her heirs and assigns.

But Mary Emery was one woman in Cincinnati who was immune to Marion Devereux's attacks. She defied the tyrant by refusing to take part in the world Miss Devereux wrote about. Mary Emery could be neither extolled nor damned on the society pages because she stalwartly refused to be social. What, after all, could be said about a sweet-faced little old lady who looked like a grandmother on a chocolate box, who kept to herself and her gardens and art collection, and whose only eccentricity, if it could be called that, was that she daintily ate the plump grapes from her prize vines with a knife and fork? (She carefully sliced each grape in half with a fruit knife, extracted the seed, then placed the halves in her mouth one at a time.)

Mary Emery had made it abundantly clear that she had no use for Miss Devereux, and Miss Devereux was aware of her feelings. But when Mrs. Emery did appear at a public function, Miss Devereux could not even employ the Fashion Attack because Mary Emery, in her plain, long-sleeved black dresses and little bonnets, defied what was fashionable. Thus did she keep Marion Devereux at arm's length throughout her career. At the same time, Marion Devereux could not simply ignore the city's most important patroness—and so, whenever she mentioned her in her column, it was "Mrs. Thomas J. Emery, very Grande Dame." Even that did not please Mrs. Emery. "Listen to that," she would mutter, pointing a small finger at the printed page. "I am *not* a *Grande Dame!*" Upper-class values again. When Mary Emery announced a major project, such as the building of Mariemont, the news made the front pages, not the society columns. Marion Devereux might be the Tsarina, but Mary Emery was a lady.

Mariemont was well under way when Mary Emery died in October

1927, at eighty-three. Because her philanthropies had been, in a real sense, international, newspapers from as far away as San Francisco and Paris noted the passing of the shy, lonely little woman who had spent half her lifetime mourning and memorializing her husband and sons. In her extraordinary twenty-one page will she left a personal bequest of $500,000 to Charles Livingood, along with instructions that he "follow through" with Mariemont. She left gifts of $100,000 to each of her Emery nieces and nephews, who, after all, would never be poor, and her church and favorite charities were also generously remembered. The sum of $2,500,000 was set aside to provide a trust, out of which sixty-nine friends would be paid annuities throughout their lifetimes in amounts ranging from $200 to $5,000 a year (one of these, at $2,000 a year, was the writer Dorothy Canfield Fisher).* At the end of this list she noted, "I desire that the names of the persons mentioned in this Item be not given any publicity." It didn't matter. The newspapers printed them anyway.

To the Cincinnati Art Museum she modestly offered "so many of the oil and other paintings that I may own at the time of my death as the said Museum may care to accept." (The collection, then valued at $3,500,000, now hangs in the Emery Wing of the museum.) The bulk of the estate, some $25,000,000, was then left to create the Thomas J. Emery Memorial, and one of the Memorial's chief tasks would be the completion of "the planned community of Mariemont."

The stock market crash of 1929 and the Depression that followed slowed things down somewhat, but Mr. Livingood carried on. During the Depression, however, Mariemont began to take on a life and character of its own that its founder could never have anticipated. In the 1930s the poor, for whom Mariemont had been intended, had become the penniless, and the middle class, who had been comfortably off a few years earlier, were tightening their belts and looking for smaller homes that were easier and less expensive to maintain. It was these folk who now began snapping up the reasonably priced houses and apartments in Mariemont—albeit Marion Devereux still did not recognize Mariemont as an address.

One day in 1939, Marion Devereux walked out of her office at the *Cincinnati Enquirer* to consult a doctor about a small pimple on her cheek. She never came back. She was discovered, it was said, to be suffering

---

* Chalmers Clifton, her former musical protégé, was also remembered. He and his wife were each given an annuity of $3,000 a year.

from at least three serious ailments, one of which may have been a mental illness. Her convoluted prose style had been becoming harder and harder to follow and her temper tantrums more frequent. Aside from planning parties, attending them, and writing about them, she had seemed to have no life whatsoever, but now the woman who had enjoyed thirty years of glory and unchallenged power retired from the public eye altogether, into a deep and total seclusion. How she passed her time no one knew. She was not heard from again until nine years later when, after her seventy-fifth birthday, the *Enquirer* heralded in banner headlines:

DEATH TAKES "TSARINA" MARION DEVEREUX,
LONG ARBITER OF CINCINNATI'S SOCIAL LIFE

Of her, Cincinnati chronicler Alvin Harlow commented, "There has never been anyone else quite like her in America, and Cincinnati for one fervently hopes there never will be again."

The construction of Mariemont was halted by the Second World War, and it was not until 1965 that the model town was finally "finished," the last tree planted, the last floral border in place. A few things had not worked out. The central steam-heating system, for one, had failed. For its day it had been quite a daring idea. Central steam heating for downtown business districts had been installed successfully in the past, but such a system, involving live steam piped underground for considerable distances, had never been tried before in a residential development. The steam-generating plant had been built on the banks of the Little Miami River, and had worked well for a number of years. It had even survived the Great Flood of January 1937, when the waters of the Ohio and the Little Miami reached record heights, knocking out at least one of the plant's transformers and rising dangerously close to the boilers. Still, while the rest of Cincinnati shivered, Mariemont had heat. In the end, it was, of all things, termites that did the system in. The underground steam lines had been insulated in sleeves of wooden logs lashed together, and the termites had attacked the logs. To replace the logs with vitrified tile insulation was considered prohibitively expensive, and so Mariemont converted to city gas. As it did in any emergency, the Emery Memorial stepped in to help Mariemont residents with the costs.

But otherwise the little town was exactly as it had been in the plans John Nolan had brought to Mary Emery for her approval.

Except, of course, the plan itself had not really worked—for the simple reason that it had worked too well. The slums of the city were still where they were, and Mariemont had become a garden suburb of such quality that it had developed into one of Cincinnati's choicest residential enclaves. The Tudor central square, the landscaped mall, the intimate little tree-lined drives and lanes, the arch-covered cul de sacs, the pretty street lamps and wrought-iron street signs, the distinctive bell tower, the lovely English-style church (Episcopal), the excellent schools and hospital, the well-built houses and apartments, and above all the continued benevolence of the Emery Memorial in maintaining the public areas, had proved a powerful magnet not to the poor, but to the successful and upwardly mobile—young executives moving up the corporate ladder at Procter & Gamble, doctors, lawyers, engineers, educators, entrepreneurs . . . and all white.

Today Mariemont bustles with civic pride. Woe betide the Mariemont resident who fails to keep his lawn manicured, his hedges clipped, who leaves his garage door yawning or who fails to set out fresh spring bulbs each fall. The little shops, intended to provide the necessities, now sell Vitabath and L'Air du Temps. The theatre, designed for uplifting concerts and plays, offers Walt Disney movies. The Community Center, where Mariemontonians were to have aired their grievances, is now the scene of self-congratulatory town meetings. Mariemont matrons toil for the Art Museum, the Symphony, the Opera, and the Junior League . . . and for the betterment of Mariemont. Mariemont fathers canvass for the United Appeal, work for the Boy Scouts and the Little League.

Mariemont's rival suburb is Glendale, and in 1976 Glendale, another attractive community, was placed on the National Register of Historic Places, and was later named a National Landmark. Mariemont would like the cachet of this honor, too, and feels it deserves it. In the summer of 1981 architects and historians of the U.S. Department of the Interior were reviewing Mariemont's application. If granted, Mariemont would become the second community in Hamilton County to receive this designation.

Life teems with ironies, of course, but it is particularly ironic that Mariemont, Ohio, pop. 4,500, the dream of a little lady who shunned society—who never had her portrait painted, who turned her back whenever a camera was pointed at her—should have become an address for those whose names and faces regularly appear on the Cincinnati society pages.

PART SIX

A Woman of Mystery

18

SECRETS AND SCANDALS

THERE WAS NO DOUBT that the dominant partner in California's Big Four, the legendary quadrumvirate who built the Central Pacific and Southern Pacific railroads, was Collis Potter Huntington. It was a partnership which worked well because each of the four had a specialty that, when joined with the others', resulted in an unbeatable combination. Leland Stanford was a politician—he would become governor of California—and, because he also appeared to be very dull-witted, he created an impression of the utmost honesty. Surely such a stupid man was incapable of craftiness or guile. Stanford, with his connections in the United States Congress and along the political hustings of the raw new state of California, was thus put in charge of bribing state and federal officials into granting rights-of-way as well as government funds to finance the foursome's great railroad adventure. Charles Crocker was the workmaster. It was he who rode horseback along the miles where crossties and track were being laid, exhorting the Chinese coolie laborers to work harder and faster, and paying them in cash so that there would never really be any record of how much the railroad had cost. Mark Hopkins was the office manager, the detail man, the string saver, whose duty it was to see that the cost of operations was as low as possible. He kept such books as were kept at all.

But Collis P. Huntington was the mastermind. When Stanford came home from Washington in 1862 with a pledge from Congress to underwrite the building of the railroad to the tune of $16,000 per mile for track laid over flat land, and $32,000 a mile for track laid over mountains, it was Huntington who had the ingenious idea of redrawing the map of California to show that it had many more miles of mountains than it actually had. Naturally, nobody in Washington knew the difference, and the boys were on their way.

Huntington liked to boast that he had started out with all the advantages—no education and no money. He had been born October 22, 1821, in the village of Harwinton Township, Connecticut, either the fifth or the sixth—accounts vary—of nine children of a local tinker whose house perched at the edge of a swamp known as Poverty Hollow. At fourteen he was apprenticed out to a local farmer, for whom he worked for a year at seven dollars a month. At fifteen, his formal education over, he struck out for New York. There, for a while, he peddled watches. For the next few years there is no clear record of his wanderings, though he apparently spent some time in the Deep South, where, he later said, he was appalled by slavery. By the time he was in his early twenties he had made his way northward to the upstate New York town of Oneonta, where he joined an older brother, Solon Huntington, who operated a moderately successful dry-goods store. Now, established in a solid trade, he returned to Connecticut to marry a Litchfield girl named Elizabeth T. Stoddard, who may have been a childhood sweetheart. Litchfield is just a few miles down the road from Harwinton. Huntington was twenty-three.

He was a big man—as, indeed, were all the Big Four except the wizened Mark Hopkins. Huntington who weighed well over two hundred pounds, bragged that he had never been bested in a fight or been sick a day in his life. In 1849, lured by tales of new-found gold in California, Collis did what so many young men were doing and joined the Gold Rush, heading by steamship to Sacramento. In Panama, to pick up needed cash for the rest of the trip, Huntington did a little trading—in what commodities it isn't clear, but it may have been gunrunning—which involved several trips back and forth across the jungle of the Isthmus. "I was too poor to hire a mule," he would enjoy saying later, "and it was only twenty-four miles, so I walked it."

Once in Sacramento, he worked as a miner for exactly one day before deciding he didn't like it. The real money, he noted, was being made by men who were selling hardware and mining equipment. Taking in another transplanted easterner, Mark Hopkins, as his partner, he opened a store in Sacramento, and presently the two were joined by Charles Crocker, also a hardware and dry-goods merchant, and Leland Stanford, who had studied law and thought he knew a few things about getting around it. The Big Four were born.

The progress of the Big Four, much of it skulduggerous and all of it unscrupulous, has been well chronicled elsewhere. Suffice it to say that, by 1870, as controllers of one of the largest railroad systems in the world, all four were very rich men. But Huntington was still the dominant one. "Huntington," Camille Weidenfeld, a Wall Street broker, once said, "was the cart horse . . . [He] carried all his associates on his shoulders." This is not to imply that Huntington, or any other of the Four, made himself exactly popular along his ruthless road to riches. He had, said one associate, "no more soul than a shark," and the *San Francisco Examiner*, Huntington's lifelong enemy, was also reminded of slithery underwater things, calling him "ruthless as a crocodile." Well, Huntington might have replied, one didn't get rich by being a pussycat.

Elizabeth Stoddard Huntington, meanwhile, was a modest, self-effacing lady, plump and plain as a New England apple pie. And while her flamboyant husband was cutting such a swath across California and elsewhere in the country, Betty Huntington kept so firmly in the background that most people who dealt with Huntington were unaware that he was even married. To those who knew, Huntington explained that his wife didn't care for California. That was why he had comfortably established her in a house on Park Avenue in New York. He visited her there from time to time, when he crossed the country to deal with his bankers. He may have been embarrassed by his mousy spouse and her country New England accent full of a'n'ts and cahn'ts. The Huntingtons had no children, but when Elizabeth Huntington's sister Clarissa—who had married a man named Edwin Prentice—became widowed and was left with four small children, the Huntingtons offered to take the youngest, one-year-old Clara Prentice. Though little Clara was never formally adopted, Clara Prentice became Clara Huntington.

It was not more than a dozen years after a Huntington niece became a Huntington daughter that another Huntington "relative" appeared as though out of nowhere. She was a beautiful young widow who looked to be between twenty-five and thirty, dramatically tall, slender, full-bosomed, with dark hair, enormous and luminous dark eyes and a beautifully formed, if somewhat determined-looking, mouth and chin. She appeared in Austin, Texas, where she was said to be visiting some vaguely defined members of her family, and in December 1877, this beautiful creature broke into print with a small item in the *Austin Statesman* which reported, "Mrs. B. D. Worsham, mother, and son . . . are in the city, stopping at the Raymond House . . . Mrs. Worsham is a niece of Collis P. Huntington, the railroad man."

Ah, Austin thought, that would explain the beautiful clothes, the jewels, the poised, gracious, but slightly condescending carriage as Mrs.

Worsham strolled elegantly through Austin hand in hand with her well-dressed, well-mannered little boy. She was obviously a woman of wealth and breeding.

Obviously, yes. But she was no relation to Collis P. Huntington.

Who, then, was this Mrs. B. D. Worsham, who sometimes called herself Mrs. Arabella Duval Worsham, who was at other times Mrs. Belle D. Worsham, and who, capriciously, occasionally spelled her first name Bell? It would be a hundred years before anyone would come close to being sure, and even then there would remain teasing questions, inconsistencies, ambiguities, uncertainties as to what was fact and what was fiction, what was mere speculation, guesswork, putting two and two together and coming out with—a conundrum. For few women in American history have so efficiently managed to conceal their pasts, and to confound biographers. Mrs. B. D. Worsham, it seemed, had no past.

It has been said that a successful liar must have a good memory, but Arabella—as we shall call her, since that was the name she eventually preferred—defied that rule. Her memories changed and revised themselves, and the resulting web of confusion only served to create a smokescreen around her through which it was impossible to differentiate truth from falsehood—and that, it seems, was exactly what Arabella wished.

There is, first of all, the question of her date of birth. When she became a woman of sufficient prominence to be of interest to researchers, she gave various years. To some she said that she was born June 1, 1852. While it might be logical for a woman to lie about her age to make herself younger, Arabella defied this logic by telling others that she was born in 1847, thereby adding five years to her age. The inscription on her mausoleum strikes a compromise, giving the year as 1850 and her place of birth as Union Springs, Alabama, but no city, county, state, or church record of Alabama reveals any record to indicate that anyone remotely like Arabella was born there that year, or in any of the years before or after. Nor do any records indicate that she or her family ever lived there. Arabella also told researchers that she had been born in Virginia.

To her two-volume biography of Collis P. Huntington, Cerinda W. Evans certainly brought scholarly credentials. She was Librarian Emeritus of the Mariner's Museum in Newport News, Virginia, and in her necessarily sketchy—there was little hard evidence—section on Arabella, gathered from "relatives and associates," Miss Evans wrote, "Arabella Duval Yarrington was the daughter of Richard Milton and Catherine J. Yarrington . . . The Yarringtons were natives of Alabama and Texas, but members of the family had resided in Virginia since 1850. There was an R. M. Yarrington—presumably her father—listed in the *Richmond Directory* from 1850 to 1856."

But right away the researchers began to quarrel. In *The Twilight of Splendor*, James T. Maher, noting the "rather odd reverse migration" of the Yarringtons—since most Americans of the era were moving westward and not eastward—agrees that Richard and Catherine Yarrington were probably Arabella's parents. But Maher notes that Richard Yarrington, a sometime machinist and sometime carpenter, had presumably been living in Richmond at least since 1839, since in April of that year his marriage to Catherine, a childless sixteen-year-old widow, was recorded there.

Miss Evans was forced to be a little vague on the subject of Arabella's brothers and sisters. Mr. Maher is able to be more precise. Poring through old Richmond city records, he discovered that Richard and Catherine Yarrington had five children, three girls and two boys, and that four years after the last child was born, Richard Yarrington died and was buried in Richmond in 1859. Widowed again, Catherine Yarrington ran a boarding house to support her children.

But having learned this much, Mr. Maher runs up against a baffling stone wall. Referring to the United States Census taken in 1860, the year after Richard Yarrington's death, Maher finds listed in the Yarrington household Catherine Yarrington, the mother, and the proper complement of five children, listed as Eliza Page Yarrington, seventeen; Emma J. Yarrington, fifteen; Carolina B. Yarrington, nine; Richard M. Yarrington, seven; and John D. Yarrington, five. Where, then, was Arabella Duval Yarrington? If, indeed, she was born in 1850, she would have been too young to have left home, and she would also be about the same age as nine-year-old Carolina B. Yarrington. Could Carolina B. have later changed her name to Arabella Duval? Possibly. Or, if Arabella was actually born before 1850, she could also have been the fifteen-year-old Emma J. The answers to these riddles may never be found. All that Maher was able to discover was that no birth, baptismal record, or certificate exists in Richmond or elsewhere in the state to attest that anyone named Arabella Duval Yarrington was ever born there, though Catherine Yarrington told the 1860 census taker that everyone in her household was a native of Virginia.

Next, it is necessary to turn to the equally confusing question of how Arabella Duval Yarrington, whoever she was, became the glamorous "Mrs. B. D. Worsham," widow and mother of a seven-year-old son. Again turning to Miss Evans, who was relying solely on facts as Arabella herself chose to present them, we learn that, "In 1869, at the age of eighteen, Arabella married a Mr. Worsham of New York. He lived only a short time after the wedding, leaving the widow with a son born March 10, 1870." Significantly, Miss Evans omits the date of the wedding, which further beclouds the date of Arabella's birth. If she was born in 1850, she could have been either eighteen or nineteen when she was married, depending on the time of year.

Searching for marriage licenses or church records in both Richmond and New York for that year, Maher found himself in another blind alley: there were none. He did, however, discover a good deal about Mr. Worsham. Johnny Worsham ran a Richmond faro parlor, and since faro is a game in which the house acts as banker for the players' money, Worsham was able to designate his profession as "banker." Richmond, during the early years of the Civil War, was a wide-open, hard-drinking, fast-living town, a far cry from the city of gentility and culture it has since become. Bandits prowled the streets at night, and holdups and murders took place in broad daylight when disgruntled losers at Richmond gambling houses avenged themselves against the winners. Johnny Worsham's brother was himself gunned down in one of these high-noon shootouts. Hard by the gambling palaces, of course, were the bars and bawdy houses, and all of these establishments were popular with the Confederate soldiers stationed there.

From what Maher was able to discover, Johnny Worsham's place was one of the most popular in the city, gaudily fitted out with the customary gilt, red plush, chandeliers, and velvet hangings. Johnny himself was well liked in the "sporting fraternity," and in those happy-go-lucky days he always had money in his pockets. Just how and under what circumstances he and the beautiful Arabella Yarrington met is one of a number of uncertainties about her early life, but meeting him would not have been hard. The Yarringtons' little house was only six blocks away from Worsham's lively faro parlor.

As the war drew toward its unhappy close, however, things changed dramatically in Richmond. In April 1865, as Union troops advanced on the city, the Confederate soldiers fled. Entering Richmond, the Union soldiers put much of the town to the torch, and less than a week later Lee surrendered to Grant at Appomattox. In the next few years, Richmond's sporting fraternity dispersed, many of them, including Johnny Worsham, heading northward to New York. Arabella followed him. She was, perhaps, nineteen, or even younger.

Not long afterward, Catherine Yarrington and her other children followed Arabella—once again it is not clear why, unless Mother Yarrington felt that Arabella stood to become the family's chief breadwinner, which was not, as things turned out, a bad hunch. It was in New York that Arabella would marry Johnny Worsham, and become pregnant by him. Or at least this was how she would tell the tale.

At first Mrs. Yarrington and her children lived in a rented house on Bleecker Street, and to help make ends meet she may have taken in boarders there, though there is no actual record of this. Then, before the end of 1869, the Yarringtons moved a few blocks east to 5 Bond Street. It was still a poor neighborhood, and it was here that the census of 1870 found them all. Arabella and Johnny Worsham, now established as husband and wife, shared the house with Mrs. Yarrington and the other children, and by now Johnny and Arabella had a child of their own, whom they had named Archer (which was Johnny's middle name) Milton (her father's middle name) Worsham.

The census taker's report, however, on what must have been a thoroughly confusing household, was itself a muddle of confusion. Catherine Yarrington is listed correctly as head of the household, but John A. Worsham is identified as "John De Worsion," and Arabella is listed "Bell De Wersion." Their three-month-old baby, Archer Milton Worsham, appears as "John De Wersion." Maher concedes that sloppy census methods might be blamed for these errors and spelling inconsistencies. But he also points out that a census is an official record, and both John Worsham and Arabella may have had good reason to want to cloud that record.

In any case, Johnny Worsham's lucky streak had deserted him when he got to New York City. As a faro banker, he simply did not have the wherewithal to take on the established competition. In 1870, not long after the census taker's visit, he disappeared. This was the year, Arabella explained, of her husband's death. But the thorough Mr. Maher was able to find no record of Johnny Worsham's death. Nor, for that matter, was he able to turn up any record of the marriage to Arabella Yarrington. The reasons for this, as it turned out, were quite simple. Johnny Worsham had not died, but had simply given up and gone home to Richmond. To say that he had died, it seemed, was simply Arabella's convenient way of explaining the termination of their relationship, just as saying that they were married was a convenient way to legitimatize it. Because, back in Richmond, Johnny rejoined Mrs. Annette Worsham, the wife to whom he had been legally married all along.

Maher speculates that Johnny, down on his luck and saddled not only with a mistress but also with an infant son, simply abandoned Arabella. But it is also possible that Arabella threw Johnny Worsham out, sent him packing and told him never to darken her door again. Because by 1870 it begins to seem as though Arabella had other, more interesting, irons in the fire.

She seems to have attained a sudden new affluence. Presently she was moving to a comfortable town house at 109 Lexington Avenue, on the slope of fashionable Murray Hill, just a few blocks north of elegant Gramercy Park. Morgans and Vanderbilts and Astors were now Arabella's close neighbors. With her had moved her mother and young son, and presently, too, Mrs. Yarrington was purchasing parcels of choice Manhattan real estate, around and just off Fifth Avenue, the city's ultimate address. Mrs. Yarrington seemed to have no difficulty obtaining generous mortgages from New York banks, and she also seemed to have at her command considerable amounts of cash. It was her habit, too, once she had acquired these properties, to immediately convey them to her daughter, "for and in consideration of natural love and affection and the sum of One Dollar lawful money." No one questioned these transactions at the time, since both Mrs. Yarrington and her daughter now comported themselves as southern ladies of immense breeding and wealth. Having arrived in a city where they had no history, the ladies found it easy to invent whatever history they saw fit. But it did seem possible that Mrs. Yarrington was being used as a go-between for her daughter and some very rich person who wanted to establish Arabella as a woman of means and, at the same time, wished his identity to be unknown. At 109 Lexington Avenue, for example, it was not known that Arabella had a very rich landlord. Collis and Elizabeth Stoddard Huntington already owned a good deal of New York real estate, which they had purchased jointly. The town house at 109 Lexington, however, had been bought by Mr. Huntington alone.

Again, the time and circumstances of Arabella's meeting with her new benefactor will probably never be known. Her veil of deceptions has successfully buried them. But by 1869 Collis Huntington had acquired control of another important line in the East, the Chesapeake & Ohio. He made frequent trips on C&O business to Virginia and Maryland, and in early July of that year he was in White Sulphur Springs. This was about the time Johnny Worsham was winding up his affairs in Richmond to head for New York, his "wife"-to-be to follow him. Huntington liked to gamble, and it is certainly possible that in the course of his Virginia sojourn he visited what was left of Johnny Worsham's faro establishment. Though Maher does not draw the connection, it is interesting to note that between early July 1869 and early March 1870, when Arabella's baby was born, there is an interval of nine months. Was Huntington the father?

Who can tell? True, Arabella gave little Archer Johnny Worsham's middle name. This may have been for appearance' sake, and, of course, if she was sleeping with two men at once, she would have had no way of knowing who her child's father was.

In any case, these were the circumstances in 1877 when the lovely "Mrs. Worsham," "widow," and son arrived in Austin, Texas, as Collis P. Huntington's "niece." And these secrets and scandals, with their half-answers, half-guesses, and half-explanations would have remained interred with Arabella in her mausoleum had it not been for James Maher's enterprising diggings, which he published in 1975.

Ah, the successful courtesan. With what a rich broth of feelings do we watch the career of an Arabella—skipping, like an aerialist, along a tightrope strung across the chasm of discovery and disaster. We watch her with a mixture of disapproval and envy, scorn and grudging admiration. There, we think, but for the grace of God go we, and yet, given the opportunity, wouldn't we do the same? The failed courtesan is merely pitiful, but the successful kept woman brings a special intelligence, even class, to her craft. We may, in the 1980s, applaud the gains and goals of the Woman's Movement, but a visceral feeling tells us that to be a rich man's moll offers a luckier life than scrubbing floors.

Arabella was exceptionally successful. Hardly anyone guessed any of the details of her secret life. Did Elizabeth Huntington suspect? Perhaps. Early in the affair Huntington had his wife sign away her dower rights to 109 Lexington, and she must have known that Arabella lived there. But she said nothing. One of the few people who grasped the situation was James Henry Duveen, the cousin of Joseph Duveen, with whom Arabella would presently be doing business. James Duveen disliked her, but in *The Secrets of an Art Dealer* he wrote, "One of the most extraordinary women I have ever known was Arabella . . . extraordinary because of her indomitable mind and an outrageous spirit which compelled her to outvie all competitors. Long before I met her, Arabella was the unofficial wife of Collis P. Huntington."

It was a position she would fill for nearly fifteen years.

19

MRS. HUNTINGTON

COLLIS P. HUNTINGTON HAD ONCE BOASTED that he never spent more than $200 a year on "personal adornment." But now that Arabella had become a permanent fixture in his life he could no longer make that claim. By 1874 the house at 109 Lexington Avenue had begun to seem a bit cramped, and New York society was abandoning Murray Hill and Gramercy Park and moving relentlessly uptown, on and just off Fifth Avenue north of Fiftieth Street. The attraction was Central Park, the magnificent rectangle of green that Frederick Law Olmsted had laid out in the heart of Manhattan and through which the fashionable regularly paraded in their carriages. That year, Catherine Yarrington paid $43,000, most of it in cash, for a residence at 68 East Fifty-fourth Street and, as was her custom, immediately turned over title to the property to her daughter.*

Three years later, Arabella sold 68 East Fifty-fourth Street to one Isaac Henderson and, in the same transaction, bought 4 West Fifty-fourth Street from him. Now she was only two doors away from Fifth Avenue, and the new William H. Vanderbilt mansion—the talk of New York— was right around the corner. The price for the Henderson house was $250,000—again most of it in cash—and within a few months Arabella also bought the two vacant properties on either side, to give her new house some elbow room.

Four West Fifty-fourth Street was Arabella's first "important" house —not for its architecture, which was undistinguished, but for what she

---

* One way to translate 1870s dollars into their 1980s equivalent is to multiply by ten; it was close to half a million dollars that Mrs. Yarrington pulled out of her purse.

herself did to its interior. Her renovation was total. She gutted the house to its brick and brownstone skin, knocked out a wall, and built a new wing. Partitions were moved, rooms rearranged, and then the entire four-story structure was fitted out with rosewood paneling, brocade-covered walls, a great curving staircase at the center lit by a rooftop skylight of stained glass. An Otis passenger elevator was also installed, one of the first in New York in a private residence. On the main floor was a long *grand salon*, which opened into a smaller Moorish salon. Above was the formal dining room, serviced by a dumbwaiter from the basement kitchens. On an upper floor Arabella installed a complete Turkish bath. Indications of the success of her renovation and redecoration are the fact that 4 West Fifty-fourth Street later became the New York home of John D. Rockefeller, and the Rockefellers were so pleased with what Arabella had done that they hardly changed a detail; and that several of Arabella's rooms, through a gift from John D. Rockefeller, Jr., are now on display at the Museum of the City of New York and the Brooklyn Museum. (The site of the house is now the sculpture garden of the Museum of Modern Art.)

The renovation cost her about $1,000,000.

Where did Arabella's taste come from? She had had, as far as is known, no more than a rudimentary education. Certainly, she had the advice of a number of expert craftsmen, cabinetmakers and decorators, but the overall scheme for the house was her own. Her taste for splendor may, of course, have been inspired by the rococo opulence of Johnny Worsham's faro parlor, but even that does not entirely explain it. The fact was that Arabella read, and studied, architectural and decorating guides, and learned from these sources what she wanted. The Moorish salon, for example, would be considered a fanciful folly today, but Washington Irving had come back from southern Spain with his tales of the Alhambra, and society folk all over the country were building Moorish salons. They were very much the fashion, and Arabella knew it.

Arabella liked to keep up with things. The newspapers and magazines of the day were filled with illustrations and descriptions of the castles of the rich. Even Marion Devereux, a generation later, filled her yards of print with word pictures of what people wore and how their homes were fitted out, with hardly a mention of what any of them had to say. In post–Civil War America, décor and appearance were all; form took precedence over substance. Arabella Yarrington Worsham, though she might, *au fond*, be only a rich man's mistress, wanted to do things right.

Collis Huntington, meanwhile, cared little for art and culture. Visiting the Paris Exposition, and asked what he thought of the Eiffel Tower, which was then the pride of Europe, he replied, "American engineers could build one a mile high if they wanted to. Besides, what's the use of it?" In time, Arabella would redo Mr. Huntington's tastes as well.

Arabella's house had only one drawback. She could not open it up for grand entertainments. She was still a back-street wife. In those days, to be a hostess one had to have a host. But that would also change, in time.

Ensconced in the renovated splendor of her new house, Mrs. Arabella Worsham appeared to live a very quiet life. If anything immoral was going on at 4 West Fifty-fourth Street, her immediate neighbors had no inkling, and if Mr. Huntington came and went he managed his visits so discreetly that there appears never to have been a breath of gossip, or scandal, about either of the lovers during the years of Arabella's residence there. "No man, for any considerable period," wrote Hawthorne in *The Scarlet Letter*, "can wear one face to himself, and another to the multitude, without finally getting bewildered as to which may be the true." But Arabella managed it. New Yorkers have always treasured privacy, and her neighbors awarded Arabella hers. They accepted her as what she seemed to be: a beautiful, and respectable, young widow in her mid-twenties with a well-dressed, well-behaved little boy. Whenever she went out, she was properly escorted and chaperoned by her mother.

Arabella had always made the most of her looks. Her unusual height, for example, demanded an erect and careful carriage that was almost regal, almost imperious. (Later, a disgruntled art dealer would say of her that she "allows herself manners which even the Empress of Germany cannot afford.") To this add her distinctive speaking voice, which was soft, low-pitched, and musical, with pleasant traces of her native Virginia. She dressed quietly, with taste and care, always mindful that she was officially a "widow." She presented herself as a cultivated mixture of southern belle and New York great lady. No actress could have performed the part more convincingly, and, all the while, Arabella was grooming herself for a much larger role.

This was finally offered to her when Elizabeth Stoddard Huntington died of cancer in October 1883. It had been a long and painful illness and, though both Huntington and Arabella were no doubt impatient for the end to come, the last months of Mrs. Huntington's life must have been difficult for them both. Naturally, now, a "decent interval" had to be observed, and some nine months later, on July 12, 1884, Mrs. Arabella Duvall Yarrington Worsham became the second Mrs. Collis Potter Huntington. His sixty-third birthday was a few months off. She was, more or

less, thirty-four. As befitted the circumstances, it was a smallish ceremony, with just Arabella's mother, her son, and a few close friends in
attendance, and the next morning the newspapers put their formal imprimatur on her utter respectability. The *New York Tribune* reported that
Arabella's "family and that of Mr. Huntington [are] on terms of the closest
intimacy. She is wealthy in her own right. Her husband died several
years ago." (This last sentence was, by now, correct; Johnny Worsham
had died in Richmond six years earlier.)

The months between Elizabeth Huntington's death and the wedding
had been busy ones for both bride- and groom-to-be, involved as they
were with complicated real-estate transactions, at which Arabella was
becoming quite skillful. First, she arranged to sell the lot just east of her
Fifty-fourth Street house to William H. Vanderbilt, and negotiations to
sell the house itself to John D. Rockefeller had already begun. Next,
Arabella bought a 113-acre estate at Throgs Neck in Westchester County,
overlooking Long Island Sound. Called The Homestead, it had been built
by Frederick C. Havemeyer. Huntington, meanwhile, had deeded his
late wife's Park Avenue house to Arabella, and she immediately began
tearing apart and refurbishing both places. The idea was that Throgs
Neck would be the newlyweds' summer place in the country, and 65 Park
Avenue would be their winter address in town.

But it was becoming clear that what Arabella really wanted was a
mansion on Fifth Avenue. In a trade-off deal with the Rockefellers, Arabella accepted nine lots on the corner of Fifth Avenue and Seventy-second
Street in return for 4 West Fifty-fourth. She also bought eight more lots
at the corner of Fifth Avenue and Eighty-first Street. Finally, perhaps
because both Eighty-first and Seventy-second streets were still considered
too far uptown to be really fashionable, and because—led by the Vanderbilts—the great Fifth Avenue palaces of the era were being built in the
Fifties, Arabella settled for a six-lot parcel on Fifth and Fifty-seventh,
right in the heart of things. This was the property William H. Vanderbilt
had originally wanted for his mansion but had been unable to obtain.
Now it was Arabella's. It would be the first house she would build from
scratch.

The kindest thing that could be said of the Huntingtons' new Fifth
Avenue mansion was that it was very large. When it was finally com-
pleted in 1893, it was also very ugly. To be fair, Arabella had not been
able to get the architect she wanted. She had wanted the great Richard
Morris Hunt, who, among other notable residences, had designed the
Vanderbilt mansion. But Hunt was not immediately available, and Ara-

bella was impatient, and so she settled for an inferior talent, George Browne Post. Post spent months submitting sketches and schematics trying to satisfy her. First she wanted the house bigger, then she wanted it smaller. Rooms were added, then removed, then replaced in different positions. Again to be fair, Arabella had never built an entire house before and probably didn't know what she wanted—and wouldn't know until she saw it. At one point she tried to call in Richard Morris Hunt, who reluctantly decided that she was too far committed to Mr. Post's basic scheme for him to successfully, and ethically, take it over.

The result was a huge, three-story (plus basement and attics) pile of rough-cut Indiana limestone that was a strange cross between Romanesque, French Château, and German Renaissance. In fact, the house was of no particular style or period. Great mansard roofs were dotted with dormers, cupolas, and finials. There was a squat square tower perched at one corner, and there were a great many massive chimneys. Some windows were arched, and some were rectangular. Balustrades, pediments and crenels abounded. The building was wrapped round with a threatening-looking fence of wrought-iron spears. At one end of the house a protuberance that looked rather like a view of Chartres Cathedral extended from the rear. Everything about the house was ponderous, heavy, and it seemed to possess enough weight to send it plunging through the sidewalks.

Oddest of all, the house seemed to have an *expression*. The huge central entrance archway looked like a gaping mouth ringed with jagged, fanglike teeth. Two arched windows just above looked like flared nostrils, and the big paired windows above and to either side of the nostrils looked like enormous, baleful eyes. Viewed from the street, the house seemed literally to be snarling at the spectator. Its whole appearance was dark, grim, and forbidding. Worst, perhaps, it didn't look like a house at all. It looked like a public building. One might have entered it expecting to find a post office or a library or a police station, a strictly run girls' school or a correctional institution. How much Arabella had to do with the final design, and how much of it was Post's doing, is no longer known, since the house underwent so many revisions right up to, during, and after the groundbreaking. Nor is it clear how much Collis Huntington may have had to say about his Fifth Avenue monstrosity. But in *The Big Four*, the anthropologist Oscar Lewis pointed out that in his railroading days Huntington was responsible for putting up railroad stations in "hundreds of towns and cities in the West," and that these were "notable examples of unmitigated ugliness." In New York, wags could not resist pointing out that Mr. Huntington's new house looked like a railroad station run amok.

Rumors have long circulated that Collis Huntington refused to spend a night in his new house, that he was superstitious about it and believed that men only built new houses to die in them. Probably, however, he stayed in the Fifth Avenue house when he was in New York, but it was true that, while the house was being built, he had acquired two other residences which he preferred. He had bought the "Italian palace" Colton mansion on Nob Hill in San Francisco for Arabella—which, with her customary thoroughness, she began completely remodeling and redecorating—and he had also bought a mountain retreat called Pine Knot Lodge on Raquette Lake in the Adirondacks. But the Fifth Avenue house seems to have perfectly satisfied Arabella at the time, and she immediately began filling its rooms with furniture and art. Four top-flight muralists of the day—Elihu Vedder, Edwin H. Blashfield, H. Siddons Mowbray, and Francis M. Lathrop—were commissioned to decorate her walls (Arabella's murals are now at Yale), and by 1884 she had even succeeded in interesting her rough-hewn husband in art.

Whether she actually educated her husband's artistic tastes is unclear, but he certainly became infected with the excitement of the art marketplace. Auction fever, that emotional rush that speeds the pulse beat of the heavy bidder, consumed him, and the cloak-and-dagger aspects of the world of big-time auctions—the undercover scouts and agents, the secret bids, the use of private signals and code names—appealed to his gambler's instinct almost as much as adding imaginary mountains to California's map had done. Soon he and Arabella had an important collection of eighteenth- and nineteenth-century paintings. At the then-record $1,250,000 art sale of the Mary Jane Morgan collection in 1886, there were gasps when Jean Georges Vibert's *The Missionary's Story* went under the hammer for the then-heart-stopping price of $25,500. The buyer, it later turned out, was Collis P. Huntington. The Vibert, though not regarded as a masterpiece today, became Mr. Huntington's personal favorite—probably not for its merit, but for the fact that he had paid the biggest price at what had been the country's biggest sale.

Arabella also got her husband to attend the opera. At the opera, he confessed, he didn't always understand the "stories," but he soon learned to enjoy the music.

Arabella had also come under the familiar influence, if not spell, of that wiliest of art dealers, Joseph Duveen. Rich women did not have to work hard to meet Mr. Duveen. He sniffed them out like a bear in search of a honey tree. He magically appeared in their grand salons, witty and urbane and charming in his beautifully English-tailored suits, with his cultivated Continental accent and his carefully self-advertised taste and expertise, and showered them with blandishments, cajolery, and flattery. Arabella Huntington, he would point out, was unquestionably one of the most beautiful women in the world, a woman of undoubted culture and elegance and exquisite refinement. Surely she deserved to live surrounded by equally beautiful and important things, such as paintings by Hals, Rembrandt, Velásquez, Vermeer, Reynolds, Lawrence, Romney, and Corot, all of which Duveen could supply. But she must be quick, because Mrs. Vanderbilt, or Mrs. Belmont, or Mrs. Astor had her eye on them as well. The technique worked with Arabella as it had worked with most of the others. It worked even better, because Arabella had more to spend than most of the others and an adoring husband who supported her every whim.

In the summer of 1900, vacationing at his Pine Knot Lodge in the Adirondacks, Collis P. Huntington died, two months shy of his seventy-ninth birthday. If Arabella was in fact born in 1850, she was then fifty; whatever her age, she was, according to the hyperbole of the press, "the richest woman in the world." It may even have been true, because Arabella's share of her husband's fortune was $150,000,000. But there was more. A third of Huntington's estate was left to his favorite nephew, Henry Edwards Huntington, son of the brother with whom Collis got his start in an upstate dry-goods store. Henry E. Huntington had become the closest thing to a real son Collis Huntington ever had, and for years he had managed his uncle's railroad interests in California. (Collis's "stepson" Archer Worsham seems never to have filled the bill, since he was mainly interested in poetry and Hispanic studies, and Collis left him out of his will entirely.) Only a million dollars was left to Collis's "daughter," Clara, who was actually his niece. Clara had displeased Huntington in 1889 by marrying Prince François-Edmond-Joseph-Gabriel Vit de und von Hatzfeldt Wildenbourg, son of the German ambassador to Great Britain, and thereby attaining the longest name in the *Social Register*. Arabella had approved of the match. After all, it was nice to have European nobility in the family. But Collis had grumbled because, in return for taking Clara's hand in marriage, the Prince had demanded, and got, $5,000,000.

To complicate the Huntington family tree somewhat further, nephew Henry E. Huntington had married Clara's sister, Mary Alice Prentice.

Though the two were technically first cousins, it was pointed out at the time that it was all perfectly legal because they were not "blood cousins," both Clara and Mary Alice being the daughters of Collis Huntington's first wife's sister. In the meantime, Arabella's son, Archer Worsham, had become transmogrified into Archer Huntington in the same informal way that Clara Prentice had become Clara Huntington.

When the details of Collis Huntington's will were read, Mary Alice Prentice Huntington was unhappy—not about her husband's generous share of the estate, but about her sister's relatively tiny one. This issue would soon create unpleasantness in the Henry Huntington household.

Now, with a vast fortune at her command, Arabella embarked on an enormous art-buying spree. With Duveen solicitously at her elbow, she toured the *salons, ateliers*, galleries, castles, and auctions of Europe, purchasing every Old Master in sight. Her buying reached a frenzied zenith one afternoon in Paris in 1907 when she and Duveen snapped up, for who knew how many millions, most of the Rudolph Kann Collection, one of the greatest in Europe. A year later she bought her own palace in Paris —the fabled Hôtel de Hirsch at 2 rue de l'Elysée, the most splendid *hôtel particulier* in the city and the former residence of Baron Maurice de Hirsch de Gereuth, the famous Jewish financier and philanthropist who established the Baron de Hirsch Fund. Again, because the French press was not meticulous about reporting prices, who knew how many millions of francs this mansion cost her? As was her wont, she immediately gutted the place, renovated it, redecorated it, and filled it with paintings, furniture, and Beauvais tapestried walls, all furnished by the helpful Mr. Duveen. This acquisition gave Arabella five houses: Paris, Fifth Avenue, Throgs Neck, the Adirondacks, and San Francisco.

While all this was going on, the American press seemed at a loss to comprehend Arabella's activities. The *New York World* reported that "her tastes are quiet and her mode of living has been rather reserved." But the *American Register* noted that, while waiting for the work on the Hôtel de Hirsch to be completed, Arabella was staying at the Hotel Bristol, "where she always occupies the royal suite," and that, to the many amenities of her Paris house, she was adding fourteen additional bathrooms. Quiet and reserved indeed!

In the meantime there were numerous trips back and forth to the United States, and, in 1905, there were disturbing hints that someone, somehow, had uncovered part of the riddle of Arabella's ambiguous, secret past. The sensational libel trial of Colonel William D'Alton Mann had just got under way in New York, and Arabella's name was about to get dragged into it. Colonel Mann published the widely read weekly *Town Topics*, which was the *National Enquirer* of its day, but with a difference. If one of Colonel Mann's staff of scouts got whiff of a wind of scandal involving some prominent man or woman, he would go to the individual, tell him what he knew, and suggest that the story need not be printed, provided the individual purchased some advertising space in *Town Topics*. Or, if that person did not happen to own a product which could be advertised, a little "loan" would do. Mann's extortion and blackmail racket had been working successfully for years, and Mann had become very rich.

Now he was about to be brought to earth and put out of business, thanks, in part, to the high-mindedness of a quiet New York woman named Mrs. Emily Post, who, not many years later, would spring to prominence as America's arbiter of etiquette. Mrs. Post's husband, it seemed, had committed a "dalliance," Colonel Mann's reporters had learned of it, and Mr. Post had been invited to make the customary contribution. The dollar amount suggested was small. It usually was with the Colonel, at least the first time around. Once Mann had found a willing blackmail subject, he invariably came back for more. Confronted with this situation, Post manfully decided to consult his wife, even though this meant confessing the affair. Emily Post immediately told her husband to go to the police, which he did, and the blackmailer was arrested in a public toilet—the venue chosen for the transaction—as Post handed over the money. Later, the Posts quietly divorced.

Now, as the trial progressed, it turned out that among the people who had "lent" the Colonel money was Mrs. Collis P. Huntington. Her loans amounted to at least $15,000, and she was to be subpoenaed to testify about the matter. Naturally, the last thing Arabella wanted was to give court testimony on how and why she had been blackmailed. Alerted by her lawyer, she escaped from her Throgs Neck house moments ahead of the process server and boarded a ship for Europe.

In 1910, suddenly and without explanation, not even two years after she had finished remodeling it and redecorating, she announced her intention to sell the Hôtel de Hirsch. She no longer wanted to live in Paris, and was returning to the United States. Though she had refused to dignify them with comment, rumors about her had been circulating for some time to the effect that she had a new American romantic interest.

She and her husband's nephew, Henry, had long been quite close. They were the same age, and Henry Huntington of course had known her from the days when she was young and beautiful. In the months following Collis Huntington's death, he had helped her with the details of the enormous estate, and he had smoothly overseen for the widow the lucrative sale of the Huntington railroad interests to E. H. Harriman. In the meantime, the arguments between Henry and Mary Alice Huntington over what she considered the mean treatment of her sister Clara had become bitter and rancorous. By 1902 the couple had become estranged, and in 1906 Henry gave Mary Alice an uncontested divorce.

Rumors circulated that Arabella Duval Yarrington Worsham Huntington was about to become Arabella Duval Yarrington Worsham Huntington Huntington. Collis Huntington had once warned his nephew in a letter: "Belle, as you know, is exceedingly particular." Still, it was obvious to anyone who saw them together that the two were fond of each other. And a union made sense. The two principal parts of Collis's fortune, separated by his death, would join hands again.

20

POMPADOUR AND MEDICI

THE YEAR OF HENRY HUNTINGTON'S DIVORCE, the great San Francisco earthquake and fire destroyed Arabella's Nob Hill palazzo. She never bothered to rebuild it, and, instead, donated the land to the city to be used as a children's playground. Arabella had never cared much for California in general nor for San Francisco in particular. She was much more at home in Paris and New York, and she considered San Francisco parvenu, provincial. Nor was she amused by San Francisco's obvious and abject attempts to imitate the society of older eastern cities—putting on great formal balls and cotillions, presenting as society debutantes the daughters of men and women who had started out as bartenders and chamber maids a generation earlier. When the rumors that she would now marry a Californian first began circulating, she took pains to deny them and, uncharacteristically, since she distrusted the press, went so far as to summon "a correspondent who called on her in her New York home last night," according to an April 1906 report. The reporter wrote that she was dressed in "a magnificent black lace gown," with "a pendant of pearls and small diamonds hanging from a chain about her neck."

Though her husband had been dead for six years, she told the reporter haughtily, "Why, as you can see, I am still in mourning for my husband." Then, as though somehow clarifying the situation, she added, "Henry E. Huntington is my late husband's nephew."

In California, Henry Huntington also issued a denial, calling the rumors "absolutely without foundation."

But the fact was that Henry Huntington was already actively courting Arabella. It was she who was being coy, and holding out.

Henry Huntington had been born February 25, 1850, in the upstate New York town of Oneonta, where the whole Huntington family saga had really begun. For twenty years he had supervised the construction of his uncle's network of railroads until it had become the biggest in the world, and in 1892 he had moved to San Francisco as vice-president and general manager of the Southern Pacific and Central Pacific railroads. He was a tall, dark, handsome man with a finely sculptured moustache and sideburns; he dressed conservatively, usually in black suits. Though he obviously had a sound business head, he was also something of an aesthete and a scholar. For years he had quietly been collecting rare books, with which he spent most of his nonworking hours, and—a far more cultivated man than his aggressively know-nothing uncle—he had also become a connoisseur of painting and sculpture. Personally he was rather shy and retiring, and had few close friends. But he was crazy about Arabella.

Probably he had been for years. Even as she approached sixty, it seemed, she had not lost whatever allure it was that made her so attractive to men. Did Henry know about her long extramarital relationship with his uncle? Did he know about the secret of Johnny Worsham? One can make an educated guess and say: Probably.

Unlike Arabella, Henry Huntington was fascinated with California—though not so much with San Francisco, which was busily trying to make itself seem "cosmopolitan" and "cultured," as with a small, arid, mostly Mexican settlement in the southern part of the state that had been christened Nuestra Señora Reina de Los Angeles, Our Lady Queen of the Angels.

Confronted with America's third-largest city as it is today, it is a little hard to picture Los Angeles as it was in 1892, when Henry Huntington first visited it—a broad, sunny basin set dramatically in a semicircle of soaring mountains which, in spring, were ablaze with thousands of varieties of wild flowers and which, by midsummer, turned a rich ochre color. The air was clean and sparkling, and from the lower hills you could see for miles, out to a wide and brilliantly purple ocean and vast stretches of wide, white, unpopulated beach. The hills were alive with deer, bear, wildcat, and rabbit, and what is now Sunset Boulevard was a trail carved by grazing cattle across the hillsides. For some foresighted reason (the town's meager water supply could support only a tiny population), Henry Huntington decided that the future of California lay in and around Los Angeles.

With his uncle's sudden death in 1900, Henry Huntington found himself suddenly transformed from a high-salaried executive to a man of enormous independent means. He immediately began buying up large tracts of Los Angeles real estate. He purchased, and began expanding, the Los Angeles street railway system, with fast trains that could carry a city population from one part of town to another, and, with others, developed an irrigation system through which water could be supplied to Los Angeles from mountain streams and lakes by way of canals and aqueducts. For his own use, he bought in 1907 a 550-acre ranch, with ranch house and outbuildings. The property sprawled dramatically across the foothills of the San Gabriel mountains east of the city, and was called Rancho San Marino. Here his intent was soon clear. He intended to build a mansion and surrounding estate of such magnificence as Southern California had never seen. After all, if he was ever going to lure Arabella to Los Angeles, and get her to share his enthusiasm for the place, he would have to present her with a residence of such splendor and sumptuousness as would surpass anything she had known before.

Perhaps Arabella had made the construction of San Marino the condition under which she would marry him. Because, from the beginning, her views on the design and construction of the California house were very much taken into consideration. Much of the planning took place at Fifth Avenue and Fifty-seventh Street, in Arabella's drawing room, where she met constantly with Henry and his architect, Myron Hunt. She saw to it that Joseph Duveen was brought into the picture, and needless to say Duveen had ideas of his own—and merchandise of his own—in terms of art, tapestries, furniture, and décor. Meanwhile, the long, low house, theatrically white against the rugged mountainside, grew. Because it was to be very large, and because the terrain was difficult, it grew slowly. Begun in 1908, San Marino was still not entirely finished by 1912, and of course neither Arabella nor Henry was getting any younger. Both were entering their middle sixties, and though it was by then generally assumed that Henry and Arabella would eventually marry, the question had become: When? Someone had the temerity to ask architect Hunt, "Why does Mr. Huntington want to marry Mrs. Huntington?" The answer was simple. "He loves her," said Mr. Hunt.

Still, Arabella would not say yes.

Then, in the spring of 1913, Arabella sailed for Europe. Though she had not set eyes on the house, she had supervised the details of its progress in a series of letters, telegrams, and directives from the East Coast to the West. And now it was nearly finished. Not long after her departure, Henry followed Arabella to Europe. They met in Paris, and on July 16 they were married there at the American Church. The dynastic Hunting-ton-Huntington nuptials, and the reconsolidation of the Huntington for-tune, made headlines everywhere, though the *Los Angeles Times* appeared to have been woolgathering throughout the previous seven years of mar-riage rumors and speculations. "The wedding was entirely unexpected," it wrote.

Apparently the sixtyish newlyweds had not expected to become celeb-rities, but they were certainly that in Southern California. *Sunset* maga-zine, in a rapturous account of the house Henry had built for Arabella, described San Marino as "The most truly magnificent residence in the whole of California," and Los Angeles breathlessly awaited the date when the Huntingtons would move in. They shortly returned from their Eu-ropean wedding trip, but they remained in the East while weeks turned into months. Each new trainload of furniture and art objects which ar-rived in Los Angeles from Joseph Duveen spurred new speculation that the Huntingtons were about to appear, but the couple remained elusive and the house stayed empty except for caretakers. Finally, in January of 1914, when the Huntingtons did arrive, their private car was met with such a raucous crowd of well-wishers and the merely curious that Ara-bella was actually frightened. For this reason, perhaps, they remained only a few weeks. Then they were off again, for somewhere else.

Arabella clearly was not ready to commit herself to living in California. Nor would she ever be. For the rest of their lives she and Henry Hun-tington would limit their stays at San Marino to a month or so each year. Where Arabella led, it seemed, her adoring Henry followed. At the same time San Marino was becoming the main repository of their collective treasures.

As collectors they had become a team which has probably never been surpassed. Henry, working through such celebrated book dealers as Dr. A. S. W. Rosenbach, concentrated on his rare volumes, and presently he was building another magnificent edifice just to house his library. Ara-bella, working largely through Duveen—though she also used other dealers, much to Duveen's annoyance (he could actually turn threatening and abusive on the subject)—concentrated on art. Through Duveen she bought such celebrated works as Reynolds's *Mrs. Siddons as the Tragic Muse* and Gainsborough's *The Blue Boy.* She was assembling one of the most important private art collections in the world, while he, according to Oscar Lewis, was turning San Marino into "one of the world's most important storehouses of the literature and history of the English-speak-ing people." Huntington once told Dr. Rosenbach that "the ownership of.

a fine library is the . . . surest way to immortality." And when he died his library was "the largest ever gathered together by a single man in the United States." It still is.

James Maher describes the joint efforts of the Huntingtons this way: "If Arabella, in her great years as a collector-patron, became the American equivalent of Madame de Pompadour and Isabella d'Este, then Huntington must be accounted a latter-day Medici prince for his achievements in the Florentine humanist tradition."

Though Henry Huntington was totally serious about his collection and his bid for immortality, he also had a sense of humor. Dr. Rosenbach's biographers, Edwin Wolff II and John F. Fleming, tell of a bedside incident when Huntington, in the hospital and about to undergo minor surgery, summoned both Rosenbach and Duveen to his room. Noting that there "was no love lost between these two giants," the authors describe the following scene:

> When the nurse announced that Mr. Huntington was ready to see them, the two men soberly entered the room. Huntington lay on the bed in his hospital shirt, his head only slightly raised and his two arms extended. With a slight motion he pointed to chairs on either side of the bed. . . . The two dealers sat stiff in their chairs, looking at Mr. Huntington and each other and uttering words of encouragement in a manner . . . far from encouraging. Suddenly, Huntington, rather amused . . . turned to Duveen and asked, "Sir Joseph, do I remind you of anyone?" Nonplussed, Duveen answered, "Why, no, Mr. Huntington, I don't believe so." Then he turned his head toward Dr. Rosenbach. "Tell me, Doctor, do I remind you of anyone?" The Doctor, quite as much at a loss as Duveen, muttered that he really did not know. "Well, gentlemen," said Henry Huntington, still lying flat with his arms outstretched, "I remind myself of Jesus Christ on the cross between the two thieves." The Doctor and Sir Joseph smiled weakly.

When Henry and Arabella were not collecting, they found time to prepare their joint wills. San Marino and its contents were to become the Huntington Art Museum. The library was to become the Huntington Library. A trust fund of $8,000,000 was set aside to provide an income to maintain these institutions, which, of course, remain two of the great cultural adornments of Southern California today.

As she grew older, Arabella began losing her eyesight, and thick corrective lenses were prescribed. In 1924, when she was—if we are to believe the date on the Huntington Mausoleum—seventy-four, Oswald Birley was commissioned to paint both her and her husband's portraits. According to Maher, Birley originally intended to paint a portrait of Arabella that the average wealthy society woman would want—that is, a kind and flattering one. But Arabella, whose eyesight was still sufficiently keen to recognize what Birley was up to, would have none of it. He was ordered to start over, and to paint her as she actually looked.

At the Huntington Museum, where the Birley portrait hangs, it is possible to see the extent to which Birley followed her orders, and the result is both powerful and unnerving. Arabella's height has already been noted, and even though Birley painted her three-quarter length, seated in a brocade chair, it is obvious that here is a woman of towering strength and determination. The years had added to Arabella's girth, too, and here is a massive figure. The beauty of her youth is gone, though the chin, doubled and dewlapped, is still strong. The lips are pursed, unsmiling, arrogant, and her nostrils are flared in such a way as to suggest that she had just detected some unpleasant odor in the air. For her portrait she chose to dress all in black. A voluminous black dress covers her almost entirely, and her large white fingertips emerge from a pair of black lace half-mittens. Two strands of black beads descend across her bosom. Most extraordinary is her enormous black headdress, which rises in great folds of fabric above her head and falls in great cascades about her shoulders. The huge hat seems like a milliner's interpretation of the headpiece of the Great Sphinx at Giza.

Arabella's face is dead-white, and apparently she insisted that Birley paint her with her glasses on. Behind the thick lenses and the heavy black frames her eyes gaze out balefully, challengingly, at the viewer: *I dare you to come closer!*

Why, one wonders, did Arabella want to present herself to posterity in such an unattractive way? Was her final statement intended to be: Listen, most of the story of my life has been invention and deception, burying the facts, distorting the truth, and so now, at last, you can really see me as I am, as the tough and ruthless old woman I became? In the past, I have been dishonest. But I will give you honesty at the end.

Perhaps. But perhaps not. Even at the end Arabella was an enigma, a woman who would not offer all the answers. Arabella died not long after the Birley portrait was completed, and her husband died three years later, in 1927. The answers lie buried with them at San Marino.

Her near-blindness, for example. How much of that was fiction, how much of it was theatre, a device she employed, perhaps to gain attention, or to provide her with some inner source of amusement? Or did she find that a handicap offered a useful tool with which to further control and dominate her world?

In *Merchants of Art*, Germain Seligman, a Paris art dealer from whom Arabella also bought, recalls a visit to his gallery in 1923, the year before her death.

> She had just dropped in to say hello, she said, as she was no longer in a buying mood and had everything she wanted to own. She was in her seventies by then, but still carried her unusual height with a splendid bearing. I seated her in one of the rooms opening onto the garden where we chatted for a while and then, with no other thought than to please her, I showed her a number of objects of a type which I knew she enjoyed, among them a delightful little marble Venus by Falconet. Looking at me somewhat reproachfully through thick-lensed glasses, she said, "You really shouldn't go to so much trouble for me. You know my sight has become so bad that I can hardly see anything." Whereupon she leaned forward for a closer look at the little figure, not over a foot high overall, and exclaimed, "What a lovely thing. Isn't it a shame that the little finger of the left hand is broken!" I couldn't help bursting into laughter as I congratulated her upon her bad eyesight, for the whole hand was certainly not over half an inch long. Almost before I did she threw her head back in a hearty laugh.

Just out of curiosity, she said, just because she liked to keep up with what the art market was doing, what was the price of the little Falconet? Seligman named a figure. Arabella bought it.

21

THE *GRANDS MESSIEURS*

RICH AMERICANS of the early twentieth century did not lay out great sums of money for art and culture without certain accompanying feelings of guilt. They might speak, reverentially, of being merely temporary "custodians" of their treasures for a one-day grateful public, but they privately admitted their own greedy longings for some sort of personal immortality. They might chauvinistically proclaim that it was American capitalism's manifest destiny to claim the finest art from a decaying European aristocracy, and yet, at the same time, they were troubled by the suspicion that collecting art was, *au fond*, frivolous.

Henry Frick, for example, after paying about $400,000 for Velásquez' *Philip IV of Spain*, tried to rationalize the expense by explaining that Philip IV himself had paid Velásquez the equivalent of $600 for the portrait in 1645. Elaborately computing the interest at 6 percent between the year of the commission and 1910, the year he acquired it—as though the painting were like shares of General Motors stock—Frick could prove that the price he had paid amounted to pennies. Henry Huntington used the averaging system. To justify his paying Duveen $620,000 for Gainsborough's *Blue Boy*, Huntington would point out that for some of the paintings in his and Arabella's collection they had paid only $5,000, and for others as little as $500. "When you average 'em all up, the price for each isn't bad," he said.

Still, the new American millionaires were constantly under critical attack on both sides of the Atlantic. They and their wives were the subject of caustic cartoons and pious editorials in which they were accused of plundering and raping the great art collections of Europe just to decorate their own pompous mansions. (Even though the Europeans were welcoming the rapists with eagerly open arms, and begging them into their drawing rooms to admire the portraits of their ancestors.) Americans, without a fixed aristocracy, were accused of trying to invent one; deprived of noble or distinguished ancestors, they were trying to borrow them. Stung by the criticism, they responded defensively. What else but guilt, for example, could have goaded Mrs. Maria Hotchkiss—the widow of a munitions manufacturer whose fortune was based on an invention which had wonderfully refined the machine gun, which had wonderfully helped dispatch the lives of thousands of young men in several wars—into endowing a splendid school for boys in Lakeville, Connecticut?

And all the time, helping to assuage the collective guilt of rich Americans, there was Joseph Duveen, who eventually became Lord Duveen of Millbank and whose considerable fortune was based on the discovery that Americans had a lot of money and Europeans didn't. Behind every *grande dame*, it may already have been noted, there was usually a *grand monsieur*, and between 1886, when he embarked on his astonishing career at age seventeen, and 1939, the year of his death, that gentleman was apt to be Duveen.

The way Duveen gained his reputation for impeccable taste and expertise is interesting. In addition to his you-deserve-beautiful-things approach, he also used the opposite technique. He would tell a prospective client that he or she was "not ready" for great art, and that "you must work your way up to it." Not surprisingly, when a millionaire was told that he was not good enough to own an Old Master, he was frustrated, tantalized. Duveen would offer to start off the neophyte collector with something from what he literally or figuratively referred to as "my basement," and that was usually a painting from the Barbizon School, for which Duveen had little use. Then, when the customer had become sufficiently educated by the Barbizon piece, Duveen would offer to buy it back and replace it with a Rembrandt or a Rubens. His Barbizon paintings circulated back and forth while he prepared his customers for bigger, better, and more expensive things.

For years he refused to consider Detroit a fit city to house an art collection, until finally the newly rich automobile manufacturers Henry Ford and Horace Dodge had almost literally to come to him on bended knees, begging him to let them be his customers. He felt the same way about Pittsburgh, and Henry Frick had to move from there to his palace on Fifth Avenue in New York City before Duveen would consent to do business with him. Duveen's methods of whetting appetites until they had reached insatiability were outrageous, and one of his more useful sales tools was his wife. Having acquired a particularly important painting, he would approach a prospective buyer and shake his head sadly, saying, "No, no, I am afraid that is not for sale. I know it is probably the finest Tintoretto in the world, but I have promised it to Elsie. I cannot disappoint her." Up, up, up would go the offer, until finally Duveen agreed that he would have to break the terrible news to Elsie. (Actually, Lady Duveen had grown accustomed to entering a room and discovering that a painting she had grown quite fond of was gone.)

When customers, as they occasionally did, complained about Duveen's prices, his favorite riposte was, "My dear woman, when you are buying something that is priceless, no price is too high." Another favorite saying was, "To fill a collection with paintings worth fifty thousand dollars each is easy. But to build a collection of paintings worth a quarter of a million each—that's hard work!"

To a special customer, such as Arabella Huntington, Duveen's approach was a mixture of fawning servility and imperious command. When she traveled, Duveen took care of all her steamship and hotel reservations. He advised her on clothes, and often shopped for her. He helped select her jewels, and who knew what under-the-counter arrangements had been made with the jewelers into whose emporiums he directed her? If he didn't care for the way she was wearing her hair, he would tell her so, and she would change it. Once, when she had bought a roomful of antique furniture from a rival dealer, she called in Duveen to pass judgment on it. He pronounced it inferior, and Arabella promptly telephoned the dealer and told him she was returning it. "It's in the back yard," she explained.

In only one arena was Duveen not able to be much help to Arabella, and that was New York society. For one thing, her personal background was too shadowy and uncertain. For another, her husband Collis—whom Oscar Lewis has described as "scrupulously dishonest"—had made so many enemies that New York society did not want him in their houses. Arabella might live next door to the Vanderbilts, but she was never invited to their parties: Vanderbilt and Huntington were old and bitter railroad rivals. Down the street, Mrs. Astor also failed to give the nod—even, for many years, to the upstart Vanderbilts.

Later, when Arabella became Mrs. Henry E. Huntington, she had made herself notorious—a curiosity, a side-show freak. After all, for an aunt to marry her nephew was more than merely uncommon; it was a social gaffe worse than belching at the dinner table. (Awareness that this might be society's reaction may have been why Arabella put Henry off for as long as she did.)

But in the ancient country homes and drafty castles of England, and in the damp palaces of Rome, Venice, and Paris, Duveen was able to serve Arabella well. He saw to it that she was entertained in splendid fashion by the aristocracy and landed gentry in Britain and on the Continent, where doors were flung open to her everywhere. One wonders, of course, whether Arabella ever suspected that her enthusiastic hosts and hostesses were really inviting her into their homes in hopes that she would spot something she might want to buy.

There was, meanwhile, always a serious question as to how much Joseph Duveen actually knew about art. As a salesman, of course, he was a nonpareil, and he was a master of bluff and bluster. Once, at a gathering at the home of one of his important New York clients, to whom he had just sold a Dürer for several hundred thousand dollars, Duveen was confronted with a young French art scholar, who had been taken in hand by the host's daughter and proudly shown the Dürer. After studying the painting for several minutes, the young Frenchman whispered, "I don't think this Dürer is the real thing." To his horror, the young woman immediately turned to her father and told him that the Frenchman had declared the Dürer a fake. The shaken father then turned to Duveen. Duveen laughed his big, hearty laugh, and cried, "Oh, that is amusing. That really is terribly amusing. Do you realize, young man, that at least twenty other art experts, here and in Europe, have made the same mistake as you have, and have declared this painting not to be genuine? Oh, how amusing that you have been taken in too!" He had instantly made everyone in the room feel like artistic imbeciles, and presently the Frenchman was apologizing for his "mistake." The rest of the evening, however, cannot have been very festive.

On another occasion, during one of the many lawsuits which peppered his long career, Duveen was asked whether he was familiar with Ruskin's *The Stones of Venice*. "Of course I've heard of the picture," he said, "but I've never actually seen it." When it was pointed out to him that Ruskin was a writer—and an art critic, at that—not a painter, and that *The Stones of Venice* was a book, Duveen merely laughed again, and said that he had always thought that Ruskin was a painter, and not a very good one at that.

Duveen loved lawsuits. He loved to sue other people, and he equally enjoyed being sued. For most of his life he was involved in at least one piece of litigation, if not several, at any time. His habit of publicly denouncing his competitors as charlatans and crooks, and of marching through their galleries shouting, "Fake! Trash! Garbage!" assured him of a steady stream of libel and defamation actions, which he seemed to relish as a kind of tonic in the day-to-day routine of selling. He also enjoyed suing, and being sued by, members of his own large and contentious family, most of whom seemed also to be in the art business, and each of whom periodically claimed that he was being tricked and cheated by the others. When Joseph Duveen's art dealer father, Sir Joel Joseph Duveen, died in 1908 and left a $7,000,000 fortune to twelve children and a brother, Joseph quickly arranged to "borrow" his brothers' and sisters' inheritances in return for "shares" in the family business. From time to time Joseph would dole out a few thousand dollars to his siblings, but there were long periods when the others received no income at all from their investments. When they grumbled and complained, Joseph would laugh and say, "So sue me!" For the most part, since they knew he wanted to be sued, they didn't sue.

Obviously, the thing Duveen wanted most to avoid in his profession was to be accused of peddling a painting that was a fake or forgery. Not only did that sort of thing tarnish his reputation. When it happened, and was discovered, it meant having to refund the purchaser his money, a much more painful operation. Fortunately, in 1906, when Duveen was thirty-seven, when Arabella Huntington's art-buying spree was at its zenith, and when Duveen had cemented himself as securely as a barnacle to such other collectors as Andrew Mellon, Henry Frick, J. P. Morgan, Eva Stotesbury, and Mary Emery, he encountered and "discovered" the brilliant young art scholar whom Isabella Gardner had actually discovered some years earlier, Bernard Berenson.

Berenson, of course, had heard of Duveen, and had never been entirely sure that he approved of him. The two first encountered each other in Duveen's London gallery, where Berenson had gone to inspect a picture he was thinking of buying for Belle Gardner. On this occasion they did not formally meet, and when Berenson mentioned a price for the painting Duveen merely uttered his familiar laugh, said something to the effect that "This young man knows too much," and turned away.

What had struck Duveen was the fact that Berenson's figure for the painting was exactly what it was worth; later, he would be able to sell it to one of his rich American clients for twice as much. This gave Duveen a clever idea. He decided to seek out Berenson, and this time they met. Berenson had limited his field of expertise to Italian painting from the thirteenth through the seventeenth centuries, and Duveen had a proposal to make to him. If Berenson would authenticate Italian paintings for him, Duveen would pay him an annual retainer fee, plus a commission on sales. Berenson accepted, on the condition that he have nothing to do with sales, which was fine with Duveen. Selling, after all, was his forte. Thus began a relationship that would last for thirty years, and that would elevate Bernard Berenson to a position of influence—and affluence—unprecedented in the history of art scholarship.

From that point on Duveen would refuse to let any of his clients buy an Italian Renaissance painting until B.B., as he was called, working with his flashlight, studying brush strokes through a magnifying glass and opera glasses, had first attributed it and established its authenticity. It was a relationship that was often stormy, though they had become in effect business partners. As a salesman, Duveen used hyperbole and superlatives. Each painting he offered was "the finest of its kind in the world," "the most perfect example of the artist's work ever to come to light," and so on. Berenson's enthusiasms for certain works were sometimes more restrained. There were times, too, when Duveen, with a lively client waiting eagerly in the wings, would have much preferred to have had Berenson declare a painting authentic. But Berenson, sticking to the guns of his integrity and growing reputation, would refuse to give the work his stamp of approval.

There were also differences of taste. "Berenson may know what's authentic, but only I know what will sell," Duveen would say. And "If I were to follow Berenson, I would have a basementful of masterpieces that no one would buy." Berenson, who used to say that his tastes and sensibilities had been shaped "by two ancient aristocracies," Judaism and Harvard, tended to prefer paintings done in dark, shadowy, mournful tones. But rich Americans, Duveen had discovered, preferred bright, cheery colors. Like a successful tailor, Duveen liked to cut the cloth to suit the customer. (When Arabella Huntington first took delivery of *The Blue Boy*, she complained that Gainsborough's blue wasn't as sharp a blue as she had remembered it from reproductions she had seen; it was more of a bilious green. Duveen, suspecting correctly that the dull color was the result of soil accumulated over generations of hanging in a musty and underheated castle, had the painting cleaned and restored to its original pretty bright-blueness. Arabella was overjoyed.)

The vagaries of the American caste system also had to be considered. When Arabella was contemplating buying Sir Joshua Reynolds's *Mrs. Siddons as the Tragic Muse*, she wanted to know just who this Mrs. Siddons *was* anyway. Duveen explained that Sarah Siddons had been an actress, a member of the celebrated Kemble theatrical family in England. With this news, Arabella reconsidered. After all, in America, an actress still bore an invisible scarlet letter "A" on her bosom; it was a profession a little too close for comfort to what had been Arabella's own. It took Duveen to convince her that what she was buying was an artist, not a woman, before Arabella would write out the check. Even so, when Arabella brought the painting home to San Marino the new acquisition was considered very daring. Americans preferred ancestors to actresses.

Whenever Berenson had the slightest reservation about a painting's authenticity, he said so. Naturally there were times when Duveen wished heartily that Berenson's standards were not so exacting—that when his doubts were irritatingly niggling, B.B. would bend his rules, just slightly, in favor of a sale. But Berenson always stood firm.

There were times, too, when Berenson eventually changed his mind about a painting. When this happened he admitted it, again exasperating Duveen. Once, in one of Duveen's lawsuits, the uncompromising Berenson felt compelled to testify against his partner. A painting, which he had earlier attributed for Duveen, was now, in his final opinion, not authentic. The opposing lawyers jumped on this apparent contradiction. How could he verify a painting one day and deny it the next? "I never stick to a mistake," Berenson said calmly.

One of the factors complicating Berenson's work for Duveen was B.B.'s knowledge that many of the Italian painters, deluged by Medici commissions, personally executed only those parts of a painting which they found interesting—the face and the hands in a portrait, for instance. The more boring parts—the costume, the furniture, the background landscape—they turned over to apprentices. Thus, was a painting that had only been half-painted by Botticelli really a Botticelli? It was a complicated academic point. To deal with it, Berenson developed nit-picking, hairsplitting categories: "School of Botticelli," "friend of," "pupil of," "After," "student of," "attributed to," and so on, all of which were euphemisms for "possible fake." To Duveen, whose eye was on the bottom line, all this seemed like an elaborate waste of time. Still, Berenson's painstaking researches are considered invaluable to art historians to this day.

As Berenson's reputation grew, so did Duveen's. Though never really comfortable in their partnership, each man needed the other. The two remained locked together by the exigencies of honesty and the marketplace. Occasionally Duveen would ask Berenson to step outside his chosen specialty, the Italian Renaissance, and authenticate, say, a Rembrandt. Invariably Berenson stood firm. "I will not baptize outside my parish," he said.

Berenson could be stubborn. One of Duveen's pet clients was Andrew Mellon, and one of the Italians whom Mellon longed to have represented in his collection was Giorgione. The work of Giorgione, furthermore, is very difficult to differentiate from that of Titian. Aesthetics aside, the difference in the art marketplace between the two painters is entirely monetary. Titian lived to be ninety-nine, and during his lifetime his output was prodigious. Giorgione, who was Titian's tutor and friend, died young and left little of his work behind. Andrew Mellon had plenty of Titians, and so, when a painting which Duveen was convinced was a Giorgione fell into his hands, he went immediately to Mellon. "What does B.B. say?" Mr. Mellon wanted to know. "Never mind Berenson," said Duveen. "I tell you that this is *unquestionably* a Giorgione." Then he lied a little. "Berenson has verified it," he said.

Mr. Mellon, a cautious man, then cabled Berenson in Italy to ask whether this was true. Berenson wired back indignantly to say that he had by no means certified the picture, but would be happy to look at it. The painting was shipped to him, and he studied it for several days. Then he returned his verdict: it was an early Titian. The sale was lost, and Duveen was furious.

The uneasy partnership between Duveen and Berenson was not helped by the differences in their backgrounds either. The Duveens were Dutch Jews who, for several generations, had been prosperous city burghers in a religiously tolerant country. Berenson was from a Lithuanian ghetto, where his ancestors had been rabbis. Duveen was not above pointing out this difference in class to Berenson when it suited him. After all, Duveen's father had been made a British baronet. Duveen himself had risen to baronet, then to baron. (Though he had no interest in politics, he occasionally popped into the House of Lords, just to show that he had gained the right to do so.) And to further complicate their relationship, their respective wives liked each other. Mrs. Berenson liked Duveen, too, and, with his effervescent personality and endless capacity for enthusiasm, he was good company. "He's like champagne!" Mrs. Berenson used to say. "More like gin," her husband would mutter in reply.

Years later, after Joseph Duveen's death, Berenson would look back at their long association with rue. He, too, felt guilty, as though he had betrayed his talent, let it be crucified on a cross of gold. To be sure, his association with Duveen had afforded him luxuries—his library, his own exquisite collection of art—that are not often vouchsafed to the art historian. It had afforded him his beautiful villa, I Tatti, outside Florence, which for years was the mecca of art students from all over the world. Still, he seemed never to escape the conviction that he had sold his soul to the devil. Significantly, in his memoir *Sketch for a Self-Portrait*, Bernard Berenson never mentioned Duveen's name, nor their long partnership. But of the great art authority that Duveen had helped him to become, he did write:

> I soon discovered that I ranked with fortunetellers, chiromancists, astrologers, and not even with the self-deluded of these, but rather with the deliberate charlatans. At first I was supposed to have invented a trick by which one could infallibly tell the authorship of an Italian picture . . . Finally it degenerated into a widespread belief that if only I could be approached the right way I could order this or that American millionaire to pay thousands upon thousands and hundreds of thousands for any daub that I was bribed by the seller to attribute to a great master . . . Needless to say that every person I would not receive, every owner whose picture I would not ascribe to Raphael or Michelangelo, or Giorgione, Titian or Tintoretto, etc., etc., turned into an enemy.

Though he had always remained true to his code, he seemed unable to reconcile his art expertise with the fact that he had made money at it:

> I took the wrong turn when I swerved from more purely intellectual pursuits to one like the archeological study of art, gaining thereby a troublesome reputation as an "expert." My only excuse is, if the comparison is not blasphemous, that like Saint Paul with his tent-making and Spinoza with his glass-polishing, I too needed a means of livelihood . . . Those men of genius were not hampered in their careers by their trades. Mine took up what creative talent there was in me, with the result that this trade made my reputation and the rest of me scarcely counted. The spiritual loss was great and in consequence I have never regarded myself as other than a failure. This sense of failure, a guilty sense, makes me squirm when I hear myself spoken of as a "successful man" and as having made "a success of my life."

To atone for his guilt, perhaps, Berenson, who died widowed and childless, left everything he owned—his estate, his collection, his money —to Harvard.

For a cheerier appraisal of B.B.'s journey on this planet, it could be pointed out that his *Italian Painters of the Renaissance* survives not only as a classic but also as something of a bible in the art world, and that a majority of the curators of the world's great museums today have been either students of, or disciples of, Bernard Berenson.

As for Duveen, it could be pointed out that the majority of the great American private art collections, most of them assembled between the end of the Civil War and the beginning of the Great Depression and nearly all of them reposing today in public museums for the world to enjoy, were put together with Duveen's assistance.

And while it is true that the rich women of the era were manipulated by Duveen and others like him—Edith McCormick's mind manipulated by Carl Jung, Anna Dodge's jewel fetishism by Pierre Cartier—look what Duveen offered in return. For Eva Stotesbury, it was simply that he taught her "how to live." As for Arabella Huntington, for much of her mature life she may have been one of the most frightened women in the world. Obviously Colonel Mann and *Town Topics* knew something. Who can imagine what inner torment she suffered in dread of the day when her untidy past—at least two adulterous affairs with married men, an illegitimate child—might suddenly rise up to confront her? Joseph Duveen had helped her drown the secrets of her past in splendor.

PART SEVEN

"Walk Erect, Young Woman!"

22

INGENUE

To be invited to one of Mrs. Astor's rather stultifying evenings, it was nearly always necessary to be rich. But Caroline Astor let it be known that she also had other standards, and three of New York's richest families were never given her stamp of approval. These were the Goulds, the Harrimans, and the Belmonts.

In the cases of the Goulds and Harrimans, it was not difficult to see why. Both Jay Gould and "Ned" Harriman were, from all accounts, thoroughly unpleasant men, whose habit of snatching away railroad companies from unsuspecting stockholders—and from each other—had made them hated and feared in the financial community. It was darkly rumored that both Gould and Harriman were Jewish, though neither was. (An earlier American Gould, however, had spelled his surname Gold.) The situation with the Belmonts was a little more complex. Nearly everybody *liked* the Belmonts. On their own they gave parties and fancy-dress balls that were every bit as lavish as Caroline Astor's, and were usually much more fun. And yet there was something mysterious and alien about the Belmonts—a secret, like Arabella Huntington's past, which they preferred to keep hidden, and a topic which, in the rules of polite conversation, could not be discussed. Because the Belmonts *were* Jewish. Or at least a little bit Jewish. Who *were* the Belmonts, exactly? In *The Saga of American Society*, published in 1937, Dixon Wecter tried to sum up their anomalous position in New York:

> Since the first August Belmont set foot in America, no member of that family has ever married a Jewess, but invariably a Gentile of social standing. In this way, plus an exchange of the synagogue for

223

Episcopal communion, a constant association with non-Jews, and the adaptability of Nature which has given Belmonts scarcely any Semitic cast of feature except in their patriarchal age, a complete break with their Old World background has been successfully effected. In social acceptance no later Jewish Family can compare with them.

A hundred years before that passage was written, the situation was somewhat different. In 1837, the first August Belmont, a youth of twenty, arrived in New York from Cuba. He was small, dark, baby-faced, almost handsome, but on the plump side. He was, he announced, the new American "agent" for the European House of Rothschild, and he certainly seemed to have brought with him a Rothschildian spending capacity. The year of his arrival, meanwhile, was no accident. The panic of 1837 was under way, and in a depressed stock market young Belmont began buying shares of American companies at bargain-basement prices. Presently a shingle appeared on his office door in the financial district announcing him to be August Belmont & Company. Still, the financial community wondered, who *was* he?

He had been born December 8, 1816, in the little town of Alzey, in the Rhineland Palatinate. Alzey was in Rothschild country, a little more than twenty miles from the family's banking headquarters in Frankfurt. And at age thirteen August Belmont had gone to work for the Rothschilds as an unpaid office boy, an even lowlier position than Ned Stotesbury's first job at Drexel. From then on, however, his rise was astonishingly rapid. Soon the teen-ager was dispatched to Naples and placed in charge of Rothschild operations there. Next he was sent to Havana, and now here he was in New York, the youngest banker in town and a man of considerable power. The balance of trade had not yet shifted, and American corporations still turned to the bourses of London, Frankfurt, and Paris for financing, and that meant dealing with August Belmont.

Belmont never denied being Jewish. To do so would have been professionally unwise, for the Rothschilds were not only rich and proud but also very pious Jews. On the other hand, Belmont did nothing to identify or ally himself with the established Jewish community of New York. It was Horace Greeley, who disliked Jews and Democrats—which Belmont had become—who first published the news, in his *New York Herald*, that Belmont had been *geboren* Schönberg, and had "Frenchified" the name on the ship to America, in an effort to conceal his Jewishness. (Belmont and Schönberg, Greeley pointed out, both translated as "beautiful mountain," though a more exact French rendering would have been Beaumont, not Belmont.) Belmont denied all this, asserting that he had "documents" proving that he was the son of Simon and Fredericka Elsaas Belmont, that his parents were "large estate owners" in Germany, and that in Alzey, which was not far from the French border, families often had French-sounding names.

All this might have been acceptable, except for a few niggling questions that kept gossips in both the Christian and the Jewish communities busy. For one thing, if his family were large estate owners, why had August Belmont been farmed out to the Rothschilds at a tender age, and not been given a university education, as would befit his station? Why had the Rothschilds advanced the young man so rapidly? Why, contrary to the Rothschilds' traditional practice—which was to send a Rothschild son or close Rothschild relative to open a new branch of their banking business—had they turned over Naples, Havana, and finally New York City to a complete outsider? Was August Belmont privy to some shameful Rothschild family secret? (Belmont himself would breezily explain that the Rothschilds didn't consider New York an important enough city to waste a family member on.) Soon an even darker allegation came into circulation, to the effect that Belmont *himself* was the shameful family secret. According to a Rothschild family custom, it was said, whenever a male Rothschild traveled with a woman who was not his wife, the couple registered at hotels as "M. et Mme. Schönberg." Was it possible that Belmont/Schönberg was a pet—if accidental—result of one of these extramarital liaisons? This would explain why the Rothschilds, while feeling responsible for his care, would also want him stationed as far from home as possible. As for the documents he claimed to have which proved his Belmont parentage, August Belmont was rich enough to have documents drawn up to prove anything he wanted.

Over the years, this sort of gossip about the original August Belmont would continue to percolate, with innuendos that Belmont, for all his jolly popularity, was not quite "nice," that there was something unsavory in his past, and that there had to have been some dirty work at the crossroads back there in the Rhineland Palatinate. Among New York's Old Guard Jewish community, where name-changing has long been anathema, the story—true or not—that Belmont's name was originally Schönberg is still believed and repeated, and his family's quick transition into Christian high society is looked on with lofty disdain.

August Belmont's Christianization moved an important step forward in 1849, when he married the blond and beautiful Caroline Slidell Perry.

Though not particularly rich or social, Caroline Perry came from a distinguished eastern family. She was the daughter of Commodore Matthew Calbraith Perry, credited with having "opened" Japan to trade with the western nations, and the niece of another naval officer, Commander Oliver Hazard Perry, a hero of the War of 1812 and the Battle of Lake Erie. Presently, August Belmont established his new wife in a huge mansion with a private ballroom—the first in New York, it predated Mrs. Astor's—on lower Fifth Avenue, and another vast palace in strictly Christian Newport. Soon the Belmonts' dinner parties were the talk of society. For one thing, with their French-trained chef, they actually served good food, which was a rarity in an era when New Yorkers, if they wanted to eat well, usually went out to restaurants.

The Christianization of August Belmont continued as he took up the Sport of Kings, and soon he had built up one of the finest racing stables in America, helped build what would become the Belmont Park Race Track on Long Island, and established the Belmont racing colors, scarlet and maroon. The scarlet-and-maroon *motif* would be carried out in his coachmen's livery, their maroon jackets piped with scarlet ribbon, with silver buttons engraved with the Belmont "family crest," which had materialized from somewhere. The Belmont carriages were lacquered in high-gloss maroon, the spokes of their wheels striped with scarlet.

Nor was Culture overlooked. The Belmont collection of paintings—by Madrazo, Meyer, Rosa Bonheur, Meissonier, Munkácsy, Vibert, and Bouguereau—was unequaled in New York, and in the Fifth Avenue house an entire gallery was lined with vitrines filled with the Belmonts' priceless collection of porcelains, bibelots, and *objets d'art*.

Shortly before his marriage to Caroline Perry, Belmont had been invited to join New York's most exclusive non-Jewish men's club, the Union, and he had gone on to found the Manhattan Club and to become president of the American Jockey Club. More honors followed. In 1853, still only thirty-seven, for supporting the Democratic presidential candidacy of Franklin Pierce, August Belmont was appointed United States chargé d'affaires at The Hague. He held this post for two years, and then for the next three was the American Minister resident there. For his support of the Union cause during the Civil War—helping re-establish the Union's damaged credit in the bourses of Europe—he was even given a special decoration by a Republican President, Abraham Lincoln.

August Belmont died in New York in 1890, at the not-too-patriarchal age of seventy-four, and was given a Christian burial. If he had any regrets about his remarkable career, they might have been that—despite the elaborate trappings and apparatus of wealth and refinement with which he had managed to surround himself, despite the fact that he had once fought a duel in defense of a lady's honor he had never, not quite, attained the rank of gentleman, not even among the thousands of guests who had eagerly partaken of his courtly hospitality. Some magical ingredient of seemliness had eluded him. Mrs. Astor, in her entertaining heyday at the time of his death, had never given the nod. Nor had Belmont's wife, sadly, ever achieved the status of *grande dame*. She was beautiful, yes, and her beauty seemed not to diminish through the years. But Caroline Perry Belmont had lacked the emotional wherewithal, the special energy and stamina, the ambition—some said the intellectual equipment —to be anything more than a lovely ornament in a rich man's collection of costly symbols, which, perhaps, was all he had ever wanted or intended her to be. The Belmonts were reminders that money could buy almost, but not quite, everything.

After her husband's death, Caroline Belmont continued to live in the shadow of her flamboyant husband, and under the lingering cloud that hung over the Belmont name. It would take another generation of Belmont women to change all that.

"Walk erect, young woman!" Isabella Stewart Gardner had commanded the young Eleanor Robson, whom she summoned to her doorstep at 152 Beacon Street with no further message to convey. Miss Robson, then eighteen, had already learned to walk erect, and it is possible that Belle Gardner, sensing a touch of class in Miss Robson's poised and confident stride, was merely enjoining her to *continue* walking erect, and was not criticizing her carriage or her posture.

Eleanor Robson, furthermore, had had to learn to walk erect in a considerable hurry. She had been born in Wigan, Lancashire, England, on December 13, 1879, the third generation of a theatrical family. Her grandmother, Evelyn Cameron, was a star of the English stage, and her mother, who used the stage name Madge Carr Cook, was probably best remembered for playing the title role in *Mrs. Wiggs of the Cabbage Patch*. Her father, Charles Robson, who conducted a small orchestra in England, died when she was quite young, and her mother later married the English actor Augustus Cook and moved with him to the United States, where Eleanor attended a convent school on Staten Island. When she was seventeen she followed her mother to San Francisco, where Madge Carr Cook had been hired for a stint with the Daniel Frawley Stock Company, a traveling repertory troupe. Though young Eleanor as yet had no real interest in the theatre, it was agreed that she would perform bit parts and walk-ons—as page boys and chamber maids—for $15 a week.

About a month after her arrival, however, the ingenue star of the company, Gladys Wallis, resigned in a huff as a result of an argument with Mr. Frawley about being late for rehearsals, and a new ingenue had to be recruited in a desperate hurry. Because she was young and unquestionably pretty, with blond curly hair and wide blue eyes—but mostly because she was there and available—Eleanor Robson was drafted on the spot. In the next thirteen days she was required to learn thirteen different parts in the same number of plays, and one part was sixty pages long and called for a southern accent to boot. While the wardrobe mistress furiously put pins in her costumes, her mother drilled her in her lines, and, with an anxious mother hovering in the wings, Eleanor Robson went on stage and was letter-perfect. Afterward her mother commented that Eleanor did not seem to have to study her lines; she *absorbed* them. Furthermore, the audiences loved her. She had become that legendary thing, an overnight success. Her salary was immediately raised to $35 a week as a new star was born.

For the next few years Eleanor Robson toured in various stock companies throughout the United States, delighting audiences wherever she went and gaining a considerable national reputation, while her salary rose to $75 a week. At twenty-one she made her Broadway debut in the role of Bonita Canby, the leading lady in a play called *Arizona*, by Augustus Thomas, whose ambition it was to write a play about every state (or prospective state) in the Union. Both *Arizona* and its star were a huge critical and popular success, the star's salary doubled to $150 a week—a considerable sum for a young woman to be earning in 1900—and *Arizona* settled in for a long run.

Eleanor Robson next demonstrated that she had a shrewd and sensitive feel for material that might be suitable for dramatization. Vacationing in London in the summer of 1903, she met the English Jewish writer Israel Zangwill, whose most recent offering had been an unsuccessful play called *Children of the Ghetto*. With Zangwill she toured the London ghetto, and during the course of the afternoon he mentioned a novelette he had written about a London slavey called *Merely Mary Ann*, which Miss Robson asked to read. Touched by the bittersweet story, she suggested to her producer that Zangwill be commissioned to write a version of it for the stage. The producer agreed, Zangwill wrote the script in record time, and *Merely Mary Ann*, with Eleanor Robson in the title role, opened on

Broadway in 1904 to thunderously rave reviews. After a long run she carried the play to London, where it was also a huge success.

In London, at the time, audiences were applauding the plays of Arthur Wing Pinero, James M. Barrie, and George Bernard Shaw. Shaw was a writer who liked to keep track of what the competition was doing, and the surprise acclaim given to this "problem" play—dealing with poverty, by a Jewish playwright—particularly intrigued him. He went to see *Mary Ann* and, though not particularly impressed with the drama, was overwhelmed by its star. After seeing Eleanor Robson's performance, he wrote to her: "I have just seen Mary Ann; and I am forever yours devotedly. I take no interest in mere females; but I love all artists. They belong to me in the most sacred way; and you are an artist." It was high praise from an even higher source.

The misogynistic George Bernard Shaw's distaste for "mere females" was well known. On the other hand, he often developed passionate, if platonic, crushes on leading ladies, and his infatuation with Eleanor Robson would become one of the most ardent of these. His initial letter included an invitation to lunch at his house at 10 Adelphi Terrace, and, having once met her, he was even more smitten. He followed this meeting by sending her two snapshots of himself. On the back of one, showing him looking merry and jaunty, he wrote, "This is how I looked before I met you." On the other, which showed him looking downcast and lovesick, he wrote, "This is how I look now."

They met several times again in London, and, when she left for a holiday in Paris, he began bombarding her with a series of long, fiery, and amorous letters, which began, typically, "To the Gifted, Beautiful & Beloved — Greeting. My dear Miss Eleanor." Erratically spelled, they went on for pages, and closed, "Yours ever & ever . . . ever devoted G. Bernard Shaw."

Eleanor Robson returned to the United States to tour with the road company of *Merely Mary Ann*, which audiences couldn't seem to get enough of, and the impassioned letters from G.B.S. followed her wherever she went. In San Francisco in the spring of 1905, she received a particularly excited missive nearly a thousand words long: "Fate has done its work. I have put you out of my mind and settled down hard to my business since you left England. After weary months of mere commercial affairs & rehearsals, I have begun another play—half finished it, indeed; and lo! there you are in the middle of it. I said I would write a play for you; but I did not mean in the least to keep my promise. I swear I never thought of you until you came up a trap in the middle of the stage & got into my heroine's empty clothes and said Thank you: *I* am the mother of that play. Though I am not sure that you are not its father; for you simply danced in here & captivated me & deserted me & left me with my unborn play to bring into existence. I simply dare not count the number of months. Anyhow the heroine is so like you that I see nobody in the wide world who can play her except you. . . ."

The play was *Major Barbara*, the story of the brave and idealistic young Salvation Army officer Barbara Undershaft; her rich, materialistic gun-powder-manufacturer father; and the handsome Greek professor and poet who loves her, and joins the Army just to be with her. Shaw confessed that he had written much of himself into the character of the lover. The play was finished within weeks and, with characteristic imperiousness, Shaw then cabled Miss Robson's producer, George Tyler, demanding that Tyler release his star immediately so she could return to London and begin rehearsals for what would be a pair of matinee try-out perfor-mances. To Eleanor Robson, Shaw wrote, "One thing is essential—that you should know how to play the trombone—it would add greatly to the effect if you played it prettily. By the way, trombone players never get cholera or consumption, never die until old age makes them incapable of working the slide."

Understandably, Mr. Tyler found Shaw's demands unreasonable. He replied that he had no intention of relinquishing the star of a hit play in the middle of its run, shipping her six thousand miles to London so that she could rehearse for two performances of a play no one had even read. Shaw's response to this rebuff was typical. Calling Tyler "a most auda-cious ruffian," he added, "You'll be sorry!" As for Eleanor Robson, she was now being deluged with offers of parts and contracts. She would go on to play Juliet in *Romeo and Juliet*, Kate Hardcastle in *She Stoops to Conquer*, Constance in Robert Browning's *In a Balcony*, and the title role in Bret Harte's *Salomy Jane;* and among her co-stars would be Gerald du Maurier and John and Lionel Barrymore.

If anyone was sorry it was George Bernard Shaw. Forced to rely on another actress, *Major Barbara* opened in London to poor notices. Though the play would later have many successful revivals, and become a motion picture—and though his adoration of Eleanor Robson remained undimin-ished—he maintained for the rest of his life that the initial failure of *Major Barbara* was due to the fact that the curmudgeonly George Tyler had refused to let Miss Robson leave *Merely Mary Ann* to perform the title role.

Surprisingly, perhaps, considering their overpowering father and indolent mother, at least two of the three sons of August and Caroline Belmont had matured into rather active and independent men. With large inheritances from their father, all three might easily have preferred play to work. Perry Belmont, the eldest, married a woman named Jessie Robbins, who died young, leaving Perry a popular widower who enjoyed the clubs and parties of Newport, where he died in 1947 at the age of ninety-seven. But Perry Belmont was not a total idler. Between 1881 and 1889, he served in the United States House of Representatives, and was chairman of the House Foreign Affairs Committee from 1885 to 1887. In 1889, having switched his allegiance to the Republican Party, he was rewarded by President Benjamin Harrison with an appointment as United States Minister to Spain. Oliver Hazard Perry Belmont, the youngest, was less distinguished. He married, first, Sarah Swan Whitney and, second, Alva Smith, the former wife of William K. Vanderbilt and the mother of Consuelo Vanderbilt, later to become the Duchess of Marlborough. The second Mrs. Oliver H. P. Belmont was a political activist, a suffragette, and a doer of Good Works who helped, among other things, to form the Women's Trade Union League. This was an organization of rich women which, in the early 1900s, periodically swept downtown to join the picket lines of the "Shirtwaist Girls" who were striking for higher wages and better working conditions in the garment-industry sweatshops.

August Belmont, Jr., the middle son, had added to the family fortune by helping to finance and build the New York subway system. Like his father, however, he preferred a more aristocratic means of transportation, and was interested primarily in breeding and racing horses. He had a plantation in South Carolina; an estate in Hempstead, Long Island, and a nursery farm in nearby Babylon; a bungalow in Kentucky's Blue Grass country. He also had a cottage in Saratoga called The Curcingle, set in the middle of a small private training track that adjoined the Saratoga race course. Then there was a big place in Newport called By-the-Sea, and a big house in New York. His wife, the former Elizabeth Hamilton Morgan, by whom he had three sons, died suddenly in 1898. August Belmont, Jr., then became what in those days was called a Stage-Door Johnny. One of the actresses upon whom he showered huge bouquets of roses, and to whom he sent worshipful notes backstage, was Eleanor Robson.

In her memoir, *The Fabric of Memory*, Eleanor Robson Belmont is a little reticent about the details of her meeting with, and her courtship by, August Belmont, Jr. He drops rather casually into the pages of her book, as does her "decision" to marry him. One gathers that this decision was based on practicality more than passion. He was twenty-seven years older than she. On the other hand, he was a very rich man, and it was obvious that he adored her. In her book Eleanor Robson Belmont never fails to speak kindly of her husband, and it is clear that he was always kind to her. A father figure? Perhaps, but there was probably a little more to it than that.

By 1910, when it was clear that he had become a serious suitor, there were certain facts to which she no doubt gave serious thought. She was thirty, getting a little old to play the ingenue roles which had made her famous. A sensible woman, she certainly realized that the kind of parts she had been playing would not go on being offered to her forever. Her career had reached a delicate stage. Professionally, she was at the Rubicon. Also, she had been working since her mid-teens. She may well have felt that she had earned retirement to a life that promised a certain amount of luxury and ease.

On February 26 of that year, she and Mr. Belmont were married in a small ceremony at her New York apartment on West Seventy-seventh Street.

Her final role as an actress was as Glad in *The Dawn of Tomorrow* by Frances Hodgson Burnett. At her farewell performance, just weeks before she would become Mrs. Belmont, the audience stood up, cheering and weeping, when she uttered, in her full, rich voice, the curtain line: "I'm going to be took care of now."

23

RULES AND REGULATIONS

"THERE ARE CERTAIN RULES," James H. R. Cromwell said in 1980, "which a young woman must follow if she's going to marry a rich older man." He was referring to a former sister-in-law, a one-time show girl, who married his brother-in-law Horace Dodge. The marriage ended in a rancorous divorce with accompanying bitter lawsuits. "She knew that Horace was rich," said Mr. Cromwell. "And she also knew that he was an alcoholic, and not particularly attractive. If she had followed the rules, it could have worked out very well—but she didn't."

The rules are unwritten, of course. When a woman, not rich, marries a man who is, one of the things she may safely assume is that he is also reasonably spoiled, and accustomed to having his orders speedily obeyed. Since it is usually unrealistic, if not futile, to expect any alteration to this habit, the wise wife adapts to it. It is one of the rules. As the wife of August Belmont, Eleanor Robson seemed to come to terms with the rules of her new life intuitively. As she had done with her lines, she did not seem to need to memorize the rules; she absorbed them. "A private railroad car," she wrote, "is not an acquired taste. One takes to it immediately." The private car, named the *Mineola*, after one of her husband's favorite racing sloops, came equipped with its own French chef and black porter, and its purpose was to transport the Belmonts back and forth between their various residences scattered up and down the Eastern Seaboard, just as a chartered yacht had transported the newlyweds on an extended Mediterranean cruise.

Housekeeping, she admitted, was her major difficulty—the problem being that there were so many houses, each to be occupied during its own rigidly prescribed season. From a small place where she and her mother had made do with a single, all-purpose maid, she was now confronted with the Belmont mansion, a six-story affair which occupied most of the southeast corner of Madison Avenue and Thirty-fourth Street in Manhattan's Murray Hill. Then there was By-the-Sea in Newport, which required sixteen servants indoors, four men in the garage, three in the stable, and several gardeners. One of the rules was that the lady of such houses became the equivalent of an office manager of a large corporation, whose job it was to see to it that work flowed smoothly from department to department, that interoffice jealousies and squabbles were patched up smoothly, and that good performance was rewarded with praise and promotion.

She also had to be chief bookkeeper. In any large organization there are apt to be pilfering, kickbacks, and under-the-counter dealing. Though her chef did the ordering, it fell to her to supervise not only the menus but the accounts. In addition, she had to be a kind of travel agent, overseeing the periodic moves from place to place, keeping lists of which articles of clothing were packed in trunks and which were to stay put, when the silver and the paintings were to be put in the vault in one house, and the furniture covered with sheets, and when everything was to be unsheeted and unvaulted in the next. Obviously, she needed, and had, a private secretary to help her with the complicated details which faced her organization daily. But what must have made her duties seem particularly exhausting was the knowledge that the sole "product" of the Belmont operation was no more and no less than the comfort and well-being of Mr. and Mrs. August Belmont. "It was another world," she wrote with understatement.

At the same time she was expected to be a charming and gracious hostess, an amiable and comforting companion to her husband whenever and wherever he needed her—and to disappear quietly when he did not —and to open her arms to him in love when at night he tapped on her bedroom door.

There were also the arcane rituals of American society to be mastered. Golf, for example, was in those days the required rich person's sport. One started golfing in April, and stopped in September. Eleanor Belmont, however, could not force herself to become interested in the game. Defiantly proclaiming herself a nongolfer, she claimed to see no point in a sport which involved chasing a small ball across a great deal of acreage when, as she put it, "you had the ball in your hand to begin with." Nor did she have any taste for sports which involved bringing down small winged creatures from the sky with guns. Though she accompanied her husband on quail shoots, she always brought along a book to read.

In Newport, she quickly noticed that there seemed to be a tradition that society should be divided along generational lines. Parties were given either for young people or for the young people's parents. This struck her as a pity, particularly as her own age fell between the young group and the old. She decided to give a dinner party which would mix the generations up.

It would seem like an innocent enough experiment, but the evening was an unqualified disaster. One of the young people she invited was a woman whom, unbeknownst to her, the senior Mrs. Belmont had snubbed as long as she lived. A whole elaborate caste system was thereby thrown into confusion because, of course, the young woman quickly accepted. Then, in setting out her place cards, Eleanor seated the crusty old chairman of Bailey's Beach, Newport's private swimming club, next to a pretty young girl named Elsie Clews—not realizing that Mrs. Clews and the chairman had not been on speaking terms since she had defied his 1910 rule that ladies could not bathe at Bailey's Beach unless they wore long stockings.

In the wake of that evening Eleanor Belmont suggested to her husband that she write a book called *The Outlaws and In-Laws of Society*. He discouraged the notion. "If you don't tell the truth," he said, "there would be no point in it. If you told the truth, the points would make you and everyone else uncomfortable." He then quoted Mark Twain: "A little truth is a dangerous thing; a great deal is fatal."

Her second dinner party was more successful. For this occasion she hired Harry Houdini, the escape artist, who was then at the height of his fame and popularity. While guests gathered under a tent on the lawn, Houdini was handcuffed, bound with heavy ropes and chains, and then sealed in a large box to which heavy weights had been added. Then he was towed by launch out to the Belmont yacht, which lay at anchor in the harbor, carried aboard, and dropped from the deck into the Atlantic. Within seconds, he bobbed to the surface, free of his bonds.

And so the new Mrs. Belmont learned the new rules—from her own experience, from her husband, and from her peers. Two women in particular provided useful examples—Mrs. Cornelius Vanderbilt, Jr., and Mrs. Stuyvesant Fish. Mrs. Astor was dead, and Grace Vanderbilt had come forward to fill her place as New York's most important hostess. Her annual Christmas parties, with a gift for each guest tied to the branches of an enormous tree, were command performances for New York society. Mrs. Fish was the reigning *grande dame* of Newport, celebrated for her witty and often caustic remarks. At one of Mrs. Fish's dinner parties, for example, she had seated the Russian Ambassador, George Bakhmeteff, on her left, and the Bishop of Rhode Island on her right. The protocol-conscious diplomat was miffed about this arrangement, and made no bones about it after dinner, saying, "Mrs. Fish, please explain. I do not understand. Is it customary in America to put an ambassador on your left and a bishop on your right?" "Oh, no, Your Excellency," said Mrs. Fish. "I assure you it is *not* customary. It just depends on which you put first, God or the Tsar."

Both these older women took the new Mrs. Belmont under their wings, and years later, when Eleanor Belmont had become a *grande dame* in her own right, she would be able to deliver ripostes that would have made Mrs. Fish proud. At a 1953 dinner party at the Thomas K. Finletters' house in New York, one of the other guests was John P. Marquand, the best-selling novelist. Marquand was holding forth, as he liked to do, delivering long and entertaining verbal concertos, and on this particular evening his topic was "the lack of taste and reticence in today's youth." Suddenly he changed the subject, and began telling of his recent heart attack, for which part of the recovery procedure had been a daily abdominal massage. The young nurse who had performed this massage had, he said, after raising his hospital gown, said to him, "What a pleasure it is, Mr. Marquand, to be able to massage the lower abdominal muscles of a man like you!"

There was a silence, as Marquand paused for effect. Then, from across the table, the rich, theatre-trained voice of Eleanor Belmont was heard to comment, "Tell me, please, Mr. Marquand, because I am curious to know—where was the taste and reticence in that anecdote?"

The rules of being a rich man's wife, meanwhile, did not prevent a woman from creating and claiming an independent bailiwick of her own, an area of service or expertise in which she could personally shine. On the contrary, it very much behooved her to do so. Caroline Belmont's function had been essentially decorative, but her daughter-in-law was much too energetic and inventive to settle for a life that was no more important than a doily. Eleanor Belmont remained an Englishwoman at heart, and she shared her husband's enthusiasm for horses. Long before their marriage he had delegated to her the task of naming his race horses.

To those unfamiliar with the world of horse racing, this may not sound like a great chore, but it is a complicated process and is itself surrounded by rules and traditions. A horse is traditionally named, for example, with a name using the same first initial as its dam. Then, if at all possible, the name should convey some suggestion of the animal's breeding line. (The son, say, of a horse named Bright Day, might be named Berry O'Day, or some such.) But it is even a bit more complicated than that. The proprietors of the *Stud Book*, which oversees such matters throughout the world, insist that no race horse carry the name of any other in the entire history of racing. Each name must be unique. Owners of new-foaled horses often submit long lists of possible names to the *Stud Book*, only to have every one turned down. A certain amount of imagination and a nose for research are required.

These Eleanor Belmont was able to provide. For example, she proposed that a filly foal be named Mahubah—a greeting she had heard in Tunis which, freely translated from the Arabic, means "May good things be with you." She was confident that no other race horse had borne the name Mahubah, and she was right. The name was accepted by the *Stud Book* immediately. Later, she discovered that, though she had spelled the name right phonetically, the correct English spelling should have been Mahabah. But it was too late for a correction. Mahubah had already gone down in the annals as the dam of one of the greatest champions in racing history, Man o' War, another Belmont horse whom Eleanor had named. Other favorite Belmont entries, christened by Eleanor, were Stromboli, Hourless, and Ladkin.

The world of big-time racing was full of drama and suspense. In 1910 one Belmont two-year-old, whom Eleanor had named Tracery, was sent to England with the expectation that he would win the English Derby. Disappointingly, he came in third. Two years later, however, Tracery won the St. Léger, one of England's classic turf contests, and the following year he was entered for the Ascot Gold Cup, the most famous trophy in England, and one that had thus far eluded any horse from the Belmont stable. Coming down the home stretch, Tracery was in the lead by several lengths when a spectator, waving a suffragist banner in one hand and brandishing a revolver in the other, leaped out of the infield and onto the track and seized Tracery by the bridle. Tracery fell on top of his assailant, the jockey was thrown, and two other horses and their riders, just behind, tumbled on top of Tracery. The horse in fourth place was far enough behind to steer wide of the collision, and went on to win the Ascot.

Miraculously, no one was killed, and in the extensive press coverage of the incident the activist apparently got what he wanted—publicity for his cause.

Tracery's shoulder was badly damaged from the fall, and it was assumed that the valuable animal would never race again; for several hours the Belmonts debated whether Tracery should be destroyed. August Belmont argued that the suffering horse should be put out of his misery, but Eleanor insisted that the veterinarians be allowed to do what they could to save him. As it happened, Tracery recovered splendidly, and later, over the same course where he had been brought to grief, handily won the Eclipse Stakes, another English classic.

Meanwhile, Eleanor Belmont was expanding her field of interests to include philanthropy. In 1915 the novice philanthropist did not have to be very clever to realize that philanthropy in America was in a state of chaos. The Lady Bountiful syndrome was in full flower, and every woman of importance had her "pet" charity, to which or whom she was often exceedingly generous. But the trouble was that, with no overall organization, individual giving was random, sporadic, and idiosyncratic, with a great deal of duplication and overlapping. For example, any cause which benefited little children was popular, and any number of American women worked for, and gave to, their favorite children's hospitals. Hospitals and homes for the aged, however, were less glamorous, and got very little help. It was easy to raise money for an orphanage or home for wayward girls, but no one cared much about the fate of wayward boys. Certain diseases—such as cancer—which no one liked to think about were unpopular causes. But money could almost always be raised to aid those afflicted with less frightening ailments, such as blindness or tuberculosis. The various Christian churches had no difficulty collecting, from their wealthy parishioners, large sums of money which were used to finance missionary work around the world to Christianize the heathen. At the same time hundreds of thousands of Americans, who had already been Christianized, lived in poverty. (The Jews, who did not believe in proselytizing and had no missionaries, were able to funnel the money from their coffers directly back into the community.) In education, wealthy Americans gave impressively to create private boarding schools in New England and to endow Ivy League colleges, which, in those days, were still essentially schools for the well-to-do. Less elegant schools and colleges, ignored by private philanthropy, suffered accordingly.

A few years earlier, in 1901, the Junior League had been founded by two New York debutantes, Mary Harriman, the daughter of E. H. Harriman, and Nathalie Henderson—"for the benefit of the poor and the betterment of the city." Much of the Junior League's time was spent providing volunteers to work in New York's hospitals, which was fine as far as it went. The trouble was that most of the well-born young women whom the League invited to join their club preferred working with children's hospitals, and disliked situations involving the elderly, the incontinent, the maimed, the insane, or the terminally ill. Thus private philanthropy remained lopsided and inefficient.

There were plenty of examples, too, of private philanthropy in which huge sums of money were donated for causes that some people thought frivolous. In New York, Mrs. James Speyer, the wife of a Wall Street investment banker and a devoted dog lover, gave millions of dollars to establish the Ellin Prince Speyer Animal Hospital on the East Side. The Speyer Animal Hospital was fitted out with equipment more sophisticated than could be found in most ordinary hospitals of the day.

New York's Jewish upper crust, meanwhile, though a much smaller group, had already done a great deal to give Jewish philanthropy some cohesiveness and focus. Under the leadership of such New Yorkers as Jacob Schiff and Louis Marshall, the Joint Distribution Committee and the United Jewish Appeal had already been established. Eleanor Belmont's idea was similar—to establish a central planning agency for philanthropies which would study areas of need, and try to persuade individual donors to let their gifts be allocated and apportioned among these. It was simply an early version of what would later be called United Appeal. The name Eleanor gave her New York group, however, was wittier: the Society for the Prevention of Useless Giving.

Though Eleanor Belmont felt uncomfortable as a fund-raiser and disliked asking people for money, she was still a stage performer of extraordinary talents, and her bailiwick became the speaker's dais. From here she could eloquently present her ideas, and with significant results. Among other things, she succeeded in calling the attention of wealthy New Yorkers away from sickly children, female orphans, and "wronged" teen-age girls, and in getting them to recognize that the young working woman might deserve some attention, too. One of Eleanor Belmont's philanthropic creations was the Working Girls' Vacation Association, which was just that—a fund to help young women who worked to get out of the city a couple of weeks a year.

In 1917, when the United States entered the First World War, Mrs. E. H. Harriman invited Eleanor to apply her persuasiveness on the dais in behalf of the Red Cross. The war had brought the Red Cross from

Europe to America with an international charter "to . . . aid the sick and wounded of armies in time of war . . . to mitigate . . . the suffering caused by pestilence, famine, fire, floods, and other great national calamities." President Woodrow Wilson attached great importance to the Red Cross, and had established the War Council to take charge of its operations, with Henry P. Davison as chairman of the Council. Davison immediately announced that the then-staggering figure of $100,000,000 must be raised through contributions to the Red Cross that year, and Mrs. Harriman and Eleanor Belmont would head the New York team.

Once more, as in her theatre days, Eleanor Belmont was off on tour. During the first three months of the war she made forty-five speeches in thirty-eight cities in ten different states in behalf of the Red Cross, and, in the end, the War Council topped its goal by collecting $114,000,000. All told, in three successive annual wartime drives, over $400,000,000 was raised, including the costs of donated equipment and supplies, with Eleanor plugging from the platform all the way.

In the autumn of 1917 she was off across the Atlantic through waters filled with German U-boats and enemy destroyers disguised as tramp steamers to inspect United States Army camps in Europe and report on Red Cross needs at the front. Though there was, as she reported later, "a general feeling of tension" during the voyage, as the ship zigzagged to avoid the U-boats, she and her fellow passengers managed to keep their composure. Arriving in France, she presented a letter of introduction to General Pershing, commander of U.S. forces there. It read: "Mrs. Belmont is one of the few really able people who are also gifted with the power of expression. She wishes to help in every way, and then, on her return home, to put before our people, as vividly as only she can do, what the real needs of our troops are. She has a man's understanding, a woman's sympathy, and a sense of honor and gift of expression such as are possessed by very few either among men or women." The letter was signed "Theodore Roosevelt." Though she was only thirty-eight, a *grande dame* was clearly in the making.

She would make a number of other transatlantic crossings in behalf of the Red Cross before the war was over.

Throughout the prosperous 1920s, when most of the great American private art collections were being completed, it had become clear that, for all the glamour and prestige that an art collection conferred upon the collector, there was something a little sordid about the whole business. With prices at record highs for both Old and New Masters, the possibilities of fraud and forgery abounded, and even the meticulous B.B. admitted that he occasionally made mistakes. And, though Joseph Duveen virtually carried the booming art market on his shoulders, there was no question that he was essentially a manipulator and high-pressure salesman, with no more scruples than a side-show pitchman. The bitter jealousy and rivalry among the art dealers themselves extended to the collectors, whose infighting, of course, was abetted by Duveen. (At Duveen's death in 1939, a rival dealer delivered this ambiguous eulogy: "We miss him, but we are glad that he is gone.") Behind the beauty of the paintings, it was not a pretty scene.

Perhaps this was why, though Eleanor and August Belmont had plenty of paintings—many of them inherited from his father—they were never serious art collectors. In her memoir Eleanor Belmont wrote, "In retrospect, the past seems not one existence with a continuous flow of years and events that follow each other in logical sequence, but a life periodically dividing into entirely separate compartments. Change of surroundings, interests, pursuits, has made it seem actually more like different incarnations." One of these compartments, or incarnations, was definitely artistic—as Shaw had said, she was an artist—but the art she chose to support was not one of the plastic ones. Though she continued to toil for such diverse causes as the Red Cross—and was given its Gold Medal in 1934—the National Institute of Social Sciences, the Adopt-a-Family Committee, and the Emergency Unemployment Relief Committee, her real love remained the theatre and, in particular, opera.

Opera, after all, did not lend itself to the hucksterism of a marketplace. An aria, once sung, could not be sold at auction.

24

LEADING LADY

ELEANOR ROBSON'S FIRST TASTE of grand opera had been during her long run in New York in *Merely Mary Ann*. She had met the dramatic soprano Milka Ternina, who was singing Brünnhilde in *Götterdämmerung*, and one night, after the curtain had run down on *Mary Ann*, the young Miss Robson hurried down to the old Metropolitan Opera House on Broadway and Thirty-ninth Street to catch what she could of Mme. Ternina's performance. When she arrived, the curtain was just going up for the final act, and so she did not have to buy a ticket. But, since there were no seats, she had to stand. She nonetheless got to see and hear one of the ripest and richest scenes in Wagner, the fiery immolation of Brünnhilde. It was theatre beyond theatre, and Eleanor Robson was an instant opera addict.

For all its gorgeousness, opera in the United States just a few years earlier, at the turn of the century, had been in serious trouble. The reason, though it was not immediately apparent to those involved, was simple: opera had become the exclusive domain of the upper crust. In New York, for example, two autumn events—the opening night of the Metropolitan Opera, and the New York Horse Show—marked the "official" beginning of the winter social season. One attended these events to demonstrate that one had successfully returned from Newport, to show off one's new clothes and jewels, and to indicate that one was prepared to resume society's demanding rituals. In the press, these occasions were treated more as fashion shows than as artistic or athletic performances, and the implication that opera was only for the carriage trade had an intimidating effect on ordinary mortals.

Merely attending the opera, furthermore, conveyed no social status. It mattered where you *sat*, and the only acceptable seats were the little, and fairly uncomfortable, gilt-and-red-plush chairs in the arc of private boxes that ringed the first balcony—the Diamond, Golden, or Dress Circle, as it was variously called. No other seating in the auditorium was socially acceptable. The opera boxes, each with its owner's name engraved on a brass plaque at its entrance, provided a compendium of People Who Counted in New York society. There was not even a way for the ambitious parvenu or outsider to climb into this perfumed circle. The boxes were sold for as much as $30,000 each, but even so they rarely became available, and were passed on from one generation of a family to the next. Ownership of opera boxes was also strictly controlled by a board of directors, who saw to it that only the right people were admitted to the club. No Jews, of course.

Meanwhile, even within the Dress Circle there was stratification. Most of the boxes were owned outright by box holders, but a few less desirable ones could be leased. (Jacob Schiff, the banker, who was an opera lover and also happened to be Jewish, was made a box-holding exception, and was permitted to lease a box "for certain performances.") There was no logic to it. Some of the "best" boxes, such as Mrs. Astor's Number 7, had the poorest sight lines to the stage, and in all the boxes the acoustics were generally bad. It didn't matter. By 1900, society's rules had been laid down: if one didn't own a box at the opera, one might as well do what Eleanor Robson had done, and stand.

Opera had become something one didn't attend to hear and see music performed. One went to opera to be seen, and to see who else was there to be seen. It mattered little what was going on onstage, though there was a marked preference for Italian opera—perhaps because Italian was a language almost no one understood, and there was therefore no reason to take the trouble to follow the words. In the boxes, the behavior of the people who thought of themselves as setting the social standards had become notoriously rude. While sopranos onstage strained to reach high C, the box holders chatted and visited and waved to one another, or departed mid-aria to refresh themselves at the bar. Mrs. Astor had set the example of arriving late and leaving early, and others followed her lead. Since she had demonstrated her preference for Monday-night performances, that became the most fashionable night at the opera. During the rest of the week the boxes stood largely empty.

That the gentry should have established such an impregnable beachhead in "democratic" America on an art form which, in nineteenth-century Europe, had been popular with poor and rich alike, might seem peculiar. But the same thing was going on on the Continent as well, and opera-going was becoming an increasingly aristocratic pastime. As the kings took over the opera house, the commoners moved out. In New York, the gentrification of the Met had meant that opera performers and managers had grown more cynical. When no one was paying attention anyway, when opera was simply a high-society status symbol, why trouble to deliver a good performance? When no one cared, when the stars of the evening were the men and women in the boxes and not the poor souls struggling through the music onstage, what did it matter whom you booked or what opera you decided to put on?

Unfortunately, the situation at the Met had begun to be noticed where it hurt, not in the boxes but at the box office. Ordinary New Yorkers, who might have enjoyed an evening of opera, were discouraged from it. Sitting in their plebeian orchestra seats, they disliked being scrutinized, through lorgnettes and opera glasses, by their betters in the Dress Circle above. There were pleasanter ways in which these people could entertain themselves. Others, who had no knowledge of opera, were usually too daunted by the experience of attending once ever to want to try it twice. The language of the singers was unintelligible, the complicated plots were difficult to follow, and no attempt was made to educate or enlighten this group of prospective customers in the skimpy program notes. And so the New York opera-going public had been reduced essentially to two groups: the "swells" in the boxes, and the Bohemians—actual opera buffs who took the cheap seats in the topmost gallery. To these, a third group was occasionally added: out-of-town tourists who bought orchestra seats in order to crane their necks upward and backward to stare at the swells.

All this began to change, however, in 1903. This was the year that Otto H. Kahn was offered a place on the board of directors of the Metropolitan Opera. Kahn, also Jewish, was Jacob Schiff's partner at the prestigious downtown banking firm of Kuhn, Loeb and Company, and that a Jew should have been invited to join the Met's board was certainly unusual. But then so were the circumstances. The Met was desperately in need of money, and Kuhn, Loeb was now doing business that was on a par with J. P. Morgan's. Kahn seemed a likely source of cash, which he had plenty of, and he had access to even more Wall Street money from his partners and friends. Mrs. Astor might not approve of Kahn's appointment to the board of "her" Met, but it was something close to an emergency measure. Besides, Caroline Astor was entering her twilight years, and her vise-like grip on New York society had begun to loosen. Times, at last, were changing.

But what no one suspected in 1903 was that, for the next twenty-five years, Otto H. Kahn not only would succeed in revitalizing the Met financially, but would also revolutionize the role of the opera in the city's cultural life. The first thing he did was engage a new impresario, the talented Austrian-born Heinrich Conried, who announced that instead of sticking abjectly to Italian opera, the Met would begin offering works in German and French as well. Conried brought with him a young Italian tenor named Enrico Caruso. At first, both Conried's offerings and Caruso's performances were greeted with indifference by the critics. But in December of Conried's first season, when he presented the first American performance of Wagner's *Parsifal,* the critics went wild, and it dawned on New York that something exciting was at last happening at the stodgy old Met. Triumph began to follow critical triumph, and lines began to materialize at the box office.

When, four years later, Heinrich Conried was forced to step down because of poor health, Otto Kahn approached Giulio Gatti-Casazza, who for the preceding ten years had been the successful general manager of Milan's La Scala. Gatti agreed to come to New York, but only on one condition: that he could bring with him La Scala's celebrated conductor Arturo Toscanini. Thus, in one fell swoop, were two giant talents brought to the Met.

Otto Kahn's own great talent, however, was not simply in acquiring other talent. It lay more in the field of public relations. He was a natty, dapper little man with a bubbly, champagne-like personality, and he was a natural fund-raiser. For every gift of $50,000 to the Met, he announced, he would make a matching gift of his own. One of the first to take him up on this challenge was William K. Vanderbilt, and for several years the two millionaires were in lively competition over the size of their large checks. Also, unlike the box holders of old, Kahn did not stare balefully at his economic inferiors. He was a smiler and a hand-shaker, and he became the Met's unofficial greeter—standing outside the marquee, urging people to come in, showing them to their seats, chatting with the audience during intermissions. No detail escaped his eye. He saw to it that the "story" of each opera, no matter how unlikely it might be, was outlined in the Met's program, and that translations of the librettos were also available. When the décor of the ladies' washroom displeased him, he had it done over. Most of all, he was a genius when it came to handling the press. Many of the music critics of the day, it had to be admitted, knew rather little about music, and some had been elevated to critics' desks from writing obituary notices. Kahn nurtured a camaraderie with them. During long musical passages, or whenever he noticed a critic's eyes beginning to glaze with boredom, he would gently nudge the critic and suggest that they repair across the street for a glass of whiskey, or perhaps catch part of a vaudeville show. The critics responded by giving the Met's productions rave reviews.

While he was doing all this, Otto H. Kahn was also quite literally buying the Met. When he first went on the board, he had been given two hundred shares of Metropolitan Opera stock. As more shares became available, he bought them, and presently he owned 2,750 shares, or 84 percent of the company. Five blocks away, at the corner of Thirty-fourth Street and Eighth Avenue, stood the Manhattan Opera House, which was owned by Oscar Hammerstein I, the father of the lyricist. Kahn decided that two opera houses in the same neighborhood were too many, and so Kahn paid Hammerstein a reported $1,200,000 to dispose of this competition. Just how much of his personal money Kahn contributed to the Metropolitan Opera has never been known—Kahn did not believe in releasing too many figures about his philanthropies—but it is assumed to have been between $5,000,000 and $10,000,000.

It was not until 1917, however, that the Met's board offered Box 14 in the Diamond Horseshoe to Opera House Kahn. At the time, the press called the event "notable," and remarked that only twelve boxes had changed hands in the last eighteen years. With typical aplomb, Kahn accepted the gift. But he never used the box. It was reserved for visiting dignitaries, such as President and Mrs. Woodrow Wilson. When the dignitaries came, Kahn saw to it that the box was filled with fresh flowers.

By 1929, Kahn himself was getting on. He was sixty-two, and he and Gatti-Casazza and Toscanini had been at the Met for more than a quarter of a century. The Met's coffers were now filled with enough money to ensure funding for lavish productions long into the foreseeable future, or at least as long as any future could be foreseen. Other thoughts began to occupy him. He was toying with the idea of returning to his native Germany. He was also flirting with the notion of conversion to Roman Catholicism. That was the year he decided to retire from the Met's board, to devote himself to rest, travel, and reflection. Another, younger person could assume his mantle. Four years later, he would die.

By 1933, of course, the foreseeable future had not come to pass. Instead had come the Great Crash. The Metropolitan Opera, like the rest of the country, was again in serious trouble. The huge reserve funds, which had seemed more than ample in 1929, had collapsed with the stock market.

Wealthy individual patrons, who had once thought nothing of writing out large checks in return for the status that came with supporting grand opera, were now exceedingly scarce. Gone was the well-dressed scramble to buy $30,000 boxes; boxes were up for grabs at clearance-sale prices. At the general-admission box office, business was dismal. In a depression, it seemed, the last thing New Yorkers wanted to spend money on was opera tickets. The Met seemed likely to close its doors unless desperate and original measures were taken. That was the year the board of directors decided to invite its first woman to join. Eleanor Belmont's devotion to the opera was by now well known. She was the obvious choice.

There were certain subtle ironies here. Having lost a prominent Jewish patron, the board had chosen a new one who was "sort of," but not really Jewish. Also, just as Eleanor's in-laws had been successful in getting society in both New York and Newport to overlook, if not entirely forget, the fact that the first August Belmont had been Jewish, so had Eleanor —always the trained performer—with her mastery of society's rituals, customs, and manners, not to mention her attention to society's pet art, the opera, succeeded in getting society to overlook the fact that she had once been that less-than-proper thing, an actress on the stage.

August Belmont, Jr., had died in 1924, leaving Eleanor Belmont a still-beautiful widow of forty-five. As a youngish widow her performance had been impeccable. Not a breath of scandal had surrounded her name—no lovers, no escapades, no indulgences. Now, ten years later, she had settled firmly into the role of *grande dame*. It was as though she had accepted the chapters of her life as a series of theatrical assignments to be carried out with the same poise and grace and born-to-the-role aplomb she had applied to her work in the theatre, but the ingenue had matured into a leading lady. She had let her full mane of fine hair, which had begun to grow prematurely gray in her early twenties, go snowy white. She wore it in a simple but attractive style, pulled into a loose bun at the back of her head, with soft waves framing her face. It was a style that suited itself to hats, which Eleanor Belmont liked to wear, even in her own house. It befitted a woman who, in her own house, carried a reticule on her wrist as she moved from room to room.

She had retained her creamy Englishwoman's complexion, which, framed by the white hair, made her appearance striking. She had allowed her girlish figure to become a bit matronly, but this again was appropriate. When, in the 1920s, American women raised their hemlines, Eleanor Belmont did not. At her age it would not have been seemly. Her mature figure seemed designed for long dresses, just as her pale arms seemed designed for white opera-length gloves which were always a part of the *grande dame*'s royal wardrobe.

She had never been known to lose her temper, and yet, when asked for an opinion, she was always firm. A favorite Belmont opening was, "If you will permit me, I will be absolutely frank." If she disagreed with a suggestion, she would say, "No, I'm afraid I cannot go along with that." And so, cool, self-confident, elegant and obviously enormously self-controlled, Eleanor Belmont moved through her daily schedule of philanthropic and artistic duties. If, in the first generation, the Belmont name had been slightly tainted in society, the regal first lady of the second generation had redeemed it.

She allowed herself a few extravagances. Her attendance at performances of the opera were regular and faithful, and she would make her appearances even when ill. At these times, instead of sitting in a gilt chair, she would recline on a low chaise longue which had been especially placed in Box Number 4 for the purpose. When that happened, people said, "How devoted to the opera Mrs. Belmont is!" And "What great courage Mrs. Belmont has!" If these were the reactions Eleanor expected from her audience, then so be it. She was not only the opera's great patroness. She was also its star.

As the first woman on the Met's board, Eleanor Belmont later described her first meeting with the formerly all-male body as an event she approached with trepidation. "My first meeting in May, 1933, was almost as difficult as an opening night in the theatre," she wrote in her memoir:

> It is not possible to say who was more perturbed, I or these formal gentlemen, several of whom were friends or had been cordial dinner partners. But mixed company on boards was far from a familiar sight at the time, and when I slipped into a chair, several of the directors looked solemnly uncomfortable. Missouri might have been their home state. As for me, I felt like misplaced matter.

Still, despite this self-effacing disclaimer, there is no reason to suppose she had any real doubts that she could carry it off. As a woman, she was already a veteran of several other firsts in New York. In 1924, for example, she had been the first woman to deliver a commencement address at New York University.

If Otto Kahn's contribution to the Metropolitan Opera had been essentially financial, Eleanor Belmont's was essentially creative. It was also surprisingly down-to-earth. To a board that was wringing its collective hands about the tragedy of New York City losing a great showplace for a great and classic art, Eleanor Belmont quickly pointed out that her concern was less lofty-minded. She noted that the Met employed six hundred people regularly, plus occasional additional specialists. If the Met closed, a much greater tragedy than an artistic loss would be six hundred more New Yorkers on the relief rolls or in the bread lines. This fact had not occurred to the gentlemen on the board. She, however, knew what it was like to be an out-of-work actress.

As she usually did in any circumstance, she got briskly to work. Soliciting large gifts from donors in the private sector she immediately ruled out. Such giving was too sporadic, too uncertain, and too unreliable. Furthermore, the New York rich—including herself—no longer had the money they once had. To finance President Franklin D. Roosevelt's social-welfare programs, the rich were being taxed as they had never been before, and so other sources had to be found. One of her ideas was as simple as it was brilliant. Why not, she suggested, make use of the fairly new and enormously popular medium of radio? Saturday matinees of the Metropolitan Opera could, she proposed, be recorded and then sold to radio stations all over the United States. This would accomplish three things. It would provide soothing, and free, performances of opera to frightened Americans across the country. It would also provide immediate revenue. Finally, it would have a public-relations function, and establish the primacy of the New York Metropolitan Opera in the minds of hundreds of thousands of Americans.

Anyone who remembers the 1930s, or even the 1940s and 1950s, will recall the Saturday afternoon radio broadcasts from the Metropolitan Opera. In some cities certain radio stations still broadcast the opera to this day.

Eleanor Belmont had noticed also that a large portion of the American public was addicted to contests and give-aways. In hard economic times, obviously, give-aways were more popular than ever, and the media were full of them. Newspapers gave away silver teaspoons to new subscribers, and movie theatres gave away Fiesta Ware dishes and Shirley Temple glasses to ticket buyers. The magazines were full of contests in which the contestant was asked to describe, "in twenty-five words or less," why he or she liked a certain product, with the winners to receive prizes ranging from small appliances to large amounts of cash. With the opera established on the radio, Eleanor next proposed a contest. Listeners were invited to describe, in a hundred words or less, "What the Opera Means to Me." As a prize, the writer of the winning letter would receive a week end in New York, including tickets to a live performance at the Met. While the opera contests would not generate direct income, they would serve the Met in other ways. For one thing, they would provide an informal audience-rating system. For another, they would increase radio listenership, which would please the subscribing stations.

The opera contests were an immediate hit, and thousands of letters a day poured in, in competition for the weekly prizes. A separate agency had to be engaged to read and evaluate the letters and award the prize. Otto Kahn might have democratized the opera in New York City, but Eleanor Belmont was democratizing it on a national scale.

Inevitably, there were critics who carped and complained that Mrs. Belmont was "cheapening" the opera, as, in a sense, she was. The times demanded a more egalitarian approach. Among her innovations were group discounts for children and students. Working through the music departments of New York's high schools, she established programs whereby students could attend the opera for as little as 75 cents apiece. Members of the Old Guard elite who still sat on the Met's board were appalled by reports of wads of chewing gum stuck to the red plush seats, but Eleanor Belmont countered that what she was doing was trying to encourage a new generation to be opera lovers. If the students learned to love the opera, she argued, they would also learn to respect the opera house. And, as she had predicted, as the number of student programs increased, the cases of chewing-gum despoliation declined.

At one point, it was decided that the famous old gold curtain which had graced the Met's proscenium for more than fifty years was in such fragile condition that it would have to be replaced. The company's business manager felt lucky to have found the owner of a movie house who was willing to buy the old curtain for $100. "I'm afraid I cannot go along with that," said Eleanor. She had the curtain taken down—it weighed ten tons—had it cleaned, and, using her network of volunteers, had it cut up and sewn into such souvenir items as glasses cases and bookmarks. Sales of Gold Curtain Souvenirs netted $11,000.

In spite of these innovations, money remained a desperate problem for the Met, but there were occasional bright moments. One of the brightest occurred on the night of February 2, 1935, when the magnificent voice and figure of Kirsten Flagstad, the Wagnerian soprano, came bursting upon the scene singing Sieglinde in *Die Walküre*. The audience gave her a standing ovation at the end of the first act, and when the final curtain rang down, the audience was cheering and standing on the seats. The critics raved over the discovery of the new star, and for the next few years the news that Flagstad was singing in *any* role guaranteed a sold-out house. (Later, Signor Gatti-Casazza, who had negotiated her contract, would claim that her acquisition had amounted to a $25,000 annual legacy for the Met, and he was probably right.)

But Flagstad left the Met in 1941, amid criticism and controversy, to spend the war years with her husband in Nazi-occupied Norway. And long before Flagstad's New York debut, Eleanor Belmont had been working on what would be her most important and lasting contribution to the opera, the formation of the Metropolitan Opera Guild. Later, she would admit that she had no idea at the time whether the Guild would work, or quite how it would work. But, noting that "Cathedrals are built with the pennies of the faithful," and knowing that large individual donations would not be forthcoming, she decided to concentrate on the pennies.

Again, the idea for the Opera Guild was simple. In return for an annual membership fee ranging from $100 down to $10, a person could join the Guild. The Guild member was then entitled to certain perquisites and privileges—first crack at hard-to-get tickets, for example; discounted prices for certain performances; a subscription to a periodic opera newsletter. Most attractive, perhaps, was that Guild members could attend opera rehearsals. These were often tempestuous affairs, with displays of fiery artistic temperament by divas and directors alike, and were often far more exciting to watch than the finished performances. Thus by joining the Metropolitan Opera Guild one could, for a small sum, enjoy all the special privileges that had theretofore been exclusively reserved for the wealthy box holders in the Diamond Horseshoe.

Early in 1935 the opera board, rather grudgingly, had given Eleanor Belmont a modest budget of $5,000 to organize her Guild. She began by assembling an imposing roster of names to decorate her Honorary Committee. At the head of the list were President and Mrs. Roosevelt. The governors of nine states lent their names to the letterhead, along with New York's popular Mayor Fiorello La Guardia and some two hundred celebrated Americans—in the arts, business, and society—across the country. The psychological allure of the Metropolitan Opera Guild was therefore very powerful from the beginning. By joining, and for just a few cents a day, one could achieve, or feel one had achieved, the social status of a Vanderbilt . . . a Mrs. Astor . . . a Mrs. August Belmont.

The Honorary Committee contained her showcase names. For the slightly less illustrious members of her working committee, she was careful to include important people from the media—C. D. Jackson, the publisher of *Time;* book publisher John Farrar; David Sarnoff of RCA (Guild membership would of course be promoted on the opera broadcasts).

In its first year 2,000 people became Opera Guild members. Year by year membership climbed, and soon it topped 60,000. By 1957, over and above the hundreds of thousands of opera tickets that had been sold to Guild members, the Guild had turned over more than $2,000,000 to the Met. Furthermore, as Eleanor Belmont liked to point out with a little smile, the original $5,000 underwriting which the board had granted in 1935 had never been touched.

And throughout those years the annual highlight of the New York opera season had become the moment, at the very end, when the stately Eleanor Robson Belmont—"the woman who single-handedly saved the Met"—stepped out of the wings, walked slowly in front of the gold curtain to center stage, turned to face her audience and tilted her lovely chin upward to catch the key light, and then delivered her beautiful and moving speech in behalf of the Metropolitan Opera Guild. And, when it was over, to stand, eyes lowered, head bowed just slightly so that the light caught the glacier-white hair, to receive her standing ovation.

"She was always the consummate actress," says her long-time secretary Patricia Shaw, "and I mean that in the best, classic sense—in the sense that a great actress is happiest when she knows she is pleasing other people. Everything she did was orchestrated to give pleasure to others." Throughout the 1930s, for example, another of Mrs. Belmont's main interests was unemployment, and what to do about it, and the more she worked for Unemployment Relief in New York, the more she realized that private giving—though it was touted as "the American way"—was not the solution to the problem.

In 1933, invited to address a meeting of Jewish women for the Joint Distribution Committee, she stepped to the podium and began, "If you will permit me, I will be absolutely frank." Three thousand women, including Mrs. Franklin D. Roosevelt, hitched forward in their seats. Private charities, trying to keep 13,000,000 unemployed Americans alive, were wasteful and haphazard, she said. "The major portion of the relief program should be assigned to the city, State or Federal Government," she said, "and the amount agreed upon . . . as necessary to carry out an adequate program, should be obtained by special taxation . . . I do not believe it is a wise policy to carry on the work of serious emergency relief with voluntary contributions. The system is as wrong as that of voluntary enlistment in times of war. It simply means that you penalize the generous."

England, she pointed out, was suffering its own Great Depression, and yet it had an unemployment-insurance plan. In the United States this was sneeringly called "the dole," though it provided "a definite, though modest, relief for all." Furthermore, it "recognized government responsibility."

It is ironic, perhaps, that the widow of a preeminent American capitalist should have at that point advocated the kind of government social-relief programs which Roosevelt did indeed adopt, and which became the models for many of the American welfare programs which Ronald Reagan, in the name of capitalism, would like to see abolished.

After her husband's death Eleanor Belmont had gradually begun editing the number of her addresses. The Belmont mansion on Madison Avenue was sold, the building razed and replaced by an office building. By-the-Sea joined a number of unwieldly Newport "cottages" which are now open to the public and toured by curious visitors eager to see the grandeur of the trappings and paraphernalia of a social era that will probably never come again. Home for Eleanor Belmont became a large apartment at 1115 Fifth Avenue at Ninety-third Street, facing Central Park and the Reservoir and filled with heirlooms, photographs, and mementos of all the other Belmont houses and yachts and the private railroad car. For several years she also maintained a summer home called Ledge Rock Cottage in Northeast Harbor, Maine, but by the late 1950s she had given that up as well, and home was just the New York apartment.

As she entered her eighties she didn't go out or travel or entertain as much as she once had. (In 1949, at seventy, she had paid a farewell visit to G.B.S. at his house in Ayot St. Lawrence, in England.) Still, she liked to give little lunches, famous for their sparkling conversation, in her apartment, and she kept her full-time secretary busy with correspondence. Whenever it was physically possible, she went to the opera—often in a wheelchair now, to be lifted from it and placed on the special chaise in her box.

Her final years were also spent collecting various awards and honors. She had been named chairman of the board of directors of the Metropolitan Opera Guild, had held that position for seven years, and was then given a lifetime appointment as founder and president emeritus. She had received a gold medal from the National Institute of Social Sciences (to add to the one she had received from the Red Cross), and a medal for outstanding civic service from the Hundred Year Association, a New York philanthropic group. The Theodore Roosevelt Association also gave her its distinguished service medal. She had received an honorary Master of Arts degree from Yale and an honorary Doctor of Letters from Columbia.

In the winter of 1969 the *New York Times* writer Deirdre Carmody was about to leave her office for a vacation when she received an urgent summons from her editor. Eleanor Belmont, she was told, had just had her ninetieth birthday and was far from well. Before she could leave for her holiday, Miss Carmody was told, she would have to write Mrs. Belmont's obituary, to which the *Times* was giving the unusual distinction of a full page. Miss Carmody spent most of the night marshaling the facts of Eleanor Belmont's life and writing the long story. She filed her copy and then left for her vacation, fully expecting to see her story in the *Times* in the next few days or, at most, weeks.

But the weeks turned into months, and the months into years, and the Carmody obituary did not appear. Mrs. Belmont's health, it seemed, had improved. The appearances at the Metropolitan Opera were becoming rarer, but they still occurred.

Deirdre Carmody, in fact, would have to wait nearly ten years—until October 26, 1979—before seeing her obituary of Eleanor Belmont in print. Eleanor Belmont had died in her sleep at 1115 Fifth Avenue. In less than two months she would have been a hundred.

She had never learned to play the trombone, but she had fulfilled George Bernard Shaw's prediction that old players never die "until old age makes them incapable of working the slide."

PART EIGHT

First Lady

25

"A HARD WOMAN TO SAY 'NO' TO"

IT MAY HAVE BECOME APPARENT that among the various characteristics America's *grandes dames* have shared has been a certain imperiousness, along with a certain stubbornness. It has been said of several of them that they "thought like a man," and it was observed often that these ladies liked to get, and usually succeeded in getting, their own way. But at least one Texas woman, Mrs. Barbara Dillingham, finds sexist connotations in such observations. "You never hear that sort of complaint being made about a *man*," says she. "You never hear anyone say that Henry Ford 'likes to get his own way,' or that Ronald Reagan 'likes to get his own way,' or that Louis XIV liked to get his own way. Getting your own way is all right for a rich and powerful male. But when a rich and powerful woman likes to get her own way, then that's considered a bad sign."

Mrs. Dillingham was referring specifically to her old friend, the late and legendary Miss Ima Hogg of Houston, a woman who was frequently taken to task for "liking to get her own way." "Miss Ima wanted what she felt was *right*," says Barbara Dillingham. "When they were planning to build a freeway smack through the center of one of the city's most beautiful parks, that seemed wrong to her, and she fought it. She said, 'They built a tunnel under the Bois de Boulogne—why can't we?' Well, that was one battle she lost, but she didn't lose many."

Among other things, Ima Hogg was a battler.

When introducing herself to people, she would always pause slightly: "My name is Ima . . . Hogg." The little pause was for more than dramatic effect. The introduction, delivered in a firm, even voice, guaranteed that the recipient of this information would not laugh; Ima Hogg's name was one thing about which she saw absolutely nothing funny, and the little pause said, in effect, "Yes, you have heard me correctly. My name is Ima . . . Hogg." The little flash of her blue eyes which went with the introduction seemed to add, "And I wish to hear no further comment on this subject!"

In connection with her uncommon name, two legends that grew up about her never ceased to irritate her. One was the story that her father had given her the name out of spite, to humiliate and denigrate her. The other was that her father had been equally malefic in naming his other children—that Ima Hogg had a sister named Ura, a brother named Hesa, another sister named Shesa, and so on. Actually, she had no sisters, and her three brothers had been given down-home Texas names that were plain as Job's turkey: Will, Tom, and Mike. Also, Ima Hogg worshiped her father, and the suggestion that he would have been capable of a cruel joke distressed her. Still, the stories about the Hogg family nomenclature persisted—set in motion, she always believed, by political enemies of her father's—and have continued to this good day. There are still otherwise well-informed Houstonians who will confidently speak of Ima, Ura, Hesa and Shesa Hogg.

Ima Hogg was born July 10, 1882, in Mineola, Texas, the daughter of district attorney James Stephen Hogg and Sallie Stinson Hogg, and was named Ima in all innocence by parents who had simply seen nothing odd about the juxtaposition of the first and last names. A few years before her birth, one of her father's brothers, a writer named Thomas Elisha Hogg, had written and published a long epic poem about the Civil War called *The Fate of Marvin.* The poem's heroine was named Ima: "A Southern girl, whose winsome grace and kindly, gentle mien betrayed a heart more beauteous than her face. Ah! she was fair; the Southern skies were typed in Ima's heavenly eyes." Not long before the birth of James and Sallie Hogg's daughter, Thomas Elisha Hogg had died, and Ima was given her name to honor her uncle's memory. As her father wrote to another brother, John Hogg, "Our cup of joy is now overflowing! We have a daughter of as fine proportions and of as angelic mien as ever gracious nature favored a man with, and her name is Ima! Can't you come down to see her? She made her debut on last Monday night at 9 o'clock. Sallie is doing extremely well, and of course Ima is. . . ."

One person not overjoyed with the baby's name was Ima's grandfather Stinson. He lived only about fifteen miles from Mineola, but news traveled slowly in those days. When he learned that his granddaughter was to be called Ima Hogg, he saddled up his horse and rode as fast as he could to Mineola to protest it. But he was too late. The christening had already taken place, and, as Miss Ima would say later, "Ima I became, and Ima I was to remain."

From the beginning she bore the name proudly, even defiantly, refusing to change it—she could have become Irma, for example, by adding an "r"—or to hide under any number of possible nicknames. Equally defensive were her three brothers, who at one time or another all came home from school with blackened eyes and bloodied noses earned fighting for the honor of their sister's name. And she herself, of course, as a child was relentlessly teased by her contemporaries. She refused to be fazed by any of it. In fact, it is possible that she might never have become the sort of woman she did had it not been for the character-building experience of living with a ludicrous name that made her the butt of vulgar jokes. And when she became the acknowledged "First Lady of Texas," it was said in Houston that newcomers knew that they had become true Houstonians at the moment when Miss Ima's name no longer seemed peculiar. By then, to be sure, she was known throughout the state simply as "Miss Ima," or, as they said, "Mizima."

"What a pity she never married!" people would say as she grew older. There were several possible explanations for her spinsterhood, and her own was probably not to be taken seriously. "I am fatally attracted to handsome men," she would say, "and I know if I had married, I would have picked a handsome husband who was worthless." Then there was the fact that in 1890, when Ima was eight, her father was elected governor of Texas, the first to be native-born, and the move from Mineola to the Governor's Mansion in Austin certainly helped isolate Ima from her peers. More interesting was the rather primitive sex education she received. Her mother had been in poor health for a number of years, and in 1895 Sallie Hogg died. Ima was thirteen, and a maiden aunt moved into the Hogg household to help care for the children. "I remember," Miss Ima would recall many years later, "that my aunt took me aside and told me that I was reaching an age when boys might begin taking an interest in me. She said, 'Ima, you may find boys who will come up to you and say you're pretty. But remember that you are *not* pretty. If a boy ever tells you you're pretty, he's lying.' " Miss Ima would pause at this point in the story, and then add with a wry smile, "A few weeks after that, I wore a new dress to school, and a boy spoke to me and said, 'Ima, you look real pretty in that dress.' I screamed at him, *'Liar! Liar! I'm not pretty!'*—and I ran away from him as fast as I could."

The story is even sadder because, in fact, she was very pretty—with large, wide-set eyes, a perfectly shaped nose, full lips, a dimple at the center of her chin, and a petite figure. She looked very much like the Ima described in her Uncle Tom's poem.

Then there was her overpowering father. A huge, attractive man whom nearly everybody liked, Big Jim Hogg had come to the governorship on a ticket demanding the regulation of large corporations, particularly the railroads, which had been charging through Texas bribing public officials left and right. As governor he was unusual in that he had actually fulfilled his campaign promises, and in 1891 he established the State Railroad Commission. From the beginning little Ima served as her father's hostess. When she was nine, Ima and her older brother Will were among the guests of honor at Big Jim's inauguration as governor, and, in the years that followed, Ima—seated at one end of the table while her father sat at the other—presided over formal dinners, teas, and receptions for visiting dignitaries, politicians, and important businessmen. Until her father's death in 1906, Ima Hogg was his "official wife."

Following his term as governor, Jim Hogg bought a house in Austin, where he resumed his law practice. Here the Hogg children established a menagerie, which included a horse for Ima, a pet bear, a fawn, several dogs, and a parrot named Jane that screamed "Papa! Papa!" whenever the Governor entered the room. And here, for her father, Ima continued to reign as "the sunshine of my household." Still, he could be a tough taskmaster. When Ima was a young girl her allowance was 25 cents a week. One week she lost her quarter and, needing the money to go skating, borrowed the money from a servant. Her father got wind of this and was furious. After a long lecture on the impropriety of borrowing from servants, he advised her that he would personally pay back the quarter, but would deduct a nickel from her allowance for the next five weeks.

Though not yet rich by Texas standards, Jim Hogg was well off—well enough off to afford, among other things, a private railroad car. Once, on a trip with her father to Boston, teen-age Ima found herself alone in the railroad station while her father was off attending a political meeting. She fell into conversation with a young woman who seemed friendly and pleasant, and, thinking that she had made a new friend in a strange city, Ima chatted openly about her father's career in Texas politics. The next morning she found herself extensively quoted in the *Boston Transcript*. Once again her father was furious, and from then on she was wary of strangers who asked her questions.

At age sixteen Ima was sent off to the Misses Carrington's Preparatory

School in faraway Dallas. She had been studying piano since she was a small child, and at the Carringtons' she continued her piano lessons and even considered a concert career. Still, though physically separated from him, she still found her father the dominant influence in her life. He wrote her daily letters, and she responded as often. Big brother Will was also demanding on this score: "Dear Sis, please do not neglect your duty of writing them [brothers Tom and Mike] a joint letter once a week. Don't forget to write me once in a while and your dear daddy every day."

Jim Hogg's letters to his daughter were full of exhortation and advice. In a 1902 letter he said, "Amidst the vicissitudes of a checkered career, from orphanage in boyhood, I know I have at times done wrong, but never wantonly, wilfully. Looking back I have little to regret. Looking forward I have unshaken hopes that in you and my three boys I shall enjoy much pride and undefiled pleasure in Old Age." He also expected her to serve as an example to her two younger brothers: "With your acquaintances and large circle of friends in Texas, won by your own exemplary character and excellent behavior, you have nothing to dread in the future, provided that you do not change radically in your disposition and habits. With you or away from you I have every reason to be grateful to God for such a girl."

It was not easy to forget that Big Jim was a politician, and some of his letters rang with flights of grandstand oratory: "Home! The center of civilization. Home! The pivot of constitutional government. Home! The ark of safety to happiness, virtue, and Christianity. Home! The haven of rest in old age, where the elements of better manhood can be taught rising generations by the splendid example of settled citizenship. Every man should have a home!"

A few years later, Miss Ima enrolled at the University of Texas. Here, while she continued to concentrate on music and piano, she allowed her interests to broaden, and took courses in German, Medieval English, and —a daring new field of study in 1900—psychology. It began to seem as though Miss Ima might be in danger of becoming a bluestocking, a woman who would devote her life to scholarship and pedagogy, which was certainly a far from fashionable career for a turn-of-the-century southern belle.

At the same time, though her father remained the center of her life, it was clear that Miss Ima was developing a strong sense of personal independence and becoming a woman with a will of her own—someone definitely to be reckoned with. She had also developed an interest in painting and the decorative arts, particularly in American antique furniture. This pursuit was not fashionable at the time either. (Affluent Americans furnished their homes with French, English, and Italian pieces, and the fine things that were coming from the workrooms of Newport, Philadelphia, and Charleston would be ignored by collectors for nearly another half-century.) Once a friend invited Miss Ima to lunch, and Miss Ima suggested that they drive to a "charming little restaurant" she'd heard of, which happened to be about a hundred miles away. Distances, of course, are as nothing in Texas, but still, a hundred miles for lunch was a bit extreme. Only when the two had reached their destination did the friend discover Miss Ima's ulterior motive—a set of elaborately hand-carved Belter chairs that were going on a local auction block, and that Miss Ima had, as they say in Texas, "took a notion" to buy. "She was a hard woman to say 'no' to," the friend recalled.

By the time she had reached her early twenties, Big Jim's long-term plans for his only daughter were reasonably clear. The sunshine of his household, who had been his hostess in the Governor's Mansion, was to become his guardian-caretaker-housekeeper-companion in his old age. Fortunately for her, she was able to escape that dreary domestic fate, which so often befalls the only daughters of widowed fathers. Big Jim died in 1906, when Ima was twenty-four. Though he had not acquired a huge fortune by any means, Ima and her brothers were left comfortably off. Jim Hogg and a group of other investors, betting that one day little Houston would become a big town, and that a stretch of woodland, threaded by bayous running inland from Galveston Bay, to the west of town, would one day become the town's prime residential district, had bought most of what is now the superrich enclave of River Oaks. Jim Hogg's share of River Oaks was some 1,500 acres. In 1901 he had also bought a 4,100-acre plantation near West Columbia, Texas, which contained a two-story house and several outbuildings. For this he had paid about seven dollars an acre. By 1910 Houston was already beginning its incredible expansion, and Miss Ima's inheritance helped her to spread her wings.

Her first love was still music, and now she betook herself to New York City—unchaperoned, to the horror of her brothers and friends—where she enrolled at the National Conservatory of Music. The idea of a career on the concert stage still glimmered in her mind. After several months in New York she decided that the greatest teachers of piano were in Germany, and so, unchaperoned still, she sailed for Europe. There, when not studying or practicing or going to concerts and opera, she began buying works of fledgling painters whose names were unknown in America and barely known on the Continent at the time. Their names were Picasso, Klee, Modigliani, Matisse, and Cézanne. "Their paintings were cheap, but nice," she said years later, with characteristic understatement, when she presented her collection to the Houston Museum of Fine Arts.

Miss Ima was in Germany in July 1914 when the nephew of Emperor Franz Josef, the fifty-one-year-old Archduke Franz Ferdinand, was assassinated with his wife in their automobile at Sarajevo by a student terrorist named Gavrilo Prinzip, and when the "guns of August" signaled the beginning of the First World War. She was there to read the words of Sir Edward Grey, the British Secretary of State for Foreign Affairs: "The lamps are going out all over Europe; we shall not see them lit again in our lifetime." She was able to find a seat on the last train carrying foreign visitors out of Berlin, and to scramble aboard the last passenger steamer leaving Hamburg for the United States through the U-boat-infested Atlantic. "It was really very exciting," she said later.

Rolled up in her grip, of course, were the cheap, nice canvases of the Post-Impressionists she had bought in Europe.

In addition to an eye for art and furniture, and a knack for getting people to do what she wanted—and not to forget spunk—Miss Ima possessed an almost uncanny ability to communicate with animals and to get them to do her bidding. There was her pet brown bear, for example, and her pet ostrich, both of which she rode bareback. But horses were her favorites. Miss Ima's own horse was an elegant black Arabian stallion named Napoleon. Napoleon, she explained, was "proud cut." A proud-cut horse is a stallion that has been half-gelded. He cannot reproduce, but he does not lose his sexual appetites. Proud-cutting is almost always the result of a veterinarian accident or, more accurately, oversight when the newly foaled colt is gelded, and proud-cut horses usually mature to be totally unmanageable. "It made him very lively," Miss Ima liked to say. In fact, Miss Ima was the only person who could ride him.

Once, when she returned to Austin after an absence of nearly a year, Miss Ima asked to have her groom bring Napoleon around while she waited on the veranda. People used to horses point out that a horse is not like a dog, who will "remember" his master after years of separation and, seeing him, come bounding toward him with pleasure. Horses are not particularly intelligent creatures. And, in terms of personality, a horse is more like a cat—independent, and mostly loyal to the human being who has last fed him.

While Miss Ima waited on the veranda, her groom appeared around the corner of the building with Napoleon kicking and rearing and the groom struggling with his halter. Suddenly, seeing Miss Ima standing there, Napoleon, with one fierce jerk of his head, broke away from the groom altogether and, at full gallop, charged up the flight of steps onto the porch, laid his head on her shoulder, and nuzzled her.

Miss Ima, the groom said, "had powers."

26

BAYOU BEND

Miss Ima may not necessarily have had "powers," but she did believe in ESP, or in what she called her "hunches." It ran in the family, she said, and she had some mighty peculiar stories to back it up. Once, when she was a little girl, she said, she was on a trip to Hawaii with her father. The Hoggs were about to board the ship that was to take them back to San Francisco—their luggage and a maid were already on board—when suddenly and for no apparent reason Ima began to cry. "Something awful is going to happen!" she insisted. Showing remarkable patience, her father finally agreed to unload the maid and the baggage and book passage on a later sailing. The ship sailed with its passengers, and was never heard from again. Her aunt had had the same clairvoyant knack. She had been on a stagecoach to Dallas when she experienced an overpowering sense of urgency to get home. She had ordered the driver to turn around, and arrived home just in time to pull her baby brother out of a well. Miss Ima claimed she had had a hunch about her French paintings, too—that they'd one day be considered important and valuable.

Her father had had a hunch about his West Columbia plantation property. Not long after he purchased it, oil had been struck at Spindletop—and in far greater quantities than even the speculators had dreamed—and Spindletop was not far from the Hogg acreage. In his will Jim Hogg had stipulated that the West Columbia property could not be sold until fifteen years after his death. Thirteen years later, in 1919, a rich, oil-bearing deposit of sand was brought up, and, two years later, the West Columbia oil field was producing 12,000,000 barrels of oil a year. At last Miss Ima, at the age of thirty-nine, and her brothers were Texas-style rich.

So, at about the same time, were a great many other Texans, and

Houston was rapidly becoming the hub of the state's petroleum industry. The oil-rich Houstonians were looking for places to build expensive houses, and, as Big Jim had guessed, the River Oaks section seemed to be the logical spot. Realizing that River Oaks would be more attractive if it included a park, Miss Ima, her brothers, and the other River Oaks investors deeded 1,486 River Oaks acres—nearly twice the size of New York's Central Park—to the city of Houston for the creation of Memorial Park, in memory of the fallen in the First World War. Miss Ima and her brothers Will and Mike kept fifteen acres on which to build a place of their own, and the rest of the land was sold off for development.*

Since 1909 Miss Ima and her brothers had made their principal home in Houston, where they shared a comfortable house on Rossmoyne Avenue. After the First World War, Ima had a definite hunch that she was not cut out for a career as a concert pianist, and no doubt realized that she was getting a little old to embark on such a venture. Instead, she began giving private—and free—piano lessons to promising students and, with her new wealth, established several music scholarships at the University of Texas. She had also, as early as 1913, decided that Houston deserved a symphony orchestra, and that was the year she founded the Symphony Society. Houston, of course, was not New York, and Miss Ima could not collect the imposing roster of nationally known names to decorate her committee that Eleanor Belmont would later do with the Metropolitan Opera Guild. Miss Ima's approach was of necessity more simple and direct. She knew everybody in town, as well as pretty much what everybody was worth, and so she simply, as she put it, "went calling." Armed with a blank-paged blue-covered notebook, she rang the doorbells of her rich friends. After explaining her mission she would say, "Now, just sign your name in the book, and next to it put how much you will give to the Symphony."

The little blue book served a not-so-subtle psychological function. With the book in their hands, Houstonians could see at a glance how much their neighbors had pledged. It became a race to see which Houstonian could afford to pledge the most.

---

* The four Hogg children were remarkably close. Like Miss Ima, brother Will never married. Mike and Tom eventually did, but neither had children. In Houston, rumors persist that the Hoggs feared marriage and children because the family was prone to some inheritable illness. Big Jim Hogg's parents had both died young. So had Miss Ima's mother. Though Miss Ima never spoke of it, the problem may have been diabetes. Miss Ima's health was always robust, though as she grew older, she suffered from failing eyesight—a diabetic symptom.

When enough money had been raised to hire an orchestra and conductor, Miss Ima used the same forthright technique to peddle season tickets and subscriptions. Armed with her notebook, she trudged up and down Main Street, calling on Houston businessmen, selling advertising space in the Symphony program. At the same time, like Eleanor Belmont— though Mrs. Belmont would not emerge until the 1930s and this was still the teens—Miss Ima insisted that culture in Houston, though it might be financed by the rich, not turn into an elitist affair. She organized special Symphony concerts for school children, for the elderly in nursing homes, and for patients in mental hospitals. As she put it in a speech to Houston civic leaders many years later, "If our symphony is to qualify as an instrument of brotherhood, it must meet certain requirements and expectations. In a world struggling toward peace and universal humanitarian regard for mankind, there is no place for an aloof or exclusive institution. I must say that it has ever been the aim of the symphony to serve as a unifying agency in our region and city, that music may reach and touch every facet of our civic life." She became the Symphony Society's first vice-president, and served as its second president from 1917 to 1921.

There were some people in town, of course, who thought some of Miss Ima's notions were pretty radical. In 1916, for example, when women still did not have the vote, Miss Ima's campaign to get a woman on the school board seemed going too far. "We were all in the early movement together as suffragettes," recalls a friend, "but Ima wanted more than just the vote; she wanted to get improvements in the schools as well." As usual, Miss Ima got her way, and eventually ended up on the school board herself. Among her daring innovations: seeing to it that courses in art and music were added to the curricula of the black public schools. Such egalitarianism was almost unheard of.

With each new civic triumph, her confidence in herself grew. As she entered her forties she had become a personage of aplomb and gracious command. Though she stood only five feet two, and her once-slender figure had thickened into a series of comfortable curves, when she entered a room now there was always a little hush, and one knew that one was in the presence of a force, or Force. Miss Ima's regal presence was abetted by her voice, which was clear and bell-like, with only the softest trace of East Texas in it. Lucius Beebe once observed that when a person moves from not-so-rich to very rich, his physical appearance changes—"a new set to the jaw." This had happened to Miss Ima. Early photographs showed her with her chin tucked in, her eyes modestly downcast. Now her chin was held high, her eyes cast upward, fearless. One morning during the early 1920s she awoke to find a strange man standing in her bedroom. "What are you doing in my room?" Miss Ima demanded. "You have no business being here!" As the man turned from her dresser drawer, where he had been rummaging, she said, "What do you have in your hand? Give it to me at once." The burglar, shaken, opened his fist to reveal a piece of Miss Ima's jewelry. "Bring it to me," commanded Miss Ima. "Why are you taking my jewelry?" Handing her the piece, the burglar muttered something about being out of work, out of money, and needing her jewelry to buy food for his wife and children. "That is no way to do it," said Miss Ima firmly. "Here, hand me a pencil and paper from my desk." The burglar meekly complied. "You should look for a job," she said. "I'm going to give you the name and address of my brother's office. He's always looking for good workers. Go see him and ask for a job." She wrote down Will Hogg's name and address and handed it to the burglar. "Now, then," she said grandly, "good day."

Later, astonished friends asked her how she could have the nerve to deal so audaciously with her intruder. "He didn't look like a bad man," she replied. Another hunch, perhaps.

Meanwhile, plans were under way for her and Will's and Mike's new house on the fifteen acres in River Oaks. The land lay along the winding banks and steep ravines of Buffalo Bayou, where the slow-moving stream meandered through tall, centuries-old stands of pine and live oaks. Because of Houston's warm, moist Gulf Coast climate, Bayou Bend, as Miss Ima would call her estate, would be brilliantly green year-round. Even the water in the lazy bayou was bright green. Birds and other small wildlife abounded in the acreage, and otters played on the bayou's banks. And it was all only three miles—Miss Ima often walked the distance—from the center of downtown Houston.

In 1927 the architect John Staub was commissioned to design the principal house for Bayou Bend. Miss Ima's collection of American antiques and decorative pieces was now quite large—it spanned two hundred years, from seventeenth-century Pilgrim furniture to pieces from the Federal period of the early nineteenth century—and it included Chinese export porcelains, antique china, silver, and glass. Room for all these objects was needed, and the house Mr. Staub designed was large, with a room for each period and style. Still, because Bayou Bend was low and sprawling, built of pale pink stucco with green shutters, in the Spanish Colonial style, and with a certain amount of ornamental ironwork, and because it was nestled in the tall trees, it did not look overpowering. Also, Bayou Bend differed from its River Oaks neighbors—mansions built close to the street where they were obviously arrayed for the inspection and wonderment of passersby. Bayou Bend was hidden at the end of a long, curving tree-lined drive, invisible to the curious, where it appeared as a gradually revealed surprise to the invited guest.

While John Staub supervised the construction of the house, Miss Ima turned her attention to the extensive grounds. She was, as she put it, subject to "compulsions," and gardening had become one of these. Working with her head gardener, Alvin Wheeler, she began laying out the various flower beds and boxwood hedges and clipped monkey grass parterres, using stakes and string to assure their geometric precision. Her general idea was to compose a design that would contrast hedged-in formal gardens with natural woodland walks of wild flowers and wilderness. But it was to be much more ambitious than that. Miss Ima's overall plan called for no less than eight separate and distinctive gardens—in time there would be nine—each opening onto the next so that it pleased the eye in some new way.

With Bayou Bend completed and its gardens laid out and planted, Miss Ima quickly began to demonstrate another talent—as a hostess. Dinner parties were her favorite form of entertaining, and though her dinners were often black-tie, they were not therefore necessarily sedate or spinsterly. On the contrary. Her major-domo, Lucius Broadnax, was famous for his bourbon old-fashioneds, which he served in sterling silver mugs the size of small vases, and which, on his boss's instructions, he saw to it were constantly replenished to their brims. If one was not careful at one of Miss Ima's parties—or if one was not like Miss Ima, who appeared to possess the proverbial hollow leg—one could sit down at her dinner table in a state of woozy euphoria, willing to support Miss Ima in any endeavor. Because most of her dinner parties were not just for fun. Usually they were about something which, as she put it, "needs correcting," whether she was promoting a tax levy for the public schools, a lecture series for the University of Texas, the Fine Arts Museum, the Symphony, the Opera, the Visiting Nurses Association, a Democratic political candidate, the Boy Scouts, or the Garden Club, of which she was a founding member. Whenever opponents of any of her projects needed to be brought around to her way of thinking, Mr. Broadnax's old-fashioneds were powerful persuaders. "I went to Miss Ima's house for dinner determined to fight her on a bond issue," recalls one Houston politician. "Damned if I know what happened, but the next morning she called me to thank me for my support."

Miss Ima's correcting endeavors, and their attendant entertainments, were so numerous that, for a while, there were complaints from Miss Ima's neighbors about the amount of traffic that came and went nightly at 2940 Lazy Lane. Miss Ima simply began inviting more of her neighbors to her parties, until they too had fallen under the spell of her cajolery and the heroic proportions of Lucius Broadnax's old-fashioneds.

One of her most effective techniques was to adopt a pose of utterly unassuming modesty, an It's-jes-little-ole-me stance. "Why don't you drop by my place before your meeting, and we'll chat about it," she'd say. Or "This is probably just another crazy idea of mine, but I'll mention it anyway." Or she'd say, "If there are going to be any speeches at your banquet, I hope there won't be any honoring me." Told that there would be—by the 1930s there nearly always were—she'd become all nervous and bashful, and say, "Oh, then do please keep them short!" In this vein she once wrote, "I have no answers, only a burning desire to see something encouraging happen." And once, accepting a special award from the University of Texas, she said, "I realize, in choosing me to honor, it was not so much for my personal worth as for the fact that I represent members of my family whom you wish to remember, and through them, you have identified me with certain forces and ideas which I am gratified you hold worthy. . . ."

It was all an artful ruse, of course, but it made people putty in her hands. She loved the center of the stage as much as she loved her expensive furs and dresses, her spectacular jade earrings and necklaces, and the fact that everywhere she went in support of her various causes and enthusiasms she was now known, simply, as "The Lady." The self-effacing façade was just another way of getting what she wanted. Her daily telephone calls to civic leaders and city officials with "little suggestions" were becoming legendary. She might claim to have no answers herself, but when she had questions she wanted them answered right away. Once she telephoned the curator of a park she had given to the city to ask whether the wild flowers were blooming yet. Thinking the question unimportant, the curator quickly replied, "Oh, yes, ma'am." There was a pause; Miss Ima had obviously detected something in the man's tone that told her he was putting her off. "How many varieties?" she demanded.

She had very much admired the work of President Roosevelt's Work Projects Administration during the Depression, and so she wrote to the mayor of Houston suggesting that unemployment in Houston could be solved by the establishment of the city's own WPA. The mayor responded politely, but noncommittally, saying he would give the matter some thought, etc., etc.—a politician's letter which, in the end, said very little, though it was the sort of letter that would have satisfied most people. Not Miss Ima. The next time she saw the mayor at a party, she approached him. Shaking a long, bejeweled finger at him, she said, "You didn't answer my question! I asked you why Houston can't have a WPA."

"Yet," says an old friend, "she was arguable. If you did your homework and could show her the evidence for doing something in a way that differed from hers, she would change her mind." That was the key, of course. You had to have done your homework, and you had to produce hard evidence to convince Miss Ima. Otherwise, woe betide you. Once, during a performance by the Houston Symphony—in which Miss Ima naturally retained a certain motherly interest—of Beethoven's Seventh Symphony, the orchestra had played no more than a few bars when the familiar, throaty voice could be heard in a stage whisper from Box B-4, audible for at least thirty rows, to comment, "They're playing that much too fast!"

"The trouble was," the conductor ruefully admitted later, "that she was right."

That, indeed, was the trouble with most of Miss Ima's interventions, interruptions, crusades, and corrections. She was nearly always right. And as she approached her sixties, as she moved into her years of full and unchallenged civic, social, cultural, and political command, her jeweled hand was into almost everything in Texas.

27

"I'M DOING WHAT I WANT TO DO"

MISS IMA WAS FASCINATED by mythology and Greek goddesses and muses, and there is evidence to suggest that, as she grew older, she began to believe in her own myth—not an uncommon occurrence, it should be quickly added, with an American *grande dame*. Told so often that what she did and what she wanted were *right*, she began to believe that she could do no wrong. Of course these delusions did no one any real harm. In fact, delusions of grandeur may be the most precious assets of the *grande dame*. They enable her to sail on with confidence from one worthy project to the next, certain that each new achievement will top the last. Delusions of infallibility keep the *grande dame* on her toes, and make her unwilling to rest on her laurels. The myth, once created, must be kept alive. When one has become a legend in one's lifetime, one cannot let the legend lapse.

By the late 1930s Ima Hogg had become such a legend in Texas. No one of importance—whether it was Eleanor Roosevelt, Arturo Toscanini, or a young comedian named Danny Kaye—who passed through the state failed to make the pilgrimage to Bayou Bend to pay homage to its chatelaine. By then, no one questioned Miss Ima's claim to be clairvoyant. Her story about the fate of the doomed ship sailing from Hawaii had been printed so often in the *Houston Post* that it was accepted as gospel. And the tale of the aunt and the Dallas-bound stage was equally sacrosanct. Miss Ima had said it was so, and that made it so.

Miss Ima could usually find or invent historical reference points in her own life to justify her various enthusiasms as they came upon her. For example, she said that she vividly recalled going as a little girl with her father to state schools, prisons, asylums, and hospitals for the mentally ill. Her father, she explained, had always been interested in mental illness. But his interest had been in the social conditions in the general community, and in seeking out the responsibilities for the conditions which caused mental illness, rather than in the way it was treated in institutions once it had been diagnosed. He was more concerned with eliminating causes than in treating results. He had been influenced, it seemed, by an early book on the subject which Miss Ima discovered years later in his library: *Responsibility in Mental Illness*, by Henry Maudsley, published in 1898.

She, of course, had studied psychology in college, where her professor —and later lifelong friend—Dr. A. Caswell Ellis had been a well-known psychologist. When her brother Will died in 1930, the bulk of his estate had been left to his alma mater, the University of Texas, with the stipulation that his sister and his brothers would decide in what way the money was to be spent. As an administrator, Miss Ima decided it should be used to promote mental health, or, as it was called in those days, mental hygiene. "Most of my compulsions," she commented at the time, "are rooted and grounded in the University of Texas." Furthermore, both she and Mike decided to add funds of their own to create the Hogg Foundation. As she wrote:

> In accordance with this provision [in Will Hogg's will] and also with my numerous discussions with Will prior to 1930 of the common goals we had in mind, I have chosen the field of mental health as the area of support for both our funds. Also, in keeping with his wishes and mine, I have chosen as trustees the members of the Board of Regents of The University of Texas to administer the funds. They have established the Hogg Foundation for Mental Hygiene as the instrument for accomplishing this goal.

The Hogg Foundation was officially set up in 1940, and the following year she wrote to the trustees, "I think The University of Texas has an opportunity through a broad mental health program for bringing great benefits to the people of Texas." This letter was by way of being a gentle reminder—that the foundation was to benefit the *people* of Texas, and not, as she put it privately, "a lot of gray-beard researchers." Many creators of foundations modestly retire from the scene and leave the day-to-day administrators to follow whatever lines they choose. But not Miss Ima. It was *her* foundation, and she intended to keep personal track of its every move and expenditure. She understood the importance of research, but she had no patience with it, and was determined that her foundation was not going to support investigations that wound up filed away as musty monographs or articles in obscure professional journals. What she wanted were practical, human results—a decrease in the population of Texas's mental institutions, for example.

Foreseeably, she was able to get her trustees, the Board of Regents, to go along with her, and it certainly helped that she had the president of the university, Homer P. Rainey, in her pocket. So was the first director and president of the foundation, Dr. Robert L. Sutherland. Beginning in 1940, her letters to Dr. Sutherland, and his replies to her—"My dear Dr. Sutherland," "Dear Miss Hogg"—continued almost daily through the years. Miss Ima's letters always stressed that the foundation's emphasis was on prevention of mental illness, not on cure; on the importance of maintaining mental health, rather than on the treatment of the insane. And, though the foundation would cooperate with the University of Texas's Medical School, it would not be headquartered there, or isolated there in an academic ivory tower. One of Miss Ima's notions, in fact, was to use the foundation's funds to employ visiting lecturers to carry the message of mental health to the rural hinterlands of the state.

With the attack on Pearl Harbor in 1941, the efforts of the Hogg Foundation abruptly changed direction—toward the problems of young men suddenly drafted into the armed services, their wives and children and their widows, as well as to the difficulties of people, women in particular, who were working in heavy industry for the first time.

Miss Ima was never one to spend the foundation's money to finance an elaborate building in which to house it. Too many foundations, in her opinion, spent funds to create a luxurious "headquarters" that could be better invested in work in their fields. Just as she considered research "busy work," as opposed to real work, she disliked trappings and apparatus, and the offices of the Hogg Foundation were kept deliberately Spartan. Once, when a memorial building to her brother Will was proposed, she opposed it, politely but firmly, declaring in writing that "he would prefer any investment this would entail to be directed toward mental health work which would more closely affect the lives of the people of Texas."

When a piece of property became available to the foundation through a donation, on the other hand, Miss Ima was not averse to accepting it. Such an opportunity occurred after the war, when a prominent Houston family offered its mansion to the Child Guidance Center of Houston. It was decided that a new wing was needed, and this the Hogg Foundation offered to provide. As usual, Miss Ima supervised every detail of the construction, including inspecting the grade of concrete to be used to build the basement. Eventually, it was time to decide what color to paint the new addition, and an impromptu meeting was set up on the lawn. The architect first had his say, and then the various members of the board had theirs. Finally Miss Ima—for whom a special chair had been brought out onto the lawn, where she sat regally overseeing things—had hers. For several minutes she pondered the problem while the others waited silently. Presently a car drove by. It was, not surprisingly for Houston, a Cadillac. "Look," Miss Ima cried, as the automobile rounded the corner, "that's the color!" The car was beige with a pinkish cast and, as the Cadillac of the desired color disappeared from view, the entire assemblage rushed into the street to follow it and note its hue. "And of course," said one of her trustees later, "she was right, and that was the color we painted the building."

Miss Ima liked to keep up with the times. She had discovered that the secret of perpetual youth is not only perpetual motion but also perpetual enthusiasm. In the early 1960s, when Miss Ima had passed her eightieth birthday, four tousle-haired lads from Liverpool suddenly burst forth on the American musical scene. Most of Miss Ida's contemporaries and peers, as well as a number of people somewhat younger than she, announced themselves appalled by the Beatles and by their music, which was dismissed as so much organized noise. Miss Ima, however, became an immediate Beatles fan, and announced that she found their Liverpudlian sound both intellectually interesting and melodically beautiful. All at once it seemed as though Miss Ima was the contemporary one, and her friends the old fogies. It was a situation, of course, which she couldn't have enjoyed more.

In the 1960s she acquired still another enthusiasm, restoring old houses. In 1962 she acquired the "Honeymoon Cottage" in Quitman, Texas, which had been her parents' first home, restored it and refurnished it, and presented it, along with the surrounding property, to the state of Texas to create the Jim Hogg State Park. Then, in 1963, at the suggestion of her friend Barbara Dillingham, she bought the Old Stagecoach Inn and its outbuildings in Winedale, Texas. Her original plan had been to move the inn, which dated from 1834, to Bayou Bend, but she then decided to leave it where it was, for Winedale had been the halfway-point stage stop between Houston and Austin, which gave its location historical significance. As usual, she was meticulous in her attention to details of the restoration of the old buildings, which had fallen into considerable disrepair, and to make sure that everything was being done properly she took a small cottage on the property where she could keep an eye on things. Ever the perfectionist, she journeyed to Massachusetts to buy square-cut nails for the floorboards. All timber for the restoration was cut from the Winedale property, to be sure it would match the original. Using a small but well-preserved fragment of wallpaper as a sample, Miss Ima commissioned a hand-printed replica at great cost, so that the living room of one of the buildings would be entirely authentic. Through it all, Miss Ima, using a cane now to get about, climbed over and around piles of construction materials on her inspection tours. The roof of one old building had a noticeable sag, and a carpenter, thinking it should be corrected, put up supports to straighten the roof line. That week end, checking on things, Miss Ima suddenly cried, "Where's my sag?" When told what had been done, she issued instructions that the sag be restored immediately. In 1965, when the Winedale restoration was finally complete, Miss Ima presented the entire property, along with an endowment for its maintenance, to the University of Texas as the Museum of Cultural History.

While all this was going on, Miss Ima was quietly arranging Bayou Bend so that it too could eventually be turned into a museum. Each room of the big place was assigned its period and style of American antiques, and there would be rooms to contain the silver collection and the china collection, and one to contain her honors: the framed citations she had received, honorary degrees from colleges and universities, letters from United States Presidents, Texas governors, mayors, and other public officials and civic leaders; loving cups, ribbons, medallions; keys to cities and most-valued-citizen awards; and the first dollar bill run off under the signature of her old friend ex-Governor John Connally when he became Secretary of the Treasury, autographed to her. A very large room, fitted out with a great many illuminated glass cases, would be required.

In 1966 Miss Ima was eighty-four, and that was the year when, her collection finished and its contents arranged, she turned over Bayou Bend, its furnishings, and its fifteen landscaped acres of gardens to the Houston Museum of Fine Arts, as its decorative arts collection. Along with the gift, as usual, went an endowment to maintain it. At the dedication she cheerfully announced that she was ready "to watch the sunsets from a high-rise apartment . . . free to pursue my other projects." Still, though the property was technically no longer hers, Miss Ima managed to exercise a good deal of control over it. She used the house for parties whenever she wished, and she was allowed to "borrow" certain paintings and pieces of furniture for her apartment from time to time, which made the décor of her new home a moveable feast. She was forever popping in at Bayou Bend just to check on things, and once telephoned the curator to say, "A hurricane's coming—check the windows!" And it was she who decreed that all the docents at the museum must take an intensive two-week training course under the curator, to assure that no visitor's questions would go unanswered or incorrectly answered.

Today, Bayou Bend and its gardens can be enjoyed by the public—in small groups, on a reservations-only basis, but, as Miss Ima stipulated, at no admission charge.

In 1972 Miss Ima's ninetieth birthday was celebrated with a special concert by the Houston Symphony Orchestra, highlighted by the guest appearance of her old friend Artur Rubinstein. She had, she liked to say, survived a number of serious illnesses, including gangrene (from a fall from her horse), spinal meningitis, typhoid and scarlet fever. And yet here she was. True, her cane was never out of her reach and she occasionally accepted a wheelchair, and her eyesight was failing. But at her birthday party she downed her customary quota of man-sized bourbon old-fashioneds, and sang and played the piano. In addition to extrasensory perception, she also believed in reincarnation and, in that sense, believed she was immortal. It was her hunch.

She almost was. In 1975, her ninety-third birthday behind her, she took off on a jet for Europe. She would visit London, and then fly on to Beyreuth where a very ambitious "project" awaited her. She planned to attend the Beyreuth Music Festival and to hear, uninterrupted, the full "Ring" cycle of Wagner operas. This four-work series—*Das Rheingold, Die Walküre, Siegfried,* and *Götterdämmerung,* none of them noted for its brevity—would amount to some fifteen hours of opera. She had also considered touring Germany, where she had studied piano as a girl, but at the last minute decided against it. Her reasons were purely practical. "The mark," she said, "is too inflated." When a friend questioned the wisdom of such an extensive trip at her advanced age, Miss Ima replied, "Well, when you're ninety-three, it doesn't matter where you die."

In London, outside her hotel, Miss Ima was stepping into a taxicab when the driver, thinking she was inside, pulled away. Miss Ima fell. Rushed to Westminster Hospital, she was admitted with a broken hip. Her condition complicated by pneumonia, she died a few days later, on August 19. But she had had her last words ready. To a group of concerned friends—including the remorseful cab driver—who gathered at her bedside, worried that she was so sick so far from home, she said,

"Whatever happens, remember that it was the way it was meant to be. I'm doing what I want to do. I'm where I want to be. I have no regrets." Then she smiled and closed her eyes.

Back home in Houston they said, "Well, she had a rich, full life." "Nonsense!" says her old friend Barbara Dillingham, who worked with her on the Stagecoach Inn restoration and many other projects. "She had many years of active life ahead of her. If they'd had an intensive-care unit at that hospital, she could have been saved. But they didn't."

Among the many eulogies and tributes delivered at the time of Miss Ima's death were these words from Nellie Connally, wife of the former governor: "The governor's wife is usually called the first lady of Texas, but Miss Ima always has been and always will be the first lady of Texas."

Miss Ima would have liked that. And would have agreed.

Afterword

A VANISHING BREED

"THERE JUST AREN'T WOMEN AROUND like Mother any more," said Eva Stotesbury's son, James H. R. Cromwell, in 1980. "There aren't people who can talk about the duties and responsibilities that go with money. There aren't people who can talk about uplifting the poor and the sick, about the need to bring culture to the masses, and still be taken seriously. Today, anyone who talked that way would be laughed at. But those women had integrity, they believed in what they were trying to do, believed it was important, believed it was almost a holy obligation that went with wealth. But they're a vanishing breed. I suppose it was the social welfare programs that were started by President Roosevelt that began to put those women out of business. The government took over their jobs. I admit I was a big Roosevelt supporter, but I've since had a great many second thoughts. I worked hard for Ronald Reagan, and I'd love to live to see the day when *individual* charity will come back to replace all these social and welfare programs that the federal government has gotten itself locked into. But I doubt if I ever will. Even the word 'charity' has become a dirty word. To call someone a 'patron of the arts' today, which used to be considered a high and worthy calling, is to employ a term of derision."

It is certainly true that, in the years since the beginning of the Roosevelt era, the federal government has slowly and steadily usurped the territory that once belonged to a few public-spirited philanthropists, and caring for the needy, the dispossessed, the mentally disoriented, the ill and the aged has become a public rather than a private responsibility. Whether unfortunate people in American society are any better off for it is a little hard to tell, but the revolution would appear to be complete.

279

Indirectly, too, through the strictures imposed by the Internal Revenue Service, the United States Government has discouraged *grande dame*–ship. To prevent their estates from being ravaged by taxes, the rich, like Miss Ima Hogg, have been forced to funnel their wealth into foundations, where decisions are no longer made by an individual legatee but by a board of trustees—the grand committee substituted for the *grande dame*. Today the country bristles with foundations, employing many people, all busily doing good works—the Guggenheim Foundation, the Rockefeller Foundation, the Rockefeller Brothers Fund, the Rockefeller Family Fund, the Martha Baird Rockefeller Fund for Music, and so on—all created by lawyers and business advisers for tax purposes. (The giant Ford Foundation was not set up out of a burning desire to cure the world's woes, but by canny Wall Street bankers who saw a way to save the heirs of Henry Ford from a staggering tax bill.) The IRS may also have dampened interest in collecting art and antiques—by making costs non-tax-deductible unless and until works are donated to museums.

But Big Government cannot assume all the blame for the fact that the torch that was once the *grande dame*'s has fallen into other, somewhat anonymous, hands. Big Business has also done its share and has, not always with the best intentions, assumed a certain proprietary concern for Culture. In Cincinnati, where Mary Emery gave so much time and money to support the symphony, the opera, and the art museum, these institutions receive much larger donations from Procter & Gamble, whose officers, as a matter of corporate policy, are expected to serve on their boards. (Annually, Procter & Gamble gives a Christmas turkey to each of its employees, much the way Eva Stotesbury used to deliver her Christmas parcels to the poor of Philadelphia.) In New York in 1981, the stockholders of the Kimberly-Clark Corporation voted to give $10,000 to the Metropolitan Museum of Art. It was the kind of gift Eleanor Belmont routinely made a few years earlier. In accepting the money, William V. Macomber, the museum's president, said, "It's thrilling to see what corporate America does to improve the quality of life." Thrilling, perhaps, but also a bit impersonal.

For over two hundred years Americans have boasted that the country has no aristocracy. Then how does one explain this "vanishing breed" of women, all of whom were born before the turn of the century, who stretched out their arms with great enthusiasm and grasped the burden of philanthropy and culture and gave these terms new meaning, who underwrote symphony orchestras, lent their prestige to social action, succored opera companies, and set styles in living? Painting, architecture, interior decoration, landscape design and horticulture, music, the theatre, literature, science and medicine, fashion, education, and politics all felt the impact of their presence. Sticking to the no-aristocracy rule, we fall back on French and call them *grandes dames*, which can be conveyed in somewhat depreciatory italics and loosely defined. Yet they combined to form our republic's closest approach to an aristocracy—one not of family, but of taste, panache, and style.

These women had no common denominator of birth. Eva Stotesbury's lawyer father was respectably prosperous but not rich. Edith Rosenwald's father was almost poor, and became rich while she was growing up. Mary Parkman Peabody was a Boston Brahmin, that caste which Oliver Wendell Holmes called "the harmless, inoffensive, untitled aristocracy." (When she was jailed in Florida, her aplomb and poise so impressed her jailers that when a reporter tried to telephone her at the jail he was told, "I'm sorry, but Mrs. Peabody is resting and cannot be disturbed.") Eleanor Belmont was a working actress. Arabella Huntington came from —well, who knows, really? What these women had in common was not birth but flair—a confident view of life and the vitality to express it and impress it on others whom they met. They also shared a profound toughness, an ability to scythe through the thick underbrush of lethargy and indifference without incurring a single scratch, to be invulnerable to criticism and jealousy—immune to it as some are to poison ivy.

Although some were brighter than others, these women also shared a naïve, almost childlike faith in their own infallibility, a belief that what they thought was right was *right*. In a sense, too, though they were often among the *avant-garde* in matters of taste or conscience, they were also old-fashioned women, or so they might seem to women of the 1980s. They all leaned on men for financial support and advice—with the possible exception of Miss Ima, though there was always the tall shadow of her father haunting the wings. They were none of them, in the current sense, feminists. But they were all, refreshingly, female. And, though being a *grande dame* was obviously nourishing to the ego—*grandes dames* were always very aware that they were *grandes dames*—it may have been nourishing to the physical self as well, as longevity is another common trait.

A dying breed. Throughout the 1970s we read, one by one, of the deaths of these members of America's only aristocracy, and in each obituary we were reminded that "one of the last of America's *grandes dames*" had departed. Marjorie Merriweather Post, nearly ninety, was "one of the last." Alice Roosevelt Longworth, ninety-five when she died in 1980, was another—though Mrs. Longworth was more of a Washington party goer, wit, and mimic (her imitations of her relative Eleanor Roosevelt were famously side-splitting) than a social or cultural force. Her death was followed by that of Mrs. Robert Low Bacon, eighty-eight—hostess, stalwart of the Republican Party, trustee of Adelphi University and an Eisenhower appointee to the Advisory Committee on the Arts for the National Cultural Center.

All these ladies are gone, and they seem irreplaceable. With them, it sometimes seems, has died a certain exuberant spirit and élan that flashed across the American social scene for a couple of generations. And the dream of a Great American Renaissance—in art, architecture, music, design—which showed such promise when it first came into flower around 1875—seems to have died somewhere between two world wars.

To be sure, there are still younger women of consequence who grasp the social or cultural nettle—Brooke Astor, widow of Vincent, who recently donated the traditional Chinese garden known as the Astor Court to the Metropolitan Museum in New York; Muriel Kallis Steinberg Newman of Chicago, who has promised her definitive Abstract Expressionist collection to the same museum; Mary Lasker, president of the Albert and Mary Lasker Foundation in New York, who supervises the expenditure of millions of Lasker dollars on medical research; and others. But would it be niggling or ungallant to suggest that none of them quite possesses the exuberance—the daring, the extravagance, the scale, the supremely self-confident high-handedness—that characterized some of their counterparts of an earlier era? Against that gaudy turn-of-the-century backdrop, some of today's *grandes dames* appear a little wan, a little too eager to please. (The turn-of-the-century *grande dame* was too fiercely convinced of her own invincibility to care whether she pleased or not.)

Perhaps the feminist movement of the 1970s has somewhat daunted today's rich women, and made them wonder whether they have merely become interesting anachronisms, whether the terms "philanthropist," "patroness of the arts," and "social leader" have become passé. Who today, for example, would have the temerity of Alida Chanler Emmet, who, when her friend Stanford White designed a house for her which she didn't like, moved out of it and hired another architect, Charles Platt, to design and build a new one? "You can design my barns," she told White. And he did. In any case, members of the Old Breed today are very few and, of course, getting on in years.

Nevertheless, there are still women who are *trying* to be *grandes dames*, and who seem to believe in the concept. Even more interesting is the fact that dedication to the special principles of American upper-class values —those values which must never be given voice, but must always be observed—has not died out. Not entirely. The American upper class still believes that a certain amount of time and money should be devoted to bettering the lot of the ill and needy; that an appreciation of painting and music and other beautiful things should be both shared with, and taught to, the general populace—that in art lies the power to uplift and purify the human tribe; that there is such a thing as *noblesse oblige*, and that the French usually had a better term for everything; that, when an occasion arises, one rises to it with the upper lip stiff; that gallantry and style will usually carry the day.

And so, as long as there are women around who subscribe to such notions, our very peculiar and particular brand of American aristocracy may survive, however long it may remain untitled. The nobility will oblige.

Bibliography

Altrocchi, Julia Cooley, *The Spectacular San Franciscans*. New York: Dutton, 1949.
Amory, Cleveland, *The Last Resorts*. New York: Grosset & Dunlap, 1948.
———, *Who Killed Society?* New York: Harper, 1960.
Baltzell, E. Digby, *Philadelphia Gentlemen*. New York: Free Press, 1958.
Behrman, S. N., *Duveen*. London: Hamish Hamilton, 1953.
Belmont, Eleanor Robson, *The Fabric of Memory*. New York: Farrar, Straus, 1957.
Biddle, Cordelia Drexel, *The Happiest Millionaire*. New York: Pocket, 1963.
Burt, Nathaniel, *The Perennial Philadelphians*. Boston: Little, Brown, 1963.
Burt, Struthers, *Philadelphia, Holy Experiment*. Garden City, N.Y.: Doubleday, 1945.
Carter, Morris, *Isabella Stewart Gardner and Fenway Court*. New York: Arno, 1972.
Dedmon, Emmett, *Fabulous Chicago*. New York: Random, 1953.
Duveen, James Henry, *The Rise of the House of Duveen*. New York: Knopf, 1957.
———, *Secrets of an Art Dealer*. New York: Dutton, 1938.
Evans, Cerinda W., *Collis Potter Huntington*. Newport News, Va.: Mariners Museum, 1954.
Harlow, Alvin F., *The Serene Cincinnatians*. New York: Dutton, 1930.
Harris, Leon, *Merchant Princes*. New York: Harper, 1979.
Iscoe, Louise Kosches, *Ima Hogg: First Lady of Texas*. Houston: Hogg Foundation, 1976.
Lewis, Oscar, *The Big Four*. New York: Knopf, 1938.
Lippincott, Horace Mather, *A Narrative of Chestnut Hill*. Jenkintown, Pa.: Old York Road, 1948.
Maher, James T., *The Twilight of Splendor*. Boston: Little, Brown, 1975.
Martin, Ralph G., *Cissy*. New York: Simon and Schuster, 1979.
Moffat, Frances, *Dancing on the Brink of the World*. New York: Putnam, 1977.
Nickerson, Marjorie L., *A Long Way Forward*. Brooklyn, N.Y.: Packer, 1945.
Parks, Warren Wright, *The Mariemont Story*. Cincinnati: Creative Writers, 1967.
Roberts, George and Mary, *Triumph on Fairmount*. Philadelphia: Lippincott, 1959.
Seligman, Germain, *Merchants of Art, 1880–1960*. New York: Appleton-Century-Crofts, 1961.
Tharp, Louise Hall, *Mrs. Jack*. Boston: Little, Brown, 1963.
Wecter, Dixon, *The Saga of American Society*. New York: Scribner, 1937.

Index

Index

Index

Ward, Sam, 73
Warren, Frances, 126
Washington, Booker T., 105
Washington Post, 118
Washington society, 31
Waterford Jack (Frances Warren), 126
WDSU Broadcasting, New Orleans, 118
wealth:
  in Boston society, 55, 60
  in Depression, 43
  noblesse oblige and, 40, 169–70, 283
  values associated with, 169–70, 178, 283
Wecter, Dixon, 223–24
Weeks, Edward, 91
Weidenfeld, Camille, 187
Wellesley College, 9–10
Wharton, Edith, 58, 74, 75
Wheeler, Alvin, 269
Whistler, James McNeill, 67–68
White, Stanford, 74, 75, 282
Whitemarsh Hall, 35–36, 37, 43, 44, 46–47, 48, 107
Whitney, Sarah Swan, 231
Whittier, John Greenleaf, 91
Who's Who: A Society Register . . . for Cincinnati (Devereux), 173–74
Who's Who in America, 118
Wilde, Oscar, 131–32
Wildenbourg, Prince François-Edmond-Joseph-Gabriel Vit de und von Hatzfeldt, 200
Wilson, Adah, 149
Wilson, Woodrow, 240, 246

Wingwood House, 42, 43
Wolff, Edwin, II, 208
Women's Trade Union League, 231
Working Girls' Vacation Association, 239
Works Progress Administration (WPA), 270–71
World's Columbian Exposition of 1893, 100, 126, 127
World War I, 239–40, 263
World War II, 34
Worsham, Annette, 191
Worsham, Arabella Duval, *see* Huntington, Arabella Duval Yarrington Worsham
Worsham, Archer Milton, 191, 193, 200–201
Worsham, Johnny, 190, 191–92, 195, 197
Worth, Graham A., 156

Yarrington, Arabella Duval, *see* Huntington, Arabella Duval Yarrington Worsham
Yarrington, Catherine, 189, 190–91, 192, 194
Yarrington, Richard, 189
Young Men's Christian Association (YMCA), 163, 164

Zangwill, Israel, 228–29
Zaza (Leoncavallo), 139
Zorn, Anders, 90–91
Zurbarán, Francisco de, 83